Peasants' Resentments and Resistance:

A Glimpse on Rural Past of Sikkim 1914-1950

Rajen Upadhyay

KALPAZ

First Published, 2017

Published by

Kalpaz Publications
C-30, Satyawati Nagar,
Delhi – 110052
E-mail: kalpaz@hotmail.com
Ph.: 9212142040

Printed at: G. Print Process, Delhi

Cataloging in Publication Data—DK

Courtesy: D.K. Agencies (P) Ltd. <docinfo@dkagencies.com>

Upadhyay, Rajen, author.

Peasants' resentments and resistance : a glimpse on Sikkim's rural past 1914-1950 / Dr Rajen Upadhyay.

pages cm

Includes bibliographical references.

ISBN 9789351282655

1. Sikkim (India)—History. 2. Peasants—Political activity—India—Sikkim—History. 3. Patronage, Political—India—Sikkim—History. 4. Agriculture and state—India—Sikkim—History. 5. Sikkim (India)—Politics and government. I. Title.

DS485.S55U63 2017 DDC 954.167 23

Contents

List of Figures

To

My Little Angel

Richa Rajyashree

With Love

Baba

Acknowledgements

A researcher is inspired and influenced by a number of factors which make up the synchronisation of the investigated area. Certainly, the role played by various persons and agencies deserve to be validated as poignant when one approaches the culmination of one's findings. Indeed, during a tiresome work of studying and figuring out something, any sort of help and suggestion is not less than mentoring. Therefore, on the threshold of publishing my book **Peasants' Resentments and Resistance: A Glimpse on Rural Past of Sikkim 1914-1950,** which, undoubtedly is the seed of the womb of my efforts and long labour, I, sincerely do acknowledge the contribution of many a people without whose solid guidance, inspiration, motivation and help, my work would have neither started nor accomplished.

At the first place, I am greatly indebted to my parents- Mrs Kaushila Devi Upadhyay and Mr Krishna Prasad Upadhyay for motivating and supporting me on various junctures and always remaining as idols. Again, I extend my utmost gratitude towards my better half Mrs Premika Sharma who was like the flesh and nail with me during the entire duration of my work and took all the pains to support me even in the worst of the situations. My deep sense of affection goes to my daughter Richa Rajyashree on whose face I could see a spontaneous stream of inspiration which is bestowed upon with all the radical innocence of the Creator.

My work is also a milestone for my respected Supervisor, Dr Girija Pande, an eminent historian currently Professor and Director, School of Social Sciences, Uttarakhand Open University, Haldwani. Without his constant suggestion, it would have been like trying to discover stars in the cosmos with naked eyes; but, the telescope which he provided gave me a subtle viewpoint to sort out the newer findings. In other words, this work would have been incomplete without his guidance and encouragement. I take this opportunity to convey my words of gratitude and benevolence to that esteemed teacher who always remained by my side to help, support and suggest me. Simultaneously, I am grateful to Professor Rekha Pande, Professor of History, and Joint Faculty at Women Study, University of Hyderabad for her constant advice during the course of writing this book.

The persons who continuously inspired and supported me come from a varied platform. As such, I earnestly acknowledge the encouragement and support I received from *Gyalmo* Hope Cooke, the former queen of Sikkim, who always boosted my temperament for this mammoth task. Again, I owe a great to the personalities like Mr Uttam Kumar Upadhyaya, Assistant Professor in English at Namchi Government College; Dr Satyadeep Singh Chettri, Assistant Professor in Chemistry at Sikkim Government College, Tadong; Dr Saurav Kafley, Head, Chemistry Department, Namchi Government College; Dr P.R. Paudyal, Assistant Professor in Nepali at Namchi Government College; Dr Keshav Gautam, Post Graduate Teacher in History at B.P.S.S School Ranipool, Mr Bikash Karki, a PhD Scholar, Centre for Himalayan Studies, NBU, Ms. Jennifer Bentley, a PhD scholar, Zurich University, Switzerland for allowing me access to the Nepali documents, and Mr Binod Bhattarai, a PhD scholar, Pondicherry University all of whom had genuinely supported me on various levels. I am also greatly indebted to Dr Tshwang Gyatsho Bhutia and Mr Tshering Chopel Bhutia, Assistant Professors, Department of Bhutia, Namchi Government College for translating the Bhutia Documents used in this work. Likewise, it will be unjustified if I forget the contribution rendered by Dr A.B. Karki, SDM, Gangtok, Mr Shital Pradhan, a teacher and a prominent blogger of Sikkim History, Dr B. Anil Kumar Sharma, Assistant Professor in Geography, Moirang College, Manipur for constantly motivating me to finalise this book and Mr Arabam Noni Assistant Professor in Political Science, Moirang College, Manipur for his suggestions in finding publisher and towards the completion of this book.

In addition to the stated above, I am also honestly thankful to the librarians and other staff of the libraries of Namchi Government College; Centre for Himalayan Studies, North Bengal University; Namgyal Institute of Tibetology, Deorali; District Library, Namchi; District Library, Gangtok and Central Library, Kumaun University, Nainital for providing me adequate support in terms of books, magazines and journals. Museum is an inevitable part of History as it preserves the heritage and tradition from time immemorial. I do honestly convey my sense of gratefulness to Mr Ganesh Kumar Pradhan, proprietor, Ram Gauri Sangrahalaya, Rhenock; Sikkim State Archives, Gangtok and self volunteered archive of Mr Shital Pradhan as all of these gave me a pathfinder on my way to research. Similarly, I sincerely acknowledge Mr Khada Nanda Uprety, Former Education Minister, Mr Nar Bahadur Khatiwara, Former MLA Sikkim Assembly, Mr Dugo Bhutia, Former MLA, Sikkim Assembly and Mr Biraj Adhikari, President Sikkim National Peoples' Party for their utmost help in providing documents for the completion of this work.

I am delighted to mention the names of few of my beloved students (B.A. 2009-2012 batch) who took great pains to help and support me in the tedious and rigorous field survey carried out in order to frame the basics of this research. To thank them, I should mention the names like Deepmala, Mickey, Priyanka, Hari Chandra, Late Dweep Subba, Primula, and Riwaj.

In conclusion, I am once again thankful to those who directly or indirectly helped me in this endeavour of mine. If I have missed out any of the persons who supported me in this venture, I solicit their forgiveness.

RAJEN UPADHYAY

Preface

The peasant resistance in Sikkim had come across several phases had ultimately resulted in the political consciousness among the marginalised peasantry of the Kingdom provides an attractive meadow of study. The Sikkimese feudalism that had some recognised features like forced labours, excessive taxation, inequalities, social discrimination and the like got its prominence after the British control over Sikkimese administration. In the earlier days, in all intent and purposes, the King was regarded as a *de-facto* proprietor of all the territories of his Kingdom. Accordingly, time pertinent conventions were in vogue, and the subjects of the Kingdom had accepted such conventions and usages without resistance. According to Sikkimese convention, a cultivator could settle down on the unoccupied areas without any formality and no one could uproot him except the King. The peasants who were then relatively independent and had an indirect relationship with the State were thus directly brought under the State at the whims of the British. Similarly, the very face of rural Sikkim began to change after the settlement of the Nepali cultivators who were encouraged by the British to get settle in the unoccupied and waste lands of the Kingdom. The unrestraint flow of people from Nepal had subsequently resulted in an extensive demographic change along with agrarian pattern and the mode of assessment and collection of revenues.

The uncared and neglected lot of Sikkimese peasantry began to resist the feudal dictums when they were compelled to go parallel with the materialistic zeal of the State. The peasantry always had carried hidden transcripts against the hegemonic and chauvinistic acts of their masters however; they had to follow them to avert a perilous circumstance in their lives. In spite of their reluctance, when they were forced to work as porters and sometimes when they were asked to work without wages for their masters, they got agitated and began to oppose feudal nuisance in an individual manner. Such forms of monopolistic approach from the part of the officials reached its highest level during the reign of Maharaja Sir Tashi Nomgyal. They were often asked to carry *Kalo Bhari*, *Jharlangi*, *Theki-Bethi*, and *Kuruwa* by the feudal lords to support the British in sending their goods to Tibet. Therefore, to avert such torments, the Sikkimese peasantry had devised many ways and means to tackle feudal strain through various individual acts, commonly known as everyday forms of resistance. Such acts were individual and self-centred basically associated with the bread and butter issues and were not a direct confrontation against the state. Political ideas in such social set up remain in a slumber stage until the people are ready to flow in accordance with the prevailing currents and cross-currents. The political ideas begin to take shape among the Sikkimese peasantry when they start to think above the bread and butter issues. After the Second World War the everyday forms of peasant resistance of the earlier Himalayan Kingdom had become a full fledged political conflict which was a political altercation against the injustice made upon them by the state. Being a unanimous resistance, the political conflicts waged by the Sikkim State Congress were highly organised as compared to everyday form of resistance. Though, the peasants had been able to achieve unimaginable after they came under the influence of State Congress, but, they were now in the process of losing their identity as peasant folks. For a political gain and in the name of 'ethnic balance' they had been divided according to their communities and were now merely being treated as a voter by their respective parties and a subject by the State. Although, their journey from porter to voter, and from subordinate to subject, had many turns and twirls, whereupon they were guided by their leaders who were eager to uplift their plights. However, situation began to take unpleasant turns and dwindled from bad to worse when the State adopted an unbalanced parity formula.

During their course of everyday resistance, the very same peasants who were then leaderless were free to live and to resist the State by adopting several techniques discussed in the preceding chapters. Undoubtedly, that was an individual effort to resist the State and they themselves were responsible for the disturbances they created or achievement they could attain. Being leaderless they were their own guides and philosophers and worked according to their consciences in a time apposite manner. Conversely, immediately after achieving a very little from their prolonged resistance they got bifurcated into two halves as an ethnic balancing measure. Incorporating a very little interest of the peasantry by the State, they were made the victim of a political conspiracy hacked by its protecting power. The very parity formula had become a core issue in the succeeding elections and when it was still undone, the peasants rose in a revolt that had not only eliminated the remnants of feudal structure but had also swept their sovereignty. Thus, ultimately the quest of Sikkimese peasantry to have a democratic set up in the Kingdom that was started in the decolonising period ended up assimilation with its protected power in the Cold War period.

Chapter 1

Sikkim: A Short Introduction

Sikkim is a landlocked Indian state cuddled up in the Himalayas. It is least populous state in the Indian Union and the second smallest after Goa. According to the census of 2011 the total population of Sikkim is 610,577 out of which 323,070 are Male, 287,507 are Female.[1] Sikkim was an independent state ruled by the *Namgyal* dynasty until 1975, when a referendum to make it as India's 22nd state succeeded.[2] The chicken neck shaped Himalayan state borders Nepal in the West, the Tibetan Autonomous Region (TAR) of People's Republic of China to the North and East, and Bhutan in the South-East. The Indian state of West Bengal borders Sikkim to South. The official language of Sikkim is English and Nepali and the predominant religions are Hinduism and *Vajrayana* Buddhism. Gangtok is the capital and the largest town of the State.

Owing to its location at the Himalayan foothills, Sikkim is geographically diverse; terrain ranges from tropical in the south to Tundra in the north. Kanchenjunga, the world's third highest peak is located in Sikkim spanning its northern border with Nepal. Sikkim has now become one of India's most visited states owing to its status for untouched charming exquisiteness and political stability. Recently, in October 2013, Lonely Planets, best in Travel 2014 has included Sikkim as the top ten regions for travel destination. It is also a destination for all season.[3]

Sikkim became a constitutional unit of India in 1975,[4] but her political involvement with India started from early 1817. After the Anglo-Gorkha war, Treaty of Segauly was signed between Government of Nepal and Government of India (East India Company) in 1816. In 1817, again the Treaty of Titalia was signed between the both, whereby the boundary between Sikkim and Nepal was laid along with the Mahanadi and Mechi rivers and the Sang- ri-la range as the border.[5] Sikkim's political entity was decided by the Anglo-Chinese Convention of 1890, between Great Britain and China.[6] After the Indian independence, the colonial concept of protectorate continued upon Sikkim and became a virtual protected Kingdom of Independent India. In 1975, Sikkim was converted into 22nd State of the Indian Union by abolishing monarchy.[7]

Origin of Name

Sikkim or *Sikhim* means crested land in Nepali. The term which was coined by the invading Gorkhas, is derived from the Sanskrit word '*Sikhim*' which means 'crested,' and is the most widely accepted theory of origin.[8] Sikkim would thus owe its name to its almost entirely mountainous terrain. Graham Sandberg, in his of *Manual of Sikkim Bhutia Language* also indicates the word Sikkim with a Gorkha origin.[9] An alternative etymology of Kotturan suggests that the name originates from the Limbu word '*Su*', which means 'New,' and '*Khyim*', which means 'Palace'. Hence, the term Sikkim may also mean 'New Palace,' in reference to the palace built by the State's second ruler Tensung Namgyal after his marriage with a Limboo princess.[10] Early European travellers like Samuel Van de Putte[11] and Horace Della Penna used the name '*Bramasojon*'[12] for Sikkim.

Tulshi Ram Sharma a writer and an ex-speaker of the Sikkim Legislative Assembly opine that Sikkim and the Lepchas were intimately related. In their language they had the name of Sikkim as *Nye- ma-el-Ren-Iyang* which means *'Heaven'*.[13] When Bhutias' emigrated from Tibet, Lepchas' called Sikkim as '*Ren-zong*', which was insignificant in the Bhutia language therefore, they according to their appreciative renamed it as *Dya-Zong*, or the land of rice. With the lapse of time, the word, it seems got distorted and corrupted to *Denzong*.[14]

As stated earlier, the origination of the word Sikkim is sometime correlated with the Limboos as well. It is said that, the Second King of Sikkim, Tensung Namgyal fought a battle with the Limboo King Yo Yo Hang of Aryn Tambor of *Limbuwan* in which Sikkim emerged out as victorious. To give a new silhouette to the hostile relation, Tensung married the Limboo princess and brought some Limboo maids to Sikkim. As the latter was their new home and to them either of the two names of the land *Ren-Zong* and *Denzong* was meaningless, therefore they began to call it as *Su-Heem* or new home. Later, when other people from Nepal infiltrated into Sikkim, they heard the word as '*Sikhim*' and hence began to call the land '*Su-khim*', which in Nepali means 'happiness' or the place of happiness. The word '*Suk-Him*' in the course of time was mispronounced by the British as Sikkim.

The People

Mainly there are three communities in Sikkim, who emigrated from different places and settled permanently and became inseparable sections of Sikkimese population. They are the Lepchas, Bhutias, and the Nepalese. The Lepchas are believed to have been the original inhabitants of Sikkim. Their language belongs to the Tibeto-Burman family of languages. This perhaps led George Kotturan to remark that the Lepchas came from Assam and belonged to some Tibeto-Burman family.[15] The Lepchas are nimble-fingered woodsmen. Elaborating their craftsmanship propensity Richard temple writes:

> "The Lepchas, being most skilful woodsmen, will in a very short time build themselves a hut of bamboos, much after the Burmese fashion, which is watertight and sufficiently warm".[16]

There is a universal belief among the Lepchas that they are the creation of the soil of Sikkim itself; many legends and folklore are found in connection with this conviction.[17] According to a well-known Lepcha folktale, the almighty had created *Fadongthing* the first Lepcha male and *Nuzaongnyoo* the first female from the virgin snow of Mt. Kanchenjunga and therefore they worship the mountain as their deity. Likewise, in another prodigy the Lepchas believe that the main rivers of Sikkim Teesta and Rangit were lovers who started their journey to meet at a certain point. According to the anecdote, river Teesta was guided by an eagle and river Rangit was guided by a python. If we look at the pattern of river flow Teesta is straight as according to the tale, was guided by an eagle and Rangit has many curves in a way that a python moves.[18] These tales and anecdotes too provide us some space to believe the aboriginality of Lepchas in Sikkim.

Rong, Lepchas and Lapchey are different names given to the Lepchas by different communities. The idiom Lepchas itself is derived from the word '*Lap*' which means the people who lived in sacred place. However, the term *Rong* must have been given to them by the Tibetans. In their language '*Rong-Pa*' means a person living on the scopes and the glen of the mountains. Jai Dhamala and George Kotturan suggest that the word Lepcha appears to be of Nepali origin and is derived from *Lapchey* meaning vile speakers. Later, the term was modified into 'Lepcha' in English.

Conversely, Tamsang believes that Lepcha is derived from a *Rong* word *Lapchao* meaning a resting or waiting place on the way side. He further writes that with the coming of the Nepalese the Rong word *Lapchao* got distorted into *Lapchey* or *Lapcha* due to the difficulty of the former to pronounce. He affirms this hypothesis with the prevalence of Lapcha word used by the Nepalese to identify the Lepchas of Ilam.[19]

The Lepchas are simple, mild, peace loving and superstitious people and are lovers and worshippers of nature. Hence, the majority of the Lepchas are accustomed to live in remote and inaccessible areas. Rev. J.A. Graham, a Baptist Missionary points out the usage of *Boongthings* by a Lepcha Manager Raja Tenduk of Kalimpong, to propitiate an angry demon. He further believes that the Lepchas had come under the Tibetan fold through their association with the Tibetans.[20] We do not have any historical evidences or written documents, which are available about the Lepchas, and it is also said that whatever they had was systematically destroyed by the Tibetan priests in the very beginning of their arrival in Sikkim.[21]

The Stateship was instituted and the Kingship was also brought into existence in Sikkim with the advent of the Tibetans. *'Bhot'* is the Nepali synonym for the country of Tibet.[22] Hence, the Bhutias are also known to the Nepalese as *Bhotey* meaning the people of Tibetan or *Bhot* origin. It is believed that, up to the seventeenth century they were very few in numbers therefore, as such they could not affect the cultural as well as religious and traditional beliefs of the Lepchas. However, with the arrival of numerous Tibetan Lamas, the aboriginal Lepchas of Sikkim were adapted towards the Tibetan fold.[23]

However, A.C. Sinha points out that, the Tibetan traders, farmers and the Lamas were in search of new areas for colonisation long before the first century. Sikkim at that time was very sparsely populated by the primitive tribes of Lepchas and the Limbus. The Tibetan grazers and the missionary Lamas were perhaps the earliest immigrants to Sikkim in search of new pastures and converting people to their religion. They were followed by the traders in their permit of catering their goods.

It is also said that Tibetan peasants came in search of rice fields. In this process, a large number of Tibetan immigrated to Sikkim and played a major role in the State formation. Owing to their cordial relations with the Lepchas they institutionalised a monarchy in 1642 that was in power till the merger of Sikkim in 1975.

The third but the largest number of inhabitant of Sikkim is the Nepalese. It is estimated that 75 per cent of the total population of Sikkim is of Nepali origin. Nepalese settlement in Sikkim has proved to be a boom for prosperity, because the Nepalese were hard working and industrious people and made excellent cultivation and still continues to be one. The adoption of new methods for agriculture by exploiting virgin forests and espousal of terraced field cultivation by the Nepalese had radically changed the fate of Sikkim.[24]

However, the important factor which brought the Nepalese to settle in Sikkim was the rise of the *Gorkha* Kingdom in Western Nepal under the vibrant leadership of *Maharaja* Prithivi Narayan Shah. He had succeeded in establishing a new Kingdom of Nepal and filled the logic of unity and pride among the various tribes and united them under the Gorkha banner. In 1788-89, *Gorkha* General Jahar Singh made a surprise attack on Rhabdentse, the then capital of Sikkim. Since then, for some years Pemiongchi and the entire South Teesta tract paid rent to Nepal, until in 1815 the Nepalese were expelled by the British Government.[25] The number of the Nepali population widely increased in Sikkim after the Treaty of Tumlong 1861. At this point it appears that, the East India Company or later the British Indian Empire had strongly felt the need of cheap labourers to strengthen their economy and the paucity of this essential was supplied by neighbouring Nepal. As far as Sikkim was concerned the original inhabitants were mainly engaged in trading and herding activities and were not ready to provide labour services to the British for their new schemes. As a suitable alternative to this, British encouraged the Nepalese from Nepal to get settled in their dominions in India.

The Nepali community is composed of three different sub-cultural stocks. These are known as '*Tagadhari*' (Those who wear sacred thread), '*Matwali*' (Those who do not wear sacred thread and were in the habit of drinking alcohol or traditional liquor), and the '*Newars*'. The Brahmins and the Kshatriyas (*Bahun* and *Chettris* as they are known in Sikkim) of the Nepali society are considered as the '*Tagadhari*' people. Similarly, the other warrior stocks belong to the Mongoloid race of the Nepali community like *Rai, Limbu, Gurung, Tamang, Sherpa, Magar, Sunuwar, Bhujel* etc. are known as *Matwalis*. The *Matwali* also incorporates *Kamis*, *Damais*, *Sarkis* and other *Dalits* of Aryan stock as they too are fond of alcohol. The *Newars* had their own type of social order in which one can notice the existence of both '*Tagadhari' and 'Matwali'* elements.[26] These three groups were also mentioned as the *Gorkhas,* the *Kirats* and the *Newars*.[27] As soon as the Newars entered into Sikkim they thoroughly monopolised the copper mines and minting industries and they even emerged as the Nepali counterpart of the *Kazis* in Sikkim.

As stated earlier, the emergence of the Gorkha power under the leadership of King Prithivi Narayan Shah in Nepal, the Nepalese made numerous attacks towards the East and they clashed with the *Kirats* of Eastern Nepal and the Bhutias of Sikkim in the middle of the eighteenth century. With the unification of Nepal including the valley of Kathmandu by the Gorkhas in the middle of the eighteenth century, some of the Newars of the Kathmandu valley also migrated towards East. They settled in Darjeeling by the middle of the nineteenth century. Within a time, they entered Sikkim as the monopolists of the copper mines and minting industry.[28] The *Gazetteer of Sikkim* mentions about the track of Pacheykhani including the Bhotang mines belonged to Lakshmi Das Pradhan one of the earliest Newar *Thikadars*.[29]

Another important minority which constituted the Sikkimese society is the migrants from Indian plains. They are the people from States like Rajasthan, U.P., Bihar, Bengal, Punjab, Odisha etc. The *Marwaris* and the *Baniyas* have played an imperative role in the trade and commerce of the state while others have maintained themselves in academic and administrative spheres. Thus, Sikkim has served as meeting points of these above mentioned communities broadly known as the 'Sikkimese'.

The census report of 1891 is the first available authentic information regarding Sikkim's population. It has shown a total population of 30,458 inhabitants which included 5,762 Lepchas, 4,894 Bhutias and 19,281 Nepalese.[30] The rest 521 people have been categorised as the slaves and other miscellaneous groups. It is important to mention that, all such census were conducted in a haphazard manner as the first census made by H.H. Risley was made on the basis of race and caste. Likewise, C.A. Bell, the Political Officer who succeeded Mr White made a survey in 1910-11 according to the religion a subject professed. Similarly, the Administrative Report of Sikkim for the year 1921 has simply mentioned of having 81,721 people in the Kingdom of which 41,492 were males and 40,229 were females. Once again the census of 1931 was conducted on the basis of community.

Table 1.1: Temporal Changes in Population 1891-2011

Year	*Male*	*Female*	*Total*	*Sex Ratio*	*Decadal per cent Variations*	*Density of Population*
1891	11,589	10,563	22,152	912	NA	NA
1901	39,795	28,219	59,014	709	166.4	8
1911	45,059	42,861	87,920	951	48.98	12
1921	41,492	40,229	81,721	970	-7.05	12
1931	55,825	53,983	1,09,808	967	34.37	15
1941	63,289	58,231	1,21,520	935	25.42	17
1951	72,210	65,515	1,37,725	907	13.34	19
1961	85,193	76,996	1,62,189	904	17.76	23
1971	1,12,662	97,181	2,09,843	863	29.38	30
1981	1,72,440	1,43,945	3,16,385	835	50.76	45
1991	2,16,427	1,90,030	4,06,457	878	28.48	57
2001	2,88,217	2,52,276	5,40,493	875	32.98	76
2011	323,070	287,507	610, 577	889	13.86	86

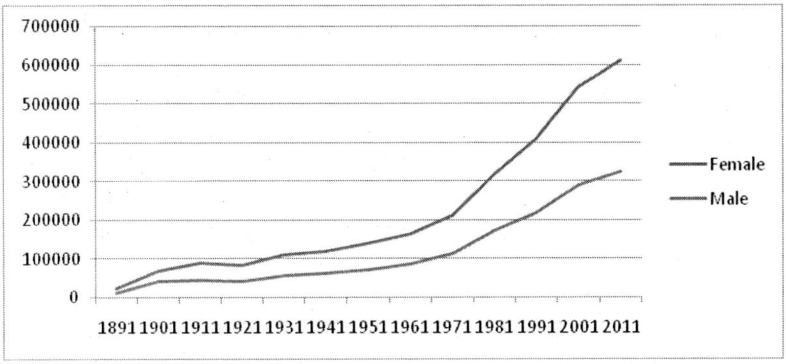

Source: Sikkim Study Series 2004, p. 58: Census of India 2001: Census of India 2011.

Graph 1.1: Temporal Changes in Population of Sikkim 1891-2011.

However, these entire censuses show an overwhelming increase in the Nepali population whereas the Bhutias and the Lepchas as has been at the same stage. According to Risley, Nepalis with 56 per cent (including Murmi) constituted majority of the population followed by the Lepchas (19 per cent) and Bhutias (16 per cent). There were other constituents like Khambus and slaves. More than a century later, the share of Lepcha population has gone down to 14 per cent whereas that of the Nepalese escalated to almost 70 per cent with the Bhutias constituting more or less the same proportion.[31]

The Bhutias and the Lepchas were all Buddhists but, nowadays the Lepchas are converting into Christianity, in spite of the fact that there are few Buddhists among the Nepalese population most of them are Hindus.[32] The Shakya Newars, Tamangs, and a couple of Gurung communities are Buddhists among Nepalese with a larger Nepali identity. The total numbers of religious institutions including monasteries, temples, mosques, and churches etc. are figured approximately 600. Nepali is the official language as well as lingua-franca of Sikkim and it is included in the VIII Schedule of the Indian Constitution.[33]

Culture

Sikkim was though, a British protectorate and even remained the same after their withdrawal from India, had remained for many centuries in splendid isolation. Sikkim's contact with India was very nominal and may be because of that many people in the plains of this country have not even heard of it. The term Sikkimese indicates a resident of Sikkim and has no linguistic or ethnological implication.[34] For the growth and development of a culture, religion, society, food and habits, manners and customs always play a key role. Hence, the culture of Sikkim is different from the rest of the country because of its distinct social set up and its isolation that it maintained in the past. It is an acculturation of three different cultures namely the Lepchas, the Bhutias and the Nepalese.

Broadly, there are two diverse cultures in Sikkim namely, the Hindu culture and the Buddhist culture. However, they run parallel in Sikkimese society. The Hindu culture which is followed by nearly 70 per cent of the total population is more appropriate to call as Nepali culture. Similarly, the Buddhist culture was implanted from Tibet long before shares similarities feature with the Sikkimese Bhutia culture.

In Sikkim, Buddha is being worshipped by a Brahmin as an incarnation of Lord Narayana. Similarly, a Buddhist Lama worships the Trinity of Brahma, Vishnu, and Shiva as the foundation pillar of his religion. A Brahmin spins the prayer wheel of the Buddhists and a Buddhist chants *sloka* of Vedas.[35] The local religious festivals are celebrated with a great enthusiasm by all the communities.

The different cultural stocks which were prevalent during the merger days are in the verge of decay today. They have forgotten their bitter past on which they held each other responsible for losing their country. Now Sikkim has been able to adopt a culture which is neither borrowed nor adopted from others. She is moving towards a novel and a universal culture i.e. the culture of amity and appreciation of every fabric of Sikkimese society.

Topography

Sikkim is absolutely a mountainous state, with a very few flat lands.[36] In the northern segments of the state are the high Himalayan peaks and acmes, at all times covered with snow. These snow covered mountains lies on the south of Tibetan plateau and play a role of natural shield for Sikkim. However, these very mountains contain certain important passes to get into Sikkim. The Chola ranges which form the eastern boundary of Sikkim with Tibet, contains the two important passes of Nathu-La (15,512 ft.) and Jalep-La (13,354 ft). Similarly, Singalila range, which forms the boundary between Sikkim and Nepal, contains the important pass of Chewabhanjang (10,320 ft). The highest peaks are Kanchenjunga (28,140 ft), Kinchinjhan (22,700 ft), Siniolchu (22,620 ft.) and Chomiomo (22,386 ft). Besides, there are some other large and small passes around Sikkim border. The Singalila range lies between Sikkim and Nepal acts as the natural boundary between these two territories.[37]

In Sikkim, there are mainly two prominent rivers-Teesta and Rangit. Teesta River originates from Lacha Lachung and Yumthang and passes through Chungthang, Singhik, Mangan, Dikchu, Singtam, and Rangpo and further from the Indo-Sikkim boundary it moves towards *Triveni* in Gorkha Territorial Administration (GTA) of West Bengal. Teesta is the longest and the largest river of Sikkim. Another significant river of Sikkim is Rangit and it flows from West Sikkim.[38]

Though, Sikkim is very small in terms of geographical area, it can be identified as the land of wide topographical contrast such as dense forests and audacious table lands, snow clad peaks, hills, dales shrubs, and grasslands. It would be appropriate to state as Kotturan says it is an artistic paradise as one can always behold here changing moods of nature in its catching forms and interplay of clouds sun shine, mist and shadow.[39]

Climate

The climate has great variations and every variety ranging from sub-tropical to temperate and arctic type types of climate can be noticed here. The rainfall is heavy and averages 137 inches a year at Gangtok, the capital.[40] The valleys and the hill regions, below 7,000 ft. from the sea level have the temperature of sub-tropical and humid type. However, the highlands above 7000 ft. up to 15,000 ft. have alpine type of climate.[41] Sikkim has its own climatic peculiarities caused by its geographical location, relief, and altitudinal variation. As such, temperature conditions vary from sub-tropical in the southern lower parts to cold deserts in the snowy north. If one feels hot at Rangpo at an altitude of 1,200 ft. from the sea level, he will find the temperature decreasing as he goes upward towards the highlands.[42] Sikkim lies in the direct path of the moist-laden South West Monsoon. So it gets a good rainfall, at times very heavy. In the lower Teesta valley the rainfall could go well above 150 inches a year. Higher up the monsoon has to penetrate through the high mountain walls, and so in the valleys of Lachen and Lachung the rainfall seldom exceeds 40 to 50 inches. Generally, there is rainfall between the month of May and November.

Flora and Fauna

Climate plays a vital role for the survival of any kind of flora and fauna. As it is known so far that, Sikkim is the land of trees and dense forest which are full of vivid creatures. The forests of Sikkim are not only lavish but are also charming which are considered as the homeland of various spices of flower and animals. Approximately 4,000 varieties of flowering plants and bushes are found including the rhododendron in various forests scattered throughout the State. About 98 per cent of the Indian species are found in the Himalayan region out of which 72 per cent are found in Sikkim.[43] In the sub-tropical lower valleys, several varieties of bamboos, ferns and tree ferns, mandamus and orchids are found.[44] There are about 480 species of orchids,[45] 30 species of rhododendron are available in Sikkim, which are eagerly sought by the botanists throughout the world. The *Gazetteer of Sikhim* has mentioned,

> "The orchid family is also extensively represented in Sikhim, there being from 350 to 400 species out of an estimated total of 5,000 for the whole world".[46]

Chandra nursery and Mainam nursery established at Rhenock Bazar and Namchi Bazaar in East and South Sikkim respectively are famous for exporting flowering plants of Dahlia, Orchid etc. all over the world. Recently, on 18th January 2016, newly found spices of orchids have been named after three important Indian stalwarts namely, Deen Dayal Upadhyay, Sardar Vallabh Bhai Patel, and the present Prime Minister Shri Narendra Modi, during organic fest organised by Government of Sikkim.

Because of its heavy rainfall, Sikkim is densely forested area and its forests are capable of yielding valuable timber. In the sub-tropical zone, which extends up to 5,000 feet, several varieties of ferns and tree ferns, *sal* and orchids are obtainable. Magnolias, conifers, larches and junipers, oaks, walnuts, silver fir, prunes etc. further beautify the landscape. The more gentle slopes at these high altitudes are often covered by a variety of beautiful flowers like the Primula which added a touch of glorious colour to the sombre grandeur of the lonely mountain sides. The floristic composition of the flora of the Sikkim Himalaya is unique of its kind.[47] Bamboo has a special value among the Sikkimese people, and most particularly it has a great importance among the Lepcha folks. They use it for building their homes, to make weapons, pots, mats, and flutes. The tender bamboo shoots are also used to prepare delicious items.[48] There are about twenty species of bamboos.

Though, a small state in area, Sikkim is quite rich in the field of wild life too. A wide variety of fauna occurs in this Himalayan state. Among the important wild animals that can be found in Sikkim are Panda, Musk Deer, Goral, Bear, Otter, Tiger, Leopard, Barking Deer, and Black Bear etc. At the altitude of 4000 ft. up to 11,000 ft the Himalayan Black Bear is found. At 9,000 ft. barking deer etc. are found and Tiger, Leopards, Wild Cats, Squirrels are found in the warmer regions. The musk deer from which *Kasturi* or musk, a valuable source of perfume is extracted is found in the higher elevations and rarely descends below 8,000 feet even in winter.[49] Similarly, over 500 species and sub-species of birds and over 600 species of butterflies have been catalogued by some naturalists in Sikkim. Multi-coloured Pheasants, Ducks, Eagles, etc. are chief birds that fly on the sky of Sikkim.[50]

Forest

Forest is an important source of livelihood for the people of Sikkim. Apart from the extraction of Timber, forest is, also the source of herbs and plants that have been traditionally used as medicine. Further, being a semi-tribal nature of the society, forest plays a vital role in the daily lives of the Sikkimese as they believed the jungles as the abode of various Gods and semi-Gods. It is probably due to its close affiliation with the forest, the erstwhile monarchy too had taken some innovative measures for the conservation of forest within their territory. *Maharaja* Sidkeong Tulku (Feb 1914-Dec1914), made certain amendments in the prevailing laws and encouraged his subjects for plantation of trees in waste lands. It was during his reign, reserved forests were categorised into two ranges namely, Eastern and Western, and they were kept in charge of the Foresters. It is worth to mention that, these forests were to be managed by the landlords as Forest Officers of their respective *Elakhas*. Strict rules and laws were adopted to abolish corruption from the forest resources and if a Forest Officer failed to execute his responsibilities accordingly were dealt with a heavier hand.[51]

Auxiliary, the traditional healing process which plays a permanent part among all the three ethnic groups of Sikkim itself is unique in its nature. The plants and herbs and the names of several Gods and Goddesses like *Jungali*, *Devi*, *Naag*, *Shimey- Bhumey*, *Ban Jhakri,* and *Lyam Lyamey* etc. confirms the close affinity of Sikkimese with forest and forest products. In the early 1970s, it was estimated that out of the total surface area of 7096 sq.km, Sikkim forest occupied 1,944.05 sq. km (27.4 per cent of the total area of Sikkim) excluding slip reserve and road reserve forest. The higher attention was paid in the northern zone, where forests occupied nearly 805.69 sq.km while in the stoutly cultivated eastern and western zones forests cover was only 527.59 and 610.7 sq.km, respectively.[52]

The existing customary forest laws associated to forest are still practiced in Sikkim even after her merger with the Indian Union. People have the right of free supply of timber and firewood from *Khasmal* land after obtaining formal permission from the concerned department. In *Gaucharan* lands the locals have the right of free grazing and collection of deadwood and fodder. However, owing to the degradation of forests and its resources, grazing in the government lands has been done away with in the recent years. For the protection of the wildlife and for a balanced ecological system, Forest Department of Sikkim made various rules for forest management under the Sikkim Forest, Water Courses, and Road Reserve (Preservation and Protection) Act 1988, and these are currently operational.[53]

Minerals

Several minerals are found in the state among them Coal, Copper, Sillimanite, Quartzite, Limestone, and Graphite is the most important.[54] The ores of Copper are widespread in Sikkim and are in Dalang beds. Dolomite, Garnet, Talc, and Magnet are of less importance. Two deposits one at Rangpo and the other near Dikchu are being explored. Besides, Coal, Limestone, Graphite, Iron, Garnet have been found in Sikkim. They are so small and not profitable that no sound works has yet been taken up in this direction to exploit the resources full. Sikkim is poor in minerals resources, yet a number of minerals like copper, zinc, lead, graphite, mica, and coal also occur in the State but they have not been adequately exploited. The Sikkim Mining Corporation is working in a copper mine at Rangpo only, while copper deposits have been discovered at many places in Sikkim.[55]

Industries

Sikkim in the last 41 years or so, as a state of Indian Union, has undergone a multifaceted socio-economic transformation in an attempt to align itself to the Indian economy. The mountainous terrain and isolated location of the state has however been an important in the absorption of the liberalisation process that has been sweeping the rest of the country.[56] During the monarchical era the industrial sector was not well developed in Sikkim. The prevalence of craftsmanship based traditional cottage industries dates back to time immemorial. A stated above, the Lepchas have a deep connection with the bamboos and they had shown their skill in bamboo-craft. The Bhutias excelled in ancient Tibetan practice of carpet weaving with striking shades and brilliant colours. On the other hand Nepalese are celebrated for the craftsmanship of their metal work, silverware, and wood-work. In 1955, the distillation of wine and liquors was one of the first modern industries, established at Singtam (East district). Another significant industry evolved during Royal Sikkim, was the Government Fruit Preservation Factory set up at Singtam in 1956. The Palden Thondup Institute of Cottage Industries was set up at Gangtok in 1957, for the development of traditional craftsmanship on Sikkim. Immediately after the merger, a rapid development of industries in Sikkim had taken place. The Directorate of Industries, established after the merger, has undertaken important measure such as the promotion of a feasible system of incentives and subsidies, financial and technical support and industrial training.[57]

In 1977, the Sikkim Industrial Development and Investment Corporation Limited (SIDICO) were set up as the state-level principal financial institution for the promotion and financing the industries.[58] The situation where there was no industry is changing and giving place to a number of industrial units. They produce such items as fruits, jams and juices, biscuits, other bakery products, beer, matches, washing soap, electric cables, watches, leather goods, and industrial jewels etc. At present, there are 929 industrial units have been registered in the small-scale sector. Unfortunately, only a small number of units are functioning, and rests have closed down due to many reasons.[59] Besides, these industrial units, many new pharmaceuticals industries are in its initial stage. To name them, Cipla, Sun Pharmaceuticals, Zidus, Alchem, McLeod etc. have started their production and many of others are in a pursuit to start their production at the earliest. Cottage industries such as weaving of carpets and blankets and manufacturing of copper ware, bamboo, and wooden articles are also operational.

Trade

The main exports from Sikkim are cardamom, oranges, tea, potatoes, apple, liquors, wines, handicrafts, canned fruits, and timber. The trade in the past has mainly been with Tibet through the passes of Nathu-la, and Jalep-la. When Chinese invaded these parts and sealed the borders, patterns of trade between the two countries from this boundary was greatly dwindled. But, from 6th July 2006, Nathu-la is reopened after 44 years. From Nathu-la, after the re-opening of old silk route, Sikkim exports 29 items to China, among them dry fruits, dry and fresh vegetables, tea, coffee, rice, tobacco, liquor, kerosene etc. are of importance.[60] Sikkim imports many consumer goods and manufactured goods from other parts of India. Food grains, beverages, cloth, cosmetics, electrical equipments, engineering goods, synthetic goods, chemical fertilisers, sanitary goods, paints etc. are the important articles imported into Sikkim.

Agricultural Production

Sikkim is an agrarian State and is the land of villages. Agriculture is the main occupation of the people and agriculture has a history of its own. By and large Sikkim's wealth is derived from agriculture and forests. The original inhabitants were not agriculturists and were living a primitive form of life based on shifting cultivation. Further, gathering of wild roots, fruits, hunting, and fishing were their means of livelihood. The Bhutias entered into Sikkim and started a semi-pastoral economy and sedentary farming. They plough only flat pieces of land available here and there. In the earlier days the shift cultivation was in vogue. The wasteful system of cultivation was viable in those days due to the immense availability of surplus land.[61] Settled agriculture stepped into Sikkim only with the arrival of the Nepali settlers. These sturdy, hardy, energetic, and innovative people cleared large tracts of wood lands and made the land fit for cultivation. It was the Gorkha people who brought cardamom seeds from Nepal to Sikkim.[62] Rice and maize are the main crops which are grown during the monsoon. The increase of population and the subsequent scarcity of cultivable land forced the people to settle down permanently at one place and to avoid the previous system of shift cultivation.

The nature of the terrain and varied climatic conditions greatly influenced agriculture in Sikkim. Maize, paddy, wheat, barley and buck wheat are the main cereals grown in Sikkim. Sikkim has the largest and the highest production of large cardamom in India. Cardamom and potato are the two important cash crops of the State. There is only one Tea Estate in Sikkim and it is located in Temi (South Sikkim) and is known as Temi Tea Estate. It was started in the 60's of the last century and is producing a high class of tea species. The tea estate extends over an area of 400 acres. Under Horticulture Department, large qualities of orange, guava, and apple are raised. Vegetables, pine apple, and banana are other cash crops of Sikkim. Some people have started to take keen in producing cinnamon and rubber plants. Paddy is another important crop of Sikkim.

Administration

From the administrative point of view Sikkim is divided into four districts namely, East, West, North and South. Gangtok, Gyalshing, Mangan and Namchi are the district headquarters respectively. Each district has two sub-divisions. Each has a District Collector and he is assisted by his deputy. Each district has a court with a judicial Magistrate. Sikkim has 447 villages and 9 towns till recently. The total Provisional Population of Sikkim as census of India 2011 stands at 607,688 out of which 321,661 are males and 286,027 are females representing a decadal growth of 12.36 per cent during the last decade 2001-2011. The sex ratio that is number of females per 1000 males in the state shows an improvement from 875 in 2001 to 889 in 2011. The density of population means total number of persons per square kilometres. According to provisional population calculated at the census of India 2011, the density of population per square kilometre has gone up to 86 as against 76 in 2001 with no change in the state area of 7,096 sq. km. The literacy rates reflect the economic and social condition of the state. The effective literacy rate for the Sikkim as per census of India 2011 is 82.20 per cent while it is 87.29 per cent for males and 76.43 per cent for females. In 2001 census, literacy rate for the total population was 68.81 per cent with 76.04 per cent for males and 60.41 per cent for females.[63]

There are *Panchayats* with elected representatives for the implementation of different schemes enunciated by the government at the grass root level. There are all together 94 numbers of Zilla Panchayat Wards, 163 units of numbers of Gram Panchayats, 452 numbers of Revenue Blocks. The total number of Assembly seats in the Legislative Assembly is 32, one seat in Lok Sabha and one seat in Rajya Sabha. The following table shows the district-wise administration in Sikkim.

The main resources of the revenue of the state government are forest, the Sikkim Nationalised Transport, land, house and excise taxes. Very few Sikkimese were engaged in trade and business. All trade and business are concentrated into the hands of the people hailing from the other states of India.

Geo-Politics

The relationship between the non-human environment and human behaviour has been speculated from time immemorial. Many attempts have been made by several individuals to explain and to predict the political behaviour of the people of a country and their relationships with reference to geographical factors. Such interpretations as the above are classified under the term Geo-politics.

Being a Himalayan state the geo-political situation of Sikkim is very important from the perspective of Himalayan studies. Keeping this fact in mind, the geo-political position, and the strategic importance of Sikkim can hardly be under mind. As Sikkim lies in the centre of the Himalayan border of India at one of the most vulnerable points, it constitutes a vital zone in her defence system.[64]

In the past, Sikkim played an important role in the formation of mutual relations between the two great powers of Asia i.e. India and China. It was a trade line between Indian sub-continent and China. The easy passes of Sikkim towards Chumbi valley of Tibet lead directly to the core region of Tibet around Lhasa. Therefore, the geo-political problems of Sikkim as one of the critical regions of the world can be analysed as an example of Geo-strategic location.[65]

Though, Sikkim merged with India in 1975 as its 22nd state, the strategic role which is played during its protectorateship has not at all decreased, rather, it has increased with respect to India. In the present context concerning Indo-China relations the strategic importance of Sikkim in India's security system cannot be miscalculated. Therefore, although small in size, Sikkim, the land of the Himalayas with all sort of geographical variation has become a point of high strategic importance and on the other she acquired significant historical importance.

Peasants' Resentments and Resistance (1914-1950)

Resistance of the peasantry is a universal phenomenon which is originated due to the suppression and exploitation from the mechanism and it is a human behaviour to defend him from the unnecessary encroachment or interference of the state. This book, an outcome of my PhD thesis submitted to Kumaun University in 2014, highlights several *modus operands* adopted by the Sikkimese peasantry to resist feudalism during World War period. To provide a clear sketch about Sikkim, Chapter One gives detail information about the State. Apart from rewriting what it has already been written, even if in an epigrammatic manner, Chapter Two has attempted to peep inside the early history of Sikkim before the Tibetans, in the light of new and fresh documents collected through different sources. Similarly, this Chapter also justifies Sikkim as a Tibetan protectorate. A detail study of Anglo-Sikkim relations, Nepalese Settlement, and its relation with independent India has been made in Chapter Three. Chapter Four illustrates about the introduction of new agrarian arrangement after the appointment of First British Political Officer. Chapter Five highlights about the hidden transcripts of peasants including other major causes for the resentment and resistance. Several forms of hidden transcripts of the rural lots have been observed in Chapter Six and study of folksongs has been made to understand the concealed feelings of the peasantry against monopolistic mechanism. Chapter Seven traces out the assorted modes of everyday resistance by the peasantry in the light of the collected data secured during field survey. Likewise, it also focuses on several forms of hidden transcripts of Sikkimese peasantry against feudal mechanism. Chapter Eight incorporates expansion of individual everyday resistance into a cohesive resistance and makes a sketch of pre-Congress rural Sikkim. Foundation of Sikkim State Congress and its achievements and popularity among the rural folks have been discussed in Chapter Nine. Chapter Ten examines sidelining of the rural issues from the purview of the political parties and their leaders.

Methodology

Being a part of my PhD research work, the data used in this book are from the fieldwork that I made during the course of my study. For the said purpose, data have been secured through different sources. Since the core issue of this study is related to the rural life of feudal Sikkim written documents have not copiously found. Apart from a few documents available in the State archives, Namgyal Institute of Tibetology and a private archive maintained by an enthusiast Ganesh Kumar Pradhan, I could not secure much related to the matter. Insufficiency of documents in the form of orders, letters, tax receipts, deeds, and agreements seemed to be the most challenging part of the research. As it is a known fact that, for the peasants, one loaf of bread is much more important than keeping and preserving records. Probably, owing to this mind set, I came across several instances of the neglecting attitude of the peasantry in maintaining records during field surway. However, even being illiterates, some of such peasants appear to be conscious about the importance of documents. They have maintained their family records since nearly a century in the form of tax receipts, letters, official notices, membership cards, ration cards and the like. Apart from such sources of information, I have to depend on the verbal sources from the descendants of the former 'flesh and blood' peasants. Few of the resisters were still alive during the field study that could substantiate me with the information about their mode of resistance and the then agrarian structure. However, it has been impossible to separate facts from their assumptions and postulations; the description that had seemed most trustworthy to me has been included in writing this book.

As stated, the real affairs related to the peasant resistance were not documented and since many of the protagonists of the resistance era died long ago, I have often had to rely on just a single piece of information. The information has been secured through personal interviews conducted in various schedules from October 2011 to February 2012. The field study has greatly supported me to understand many unheard and neglected aspects of Sikkimese feudalism through horse mouth information from the peasants. Since I was free to gather information from the elderly peasants scattered throughout Sikkim, I selected the villages where the number of such people was in a greater number. Therefore, villages like Gerethang, Chongrang, Labing, Lasso, Nesa in the vicinity of Tashiding in West Sikkim were selected. Similarly, villages in the vicinity of Uttarey, and villages under Soreng and Sombarey subdivision in West Sikkim were selected to find out the nature of peasant resistance in West Sikkim. In South Sikkim, villages like Denchung, Omchung, Nandugaon, Namchi, Dambudara, Assangthang, Sumbuk, and Timi Tarku were randomly chosen with a motive to get first hand information. Similarly, the surveyed villages of East Sikkim includes, Linkey, Parakha, Mamring, Manpur, Bering, Angkuchen, Dongrong, Aho, Kadamtam, Assam Lingzey, Marchak, Samdur, Rumtek, Ranipool, Setipool, and Namli.

Due to the devastating earthquake of 18th September 2011, it was a challenging task to visit North Sikkim for the field survey. Hence, few nearer and accessible villages like Bey, Gor, Lingzya and Passingdang were visited to find out the nature of peasant resistance in North Sikkim during feudal era. The total number of respondents in North Sikkim is only 50 that cover 14.28 per cent of the total number of 350 respondents. Owing to it, a very little information related to the issue has been gathered from these villages in North Sikkim. From each of the other districts, information has been secured from one hundred respondents that cover 85.72 per cent of the total respondents.

The data collected through the respondents shows a picture of male domination, as 267 respondents were males covering 76.28 per cent of the total respondents. The number of female respondents from the entire four districts was 83 that cover 23.76 per cent of the total 350 respondents. The major cause of the less participation of women was because of the social belief and practice. The female respondents were not the direct resisters as they were regarded as weaker sex and were never sent to carry loads and for other physical tasks. Hence, the information provided by the female respondents is from what they have heard and seen during the peak period of feudal exploitation.

The present study is based on the nature of peasant resentments and resistance during the reign of *Maharaja* Sir Tashi Namgyal (1914-1963) that covers time duration of both the World Wars. Hence, all the respondents were the old peasants of Sikkim who had witnessed the feudal exploitation and many of them had worked as wage free labourers in the said period. The number of respondents who had taken the pains of the notorious *Kalo Bhari*, *Jharlangi*, and worked as *Bethi Khetala* and *Kuruwa* porters is 68, who presently belong to the age group between 71 to 91 years and are considered as direct resisters in the study. This age group covers 19 per cent of the total respondents whereas the remaining constitutes respondents who were between 50-70 years who had also witnessed the cupidity of feudalism but not of a higher magnitude are considered as descendents of resisters in the study. Apart from peasants, the age group covering 81 per cent of the total respondents also incorporates the erstwhile *Mandals*, *Karbaris* and others like Sikkim Guards, Ex-Armies, teachers, and the like. Hence, majority of the respondents who had not experienced feudal pressure had grown up listening to the stories from their elders. Consequently, their information about the corrupt practices of feudalism cannot be overlooked. Among our respondents were 52 Lepchas (14.85 per cent), 50 Bhutias (14.28 per cent) and 240 Nepalese (68.57 per cent). A minority of the *Madhesias* (plain men) were also inquired about their involvement in the feudal system. There were 8 (2.28 per cent) *Madhesia* respondent. The *Madhesias* had been into the trade and commerce of the Kingdom after British took an upper hand in the administration.

Thus, in contemplation and observation of the aforementioned bits and pieces, this is an endeavour to peep inside the rural past of the erstwhile Himalayan Kingdom of Sikkim. As most of the historians are still engaged in venerating what is already glorified, the struggle and resistance of Sikkimese peasantry has not got its mention in the pages of history of Sikkim. Distress and pains of feudalism in the inaccessible villages, their troubles, their strategies in defending the feudal yoke, their folksongs, their hidden transcripts, grudge, and antipathy against feudal set up, their reluctance and resistance against the monopoly, their unanimity in combating feudalism, the hidden history with abominations against the feudal machinery are some of the issues that are so far neglected and have never been highlighted by a Sikkimese historian. The everyday forms of resistance, varied techniques adopted by the Sikkimese peasantry to tackle feudal yoke and their ideas of rancour, in a tacit and concealed manner among the rural souls, their odium against repressive State and its machinery, their violent ideas to dismantle feudal edifice, and eventually their assimilation with a political organisation for a far reaching change are some of the important areas that are studied meticulously while compiling this book. Further, these unwritten and unembellished events also break the impression that, only the written documents can suffice the historical growth and expansion. Such unrecorded piece of information too speaks in a voluminous manner that, history even resides in the hamlets, remote pockets, inaccessible villages, in sludge, and in dusts.

Notes

1. Census of India 2011, Paper 1, Series 12, p. 38.
2. The Resolution of April 10th 1975 Sikkim Assembly Section "A" states, The Institution of *Chogyal* is hereby abolished and Sikkim shall henceforth be a constituent unit of India enjoying a democratic and fully responsible Government.
3. India Today online '*Sikkim world's number 1 place to visit in 2014, says Lonely Planet*' New Delhi, October 29, 2013 Date of access 17th December 2013.
4. The Constitution (Thirty Sixth Amendment) Act, 1975 Dated 19th April 1975 www.indiacode.nic.in Date of access 25th December 2013.
5. Risley, H.H., *Gazetteer of Sikhim* (1894), Bengal Secretariat Press, Calcutta, p. 19.
6. Sikkim- A Concise Chronicle, Royal Wedding Committee, Sikkim Darbar Press, Gangtok, March 20th, 1963, p. 16.
7. The Resolution of April 10th 1975, op cit, pp. 1-2.
8. Pathak, Bishnu, '*Federalism: Lessons from India*' p. 12 www.transnational-perspectives .org Article 429 Date of access 17th December 2013.
9. Sandberg, Graham (1888), *Manual of Sikkim Bhutia Language, Dejang-Ke*, Oxford Mission Press, Calcutta, p. 3 Introductory Note.
10. Kotturan, George, (1983), *The Himalayan Gateway- History and Culture of Sikkim*, Sterling Publishers Pvt. Ltd. New Delhi, p. 7.

11. Van de Putte was the only European traveller who had ever completed the journey from India through Lhasa to China during Mughals. He returned to India, also passing through Lhasa and was an eyewitness of sack of Delhi by Nadir Shah in 1737.
12. Markham, Clement R, *Narratives of the Mission of George Bogle to Tibet, Journey of Thomas Manning to Lhasa*, (1896) Trubner and Co. Lud Gate Hills, London. P. Introduction IXIV.
13. Bhadra, Madhumita (1992), *Sikkim- Democracy and Social Change*, Minerva Associates Pvt. Ltd, 7-B, Lake Place, Calcutta, p. 1.
14. Lepcha, Nayan Tshering, "*Sikkim Ek Khoj*" (Sikkim a Search), *Kanchenjunga*, Nepali fortnight Journal, Gangtok, Vol. 6, No. 26, 15th November 1965, p. 70.
15. Kotturan, (1983), op cit, p. 18.
16. Temple, Richard (1887), *Journals kept in Hyderabad, Kashmir, Sikkim and Nepal*, Vol. II, W.H. Allen and Co, Waterloo Palace, Pall Mall, London, p. 163.
17. Thakur, R.N, (1988), *The Himalayan Lepchas*, Archives Publishers and Distributors, New Delhi, pp. 25-26.
18. Lyangsong Tamsang (2008), *Rangnyoo Rangeet, Lepcha Folklore and Folksongs,* Sahitya Akademi, New Delhi, p. 3.
19. *Ibid.*
20. Rev. Graham J.A (1897), *On the threshold of Three closed Lands-The Guild outpost in the Eastern Himalayas*, Edinburg R and R Clark Ltd. London, p. 50.
21. Basnett, Lal Bahadur, (1974), *Sikkim- A short Political History,* S. Chand and Co. (Pvt.) Ltd. New Delhi, p. 7.
22. Turner, R.L., *A comparative and etymological dictionary of the Nepali language*, (1980), p. 484. Allied Publishers, New Delhi.
23. Grover, B.S.K, (1974), *Sikkim and India-Storm and Consolidation*, Jain Brothers, New Delhi, pp. 5-6.
24. Basnett, (1974), op cit, pp. 42-43.
25. Risley op cit, (1894), p. 19.
26. Subba, J.R (2011), *History and Culture of Sikkim*, Gyan Publishing House, New Delhi, p. 416.
27. Sinha, A.C. (2008), *Sikkim: Feudal and Democratic*, Indus Publishing Company, New Delhi, p. 35.
28. Sinha, A.C. *Politics of Sikkim*, Thomson Press India Ltd., New Delhi, pp. 7-8.
29. Risley op cit, (1894), p. 69.
30. *Ibid*, p. 27.
31. Lama, Mahendra P, (et al. 2004), Sikkim Study Series, Vol. I Department of IPR, Government of Sikkim, Gangtok, p. 59.
32. Kotturan, (1983), op cit, p. 14.
33. Lama (et' al 2004), op cit, p. 3.
34. Joshi, H.G., *Sikkim Past and Present,* (2004), Mittal Publication, New Delhi, p. 65.
35. The Indian *Vedas* are known as *Rikje* in Tibetan and the Lamas make recitation of it in all the major Pujas in the monasteries. Likewise, they too worship Wangchuk as Shiva, Tsangpa as Brahma, and Kyapjuk as Vishnu the supreme trio of Hindu trinity.

36. Basnett, (1974), op cit, p. 3.
37. Kotturan, (1983), op cit, p. 7.
38. Dhamala, Jaya, *Sikkim Ko Itihas* (History of Sikkim), (1983), Shyam Prakshan Darjeeling, p. 12.
39. Kotturan, (1983), op cit, p. 18.
40. Rao, P. Raghunanda, *Sikkim- The Story of its integration with India* (1978), Cosmo Publication, New Delhi, p. 2.
41. Kotturan, (1983), op cit, p. 18.
42. Sankrityayan, Rahul, *Darjeeling Parichaya* (1950), Adhunik Pustak Bhawan, Calcutta, p. 193.
43. Lama (et al 2004), op cit, p. 178.
44. Rao, op cit, p. 2.
45. Lama,(et al 2004), op cit, p. 184.
46. Risley op cit, (1894), p. 85.
47. Grover, (1974), op cit., p. 3.
48. Kotturan, (1983), op cit, p. 11.
49. *Ibid.,* p. 12.
50. Basnett, (1974), op cit, p. 6.
51. Administration Report 1913-14, I, p. 5.
52. Mahendra P. Lama-Sikkim Human Development Report 2001, Published by Esha Beteille, Social Science Press, 69 Jor Bagh, New Delhi, p. 55.
53. "Sikkim Development Report, 2008", Planning Commission, Government of India, New Delhi, Published by Academic Foundation, New Delhi, p. 170.
54. Lama, (et al 2004), op cit, pp. 153, 154, 155.
55. Dewan, Dr. Dick B. (2012), *Education in Sikkim, An Historical Retrospect Pre-merger and Post-merger Period*, Published by Society for the Procurement and sales of books, In aid of school Development (Fund), Tender Buds'Academy. Pedong, Dist. Darjeeling, (WB), p. 55.
56. Lama, (et al 2004), op cit, p. 60.
57. Lama (2001), op cit, p. 69.
58. *Ibid*, p. 70.
59. Lama, (et al 2004), op cit, p. 60.
60. *Sikkim Today*, April-June 2006, Vol. VI, No. 2, Department of IPR, Government of Sikkim, Gangtok.
61. Kotturan, (1983), op cit, p. 11.
62. Basnett, (1974), op cit, p. 43.
63. Paper 1, Series 12, Census of India 2011.
64. Sengupta, N. *Sikkim: State Government and Politcs* (1985), Sterling Publishers New Delhi, p. 45.
65. Pradhyumna P. Karan and William M. Jenkins, *The Himalayan Kingdoms; Bhutan, Sikkim, and Nepal*, D. Van Nostrand Company, Princeton New Jersey, p. 57.

Chapter 2

Sikkim under the Tibetan Patronage (1642-1861 AD)

The early history of Sikkim before Tibetan ascendancy is obscure and ambiguous. The only source to understand the same are very limited and are in the form of oral traditions and religious literature which are inadequate to narrate the early history of Sikkim. The anecdotes and tales passed through generations are insufficient to reconstruct social, political, and economic life of pre-Namgyal Sikkim. In the same manner, Lepcha and Buddhist texts, full of anecdotal accounts and stories prove challenging to the scholars to separate facts from the fictions. Buddhist texts, mostly written in Tibetan proves another adversity for the foreign and Indian scholars for an appropriate study of ancient history of Sikkim. Narration points out the presence of other tribes like Limboos, Lepchas, and Magars in Sikkim before the Tibetans. However, due to the scantiness of historical documents and testimonials one cannot reconstruct history of these petty regions in a chronological manner. Lack of native evidences in the form of monuments and testaments, absence of chronology, confusing dates, and events, perplexing tales and chronicles are some of the important issues for a neglecting glance to Ancient Sikkim from the Social Scientists. Possibly, owing to these impediments, the early history of Sikkim has not so far premeditated in a radical and historical manner.

Mutually, the Indian and Western scholars suppose that Sikkim was not a single political unit till 1642, when Phuntsog Namgyal was consecrated as the first *Chogyal* of Sikkim at Yoksam and given the eight auspicious symbols and seven objects of a *Chakravatien*.[1] Thcy seem accurate in their perceptive about the absence of a single political unit in pre-Namgyal Sikkim. The established tales and accounts also replicate the same sketch of Sikkim being ruled by several tribes in different junctures. Information of *Mun Boongthing* (the Lepcha Priest) reflects that Lepchas were the most primitive and autochthons race of Sikkim and it was being governed by

Thekong Adek, Rujo-Melong-dang, Tarvey *Panu*, Tarsong *Panu*, Tar-Eng-*Panu* and *Panu* Mun Solong.[2] Similarly, as per postulation of Dahal, the Lepchas had a magnificent history that may go beyond the reign of Chandragupta Maurya (c.322-298 B.C). He argues, Lepcha King Pohorthak *Panu*, with a motive to assist Chandragupta Maurya sent his army to Takshashila (Taxila). However, after considering the noxious weapons of the Lepcha force, Chanakya, the Prime Minister, and advisor of the Mauryan Emperor find them fatal if they had to fight against them. Thus, he got reluctant to take them in their crease and killed the Lepcha *Panu* with the help of a poison girl. It is also stated that, later the Lepchas, with an intention to avenge the death of their King, had invited Chanakya for a feast and was forced to drink *Jaad* (local brew) and in a fully drunken stage he was left in a jungle where he was killed by a tiger.[3] Likewise, Chemjong too believes political antagonism between the Mauryas and the Kirati highlanders and holds Chankya responsible for the entire anomalies. He argues, following to an agreement, the Kiratas had rendered their support to the Mauryas to uproot Nandas from Pataliputra, and after their sway over Nandas, the North Eastern part was given to the Kiratas with sovereign rights. However, soon a rift in the alliance became inevitable as the Kiratas had continued their policy of expansion and had reached till Dinajpur in modern Bengal. With a motive to put a permanent cease on Kirat expansion, the Kirat King was murdered with the help of a poison girl, and according to the Hindu convention[4], the deceased King was made to succeed by his eldest son Malayaketu. However, owing to a threat of his death, Malayaketu escaped from his Kingdom and in his absence, on the advice of Chanakya, Chandragupta Maurya appointed one of his brothers Bairochak to the Kirat throne. On the day of coronation, Bairochak too became a victim of a plan murder executed by Chanakya.[5] Similarly, Singh also holds a view that the Kiratas had played a major role for the installation of Chandragupta Maurya as the ruler of Kusumapura or Pataliputra.[6] It is to be noted that, numerous hill tribes having Mongoloid features are branded as Kiratas in the ancient Indian scriptures like Vishnu Purana, Ramayana, Mahabharata, and the like and that includes Lepchas, the Bhutias, and all other hill tribes too. Therefore, it is impossible to ascertain with whom the Mauryas had their alliance and who got deceived from the dangerous designs of the Mauryan Prime Minister Chanakya. Though, these theories seem logical, they lack chronology, and on the other hand, despite several attempts of the scholars, the cause of Chanakya's death is clouded with mystery and is not revealed exactly so far.

Likewise, the accession and succession of the Lepcha *Panus* or Kings are not chronological and one can notice a long interlude in their succession.

This loophole naturally puts a historian into a serious doubt about the authenticity of the affair. Though, whatever the historicism may be, there is no doubt that the Lepchas, before the Tibetans had a glorious past; however, due to some unknown reasons it was not documented. Sceptically, whatever the Lepchas had, were systematically destroyed by the Tibetans during the course of Tibetanisation of Sikkim. It is believed that Mun-Solang *Panu* (1595- 1642) the last Lepcha *Panu* had witnessed consecration of the first *Chogyal* at Yoksam in 1642.

Apart from the Lepchas, it is also believed that, Limboos were ruling a part of Sikkim in the west, before the Tibetans. The literary meaning of Lim-bo is people residing in the border areas, which may include all other populace as well, who had their inhabitation in the borderlands. However, in this context, Limboos were the people of Limboowan,[7] a territory bordering Western Sikkim, that had 16 *Thums* or districts and three districts of Limboowan included some areas of modern West Sikkim. Therefore, to emphasize about the existence of a *de facto* Limboo principality in present West Sikkim does not give a valid impression. Yet, we cannot ignore the presence of a significant Limboo population in these areas of present West Sikkim in this phase of time. It also comes into surface that, a Lepcha *Panu*, probably Mun-Solang, had granted a land grant, through a *Sanad* to one Ambal Singh Suphakaat (Subba) of Angpho village with a condition to serve the country with devotion and loyalty without creating chaos and commotion.[8] Similarly, Subba believes that, the Limboo headman used to be called as *Subahs* during this perplexing phase of Sikkimese history.[9] However, the designation of *Subha* for a Limboo headman appears to be a later development in the history of Nepal. *Subha* is a Persian word meaning a district or a province and therefore an in charge of a district were known as *Subbas* in the Nepali Court. According to the Nepali interpretation, the process of designating *Subba* to an individual was known as *Subhangi* and for this only influential and affluent could get the privilege of enjoying the status. Available documents indicate that, the sobriquet of *Subha* before the Shahs was designated by Hindupati Sen, a Magar King[10] of Bijayapur.[11] Therefore, the same sobriquet was continued through a Royal Order by Shah King Prithvi Narayan after the unification of Nepal.[12] Conversely, in the Sikkimese context the word '*Suphakaat*' as mentioned by Dahal, sounds very different from the word *Subba* that is commonly used by the Limboo village headmen to identify them. Thus, if we have to study the relevance of the terminology of *Subba* from Nepali perspectives, it is evident that, the aforementioned hypothesises lack reason. However, as claimed by Dahal, if the process was an initiation of Lepcha *Panu* along with the title of *Suphakat* or *Subba* to a Limboo man, than undoubtedly, this evidence would serve in a broader manner not only to deal with pre-Namgyal Sikkim but, may also suffice to identify evolution of the office of *Subba* in the entire Eastern Himalayan region. Hence, keeping this inference apart, during the pre-Namgyal period, it may be believed that, Limboo people of Sikkim were known as Tsongs which is also evident from an agreement made between the Lepchas, Bhutias, and the Tsongs known as Lho Mon sTsong gsum of 1663. The Limboos had 10 sub-divisions, known as *Thars* and they call themselves as 10 Limboos or *Dus Tharey* or *Dus* Limboos.[13] After Tibetan sway over Sikkim, they too were given lower level administrative posts known as *rTa Sa*, who was a village level official responsible for collecting the taxes in a village.[14] Correspondingly, some of the influential Limboos were also accorded with land grants by Tensung Namgyal[15] and few of them were also appointed as Nagzen (courtesan)[16] and were also allowed to use *Chyabroong* (drum) in their festival and religious ceremonies.[17]

Along with Lepchas and the Limboos, another tribe known as Magar too had their stronghold in a part of West Sikkim. The prevalence of Magar *Dzong* or Magar fort at Mangsari in Soreng subdivision of present West Sikkim confirms their presence over those tracts. However, it appears that the Magar principality too was a petty area controlled by a head of the tribe. If we have to believe on the accounts of Dahal, Magars were the part of militia called Gorakhnathgan initiated by Guru Gorakhnath, with a mission to protect the entire mountainous region from the Mughals mayhem. Such three contingents of Magar force were deployed in Sikkim by the State of Bijayapur (presently in Nepal) and they were stationed at Rhenock, Mangsari, and Kurseong.[18] This illustration indicates about absence of a genuine Magar principality and points towards the existence of Magar fortifications that were supervised and monitored by the Magar State of Bijayapur. Upon the Tibetan aggression, the Magar Chief, fought against them to oppose their supremacy, and was killed in the battle. To avenge her husband's death, his wife, invited Tibetans for the last rite of her husband. It is said that, many Tibetans were killed due to the consumption of poisoned brew served at the orders of the *Rani* during cremation.[19] Folktales of Magar *Dzong* at Mangsari indicate that to save herself and the heir, the *Rani* fled on horseback along with her baby son. However, she could not save herself from the Tibetan fury that compelled her to jump off from a water fall leading to her death. The place where she got killed is still known as Rani *Kholsa* or the Queen's rivulet. The perilous event suggests that the Magars, unlike the Lepchas and the Limboos, did not want to accept overlordship of the Tibetans and resisted till the end. However, their resistance against the Tibetan turmoil got futile after the death of their Chief and their petty region got submerged into the 'Tibetan Ocean' then flooding all over *Mayalyang*.

The Namgyals

The Lepchas as mentioned above are the original inhabitants of Sikkim and they claimed to be autochthones of Sikkim proper.[20] However, it comes to the surface that, much before sixteenth century, Tibetans started to come towards Sikkim in search of land and pasture. After the lapse of time, a prince of Minyak House[21] went on pilgrimage where he was given the name of Guru Tashe. At Lhasa he was instructed by Jo Vo Rimpoche to proceed Southwest to find a country called *Demo-Song*. It is believed that Guru Tashe along with his son had helped the Sakya hierarch in building a hall of Purul-Pahi-Lha-Khang monastery, which was to be kept standing on the support of four immense wooden pillars. According to the prevailing legends, the task was made single-handedly by Guru Tashe's son and for this he was given an epithet of *Jo-Khey Bumsa*.[22] White holds the view that *Jo Khey Bumsa* was one of the descendents of Ti-Son-Desen who ruled over Tibet in AD 730.[23] Being childless, *Khey Bumsa*, was advised by his Lamas to seek blessings from a Lepcha wizard Thekong-Tek, who was also the Chief of the tribe, at Gangtok. Determined in his motives, *Khey Bumsa* crossed into *Rong* country to meet the Chief, from whom he secured blessings of having three sons.[24] Apart from this, it is also said that, Thekong Tek had further blessed *Khey Bumsa* with regal duties by his descendents in the territories of Sikkim.[25] Following to it, they initiated a blood brotherhood at Kabi Lungtshok in North Sikkim to signify the unification of Tibetans and Sikkimese *Rongs*.[26] All the three blessed sons of *Khey Bumsa* migrated to Sikkim and got settled. The youngest son of *Khey Bumsa*, Mipon Rab occupies prominence for having four sons, among them Guru Tashi was the youngest. The eldest son of Guru Tashi is known as Jowa Apha.[27]A Son of Jowa Apha was named as Guru Tenzing who had a son Phuntsog Namgyal who was later consecrated as the first ruler of Sikkim.[28]

The race of the former Sikkimese rulers is said to be gNyans caste but there is no genealogical record on the issue. As per the narratives, Sikkimese rulers happened to be the descendants of a ruling family of Kings of Tibet Khri-srong lDeu-bTsan.[29] Mythological interpretation indicates their Indian origin that maintains of having their kingdom in Eastern India. In the course of time, as it is said, Indian ancestors of the Namgyals migrated to Minyak in Tibet and ruled over the province for 25 generations.[30] Therefore, in the light of aforesaid traditions, it is sometimes believed that the *Rajas* of Sikkim had Indian origin by descent through the first King of Tibet Nah-ThiTsanpo.[31] If the mythological account is believed to be true then we can consider race of the Namgyals as Indo-Tibetan race until a detail anthropological study is made.

Foundation of the Kingdom of Sikkim

The most remarkable personality of the Namgyal house seemed to be Phuntsog Namgyal (1642-1670) who is credited as the founding father of Namgyal dynasty. Arguably, he was born in 1604 and passed his early days near Gangtok. The three Tibetan Lamas namely Lat-tsun Namkha Jigmed, Khatog Kuntu Bzangpo and mNag-bDad Sem-pa Phuntsog Rinzing[32] consecrated him as the first ruler *Chogyal* or *Dharma Raja* of Sikkim in 1642, investing him with spiritual authority along with the temporal. Very little is known about the achievements of the reign of Phuntsog Namgyal. Probably, he was chiefly engaged in subduing or winning over the chiefs of petty clans inhabiting the country east of present day's Nepal. The *Lho Mon gTsong gsum* Agreement between the Bhutia, Lepchas, and the Limboos of 1663 gives a clear sketch to a war that got eventually into the court of Phuntsog Namgyal, the protégée of Tibetan Lamas.[33] The agreement further states that all the locals must accept the overlordship of Phuntsog Namgyal.[34] It is said that with the help of Lat-tsun Lama, Phuntsog overcame one Sintu Satichen or Mangal Gyelpa, who is considered as a Lepcha.[35] With the Tibetan assistance, boundary of the newly created Kingdom was fixed as Dibdala in North, Walung in West, Titalia in the South and Tagong La in the East.[36] Likewise, in all probabilities, the signatories of the *Lho Mon gTsong gsum* were allowed to maintain the control of their respective areas in lieu of their submission to Phuntsog.[37]

Chogyal Phuntsog Namgyal instituted the first centralised administration on the advice of the leading Tibetan Lamas. The territory of Sikkim was divided into twelve *Dzongs* or districts. Each district was placed under Lepcha *Dzongpons* or governors.[38] As the *Dzongpons* were appointed from the leading Lepcha families, the ministers in the council *Kaleons* were appointed from selected twelve families from the twelve Bhutia clans.[39] The *History of Sikkim* also affirms that *Chogyal* Phuntsog Namgyal had received a letter of his recognition as the ruler of Sikkim from the Dalai Lama with an assurance of Tibetan protection during external aggression.[40] Thus, it appears that, with the signing of *Lho Mon gTsong gsum* Tibetans secured assistance of native Lepchas and Limboos in planting a 'Tiny Tibet' in the land of Kanchenjunga.

It is palpable that a feudal bureaucracy was established in Sikkim after the accession of *Chogyal* Phuntsog Namgyal. However, it is interesting to note that instead of creating new landed aristocrats; Phuntsog Namgyal incorporated existing elites into the State, probably, with a motive of consolidation. The earliest initiative of the first Buddhist King of Sikkim later proved fatal that paved its way for a struggle between the aristocrats and the crown. Nevertheless, his successors tried to reaffirm their power over the landed aristocrats but the struggle to maintain a balance in power relationship between them continued till arrival of the British. After interference of the paramount power, the landed aristocrats kept the figure of temporal and religious head aside and got their upper hand in administration of Sikkim that eventually led to the birth of peasant resistance in the erstwhile Himalayan Kingdom.

Tensung Namgyal (1670-1696) succeeded his father as the Second *Chogyal*. Immediately after his coronation, the new ruler shifted his capital from Yoksam to Rhabdentse and built a palace there. It is believed that, during his reign, the region witnessed a fierce battle between Sikkim and Limboowan principality. In this ambiguous battle, as the period is blurred, it is believed that Tensung subdued the Limboo King Yo Yo Hang and married a Limboo princess. This matrimonial alliance played a significant role in pacifying the two hostile families of the region. Other seven Limboo ladies who accompanied the *Rani* as maidens were taken as wives by the highest *Kazis* and ministers of Sikkim.[41] It is also said that the name *Sukhim* was given to the State by this Limboo Rani; earlier, it was known as *Denzong* or *Demasong* only.[42] This very word *Sukhim* later got distorted and began to be pronounced as Sikkim.

Matrimonial alliance appears as a time pertinent policy adopted by Sikkim to forbid any external and peripheral threats. Probably owing to this fact, *Chogyal* Tensung married three ladies from three different regions of Bhutan, Tibet, and Limboowan. From the available sources, it is evident that he remained busy in strengthening the toddler Kingdom of Sikkim. In all probabilities, to curb internal danger from the nobility, he reduced the council of ministers from twelve to eight.[43] Though, Tensung got succeeded in sealing Sikkim from both external and internal threats, signs of internal intimidations appeared immediately after his death. He died in 1696 leaving behind a disputed throne involving his son and daughter as its aspirant. The dispute ultimately culminated into a war of succession between his daughter Pende Ongmo and the heir apparent Chakdor Namgyal. As the matter got complex, due to her maternal relations with the princess, Bhutan supported the claim of Pende Ongmo. The unspoken and unseen tug-of-war for power between the crown and landed aristocracy appeared in a detectable mode during this course of event. The Sikkimese court comprised of leading Lamas and landed aristocrats got divided into pro-Bhutanese and pro-Tibetan section to affirm their claims on the Sikkimese throne. Mullard presumes, after the defeat of Bhutanese, the pro-Bhutanese aristocrats of Sikkim were dispossessed of their landed estates. Some of these estates were donated to the principal monasteries whereas others were bestowed upon newly ennobled families.[44]

The War of Succession and the Bhutanese Incursion

The war of succession had undoubtedly invited a hazardous situation for the newly established Kingdom of Sikkim. Further, it had a deep impact in the Sikkimese polity that ultimately delayed accession of Chakdor Namgyal (1700-1717) for four years. As discussed, Chakdor's step sister Pende Ongmo, considering herself as legitimate heir to the throne, provoked Bhutanese to invade Sikkim and attack her step brother.[45] The teenaged *Chogyal* could not stand before the invaders and fled to Tibet via Ilam, leaving his territories at its own fortune.[46] As the safety of the King was ensured, Sikkimese Generals had dealt the Bhutanese in a rigorous way. In a fierce battle Karma Dargye, a Sikkimese General had killed his Bhutanese counterpart, later he was rewarded with the position of *Phyag mdzod* (Chancellor).[47] However, Sikkimese resistance could not last long and the invaders captured the Capital Rhabdentse that remained under Bhutanese for eight years.[48] *Sikkim- A Concise Chronicle* states that during his asylum in Lhasa, *Chogyal* Chakdor distinguished himself in Buddhist learning and Tibetan literature.[49] Dhamala indicates that due to his merit and calibre, the Sixth Dalai Lama of Tibet appointed him as the State Astrologer.[50] It is also believed that, the King was allotted the estates of Padi Dzong, Nagartse Dzong, Tinke Dzong, and Gyalkharnangpa as *Jagir* by the Tibetan Government.[51] Eventually, with the mediation of Tibetan government, the Deb *Raja* of Bhutan withdrew himself from Sikkim.[52] Through a Letter, the Tibetan Government convinced Bhutanese that they were the parent figures of Sikkim and all of them should always have healthy relations.[53]

After the intervention of Tibetan government, *Chogyal* Chakdor Namgyal returned to Rhabdentse in 1707.[54] As a reward for Karma Dargey's valour against the Bhutanese, a land grant was made to him through a *Sanad* at Bermiok and Barthang that led to birth to another influential aristocratic family known as Brag dkar pa in Sikkim.[55] Chakdor founded the great monastery of Pemiongchi, and he is also credited with the popularisation of a Sikkimese dance known as *Rongcham* which is performed by the local warrior class. He also studied Lepcha language and introduced a new script for it.[56] Under his reign, he introduced several changes in administration and directed that the second of every three sons of a Bhutia family must be ordained a monk of Pemiongchi monastery.[57]

It is worth to mention that while *Chogyal* Chakdor re-established as the ruler of Sikkim the consternation with his step sister Pende Ongmo was not yet over. She was still looking for an opportunity to overthrow Chakdor and to grab political and administrative power. Therefore, in 1716, she conspired with a physician when the King being sick was convalescing at Ralang hot springs. At the orders of Pende Ongmu, the physician opened *Chogyal's* veins that led to his death. However, the conspiracy soon revealed and she was brought under punishment. Following this, Pende was strangled at the orders of *Durbar* and her corpse was burnt at a place called Pende Laptse at Namchi.[58] Lama Jig-Med Pao, who accompanied Chakdor during his retreat from Tibet, became regent in the name of *Chogyal* Gyurmed Namgyal.

Commencement of Tibetan Regency

Nothing could be secured from the war of succession apart from instability and insecurity germinated through the mouldy seeds of jealousy and distrust. After the conclusion of whole episode Gyurmed Namgyal, a minor, was coroneted as the King in 1717. In the due course, appointment of regent Jig Med Pao led to multiplication of Tibetan influence in the Sikkimese Court. In 1721, *Chogyal* Gyurmed married Mingyur Dolma a daughter of Mindoling abbot, a fugitive in Sikkim due to Tartar Mongol's invasion.[59] However, due to some unknown reasons, the *Chogyal* shifted himself from the palace to Di-Chhen-Ling monastery.[60] It is also said that Gyurmed did not find feminine magnetism on the queen and never had any relations with her.[61] Even after the prolonged war of succession, threat of internal rebellion was yet to be terminated. During the reign of *Chogyal* Gyurmed Namgyal, Tishe Bidur, a Lepcha subject, claimed himself as an incarnation of Guru Rimpoche (Guru Padmasambhava in *Sanskrit*) became an eyesore to the Kingdom. With the assistance of a Magar Raja, Bidur tried to rebel against the State, though; his motives behind the rebellion are not known.[62] However, intentions of Bidur were severely crushed by Yuthing Desit who fought a long battle against Bidur and killed him along with all the followers at Chakung.[63]

After the rebellion, with an idea of building a pathway between Di-Chhe-Ling (where the *Chogyal* was living) and Rhabdentse palace, the *Chogyal* engaged himself with building schemes. Throughout this period, it is said that, he harassed the Limboos of neighbouring Limboowan. Continuous suppression of the Limboos resulted into the breaking off their allegiance with Sikkim. Sad with the death of his regent and fed up with all conspiracies and instabilities, *Chogyal* Gyurmed Namgyal disguised himself as a religious mendicant and left for pilgrimage to Tibet. The new circumstances also discouraged and disheartened the queen at Rhabdentse and she also decided to proceed towards Tibet. Later, the King was convinced by the Tibetan Government for his return to Sikkim. The process of land grants remained continued in the reign of Gyurmed Namgyal as well. In 1730, through a *Sanad*, he made grants to Pemiongchi Monastary at Phulbari in the Sikkimese lowlands.[64] However, individual land grants to the aristocrats are not known during his reign.

It is believed that, the King fell ill in 1733 and during his sickness; he disclosed that a nun Nyer Gaden from Sanghachelling, was pregnant from him and that his heir would be born to her. Apparently, a son Namgyal Phuntsog was born to the nun soon after the death of Gyurmed Namgyal.[65] *Chagzod* Tamding, the treasurer of Gyurmed Namgyal, opposed the idea to install new born from a nun as the King as he considered him to be an unnatural heir.[66] Lack of an acceptable heir to the throne resulted in the division of Sikkimese court into Bhutia and Lepcha faction that finally led to exile of the baby King for a brief period.

Usurpation and Appointment of Rabden Sarpa as Regent

The 'controversial' son of a Sangachelling 'nun', Namgyal Phuntsog (1733-1780) had to fight with adversaries since the day of his succession. The unstable political situations in Sikkim soon encouraged *Chagzod* Tamding, a Bhutia aristocrat and the treasurer of Gyurmed Namgyal to take control of the Kingdom. In this venture, Tamding was supported by a number of leading Bhutia aristocrats like Gelong Rinzing and Norbu. He practically ruled Sikkim for nearly three years from 1738 to 1741 therefore he is also referred as *Gyalpo* Tamding. To avert danger from the Tamding faction, *Chagzod* Karwang took the young Namgyal Phuntsog into exile.[67] In the course of time, rebellion of the Lepcha aristocrats headed by *Chagzod* Karwang forced *Chagzod* Tamding for an asylum in Tibet.[68] Tamding's request to the Tibetan Government to reinstate him to his previous position went unheard. Meanwhile, *Chagzod* Karwang too made a representation to Tibet with a request for the appointment of a Tibetan Regent. Consequently, virtually eliminating all the claims of Tamding, the Tibetan Government appointed Rabden Sarpa in 1747 to act as a regent in Sikkim.[69] Appointment of the new regent marks a turning point in the revenue history as annual taxation was introduced by him in the form of grain wine.[70]

The period of Namgyal Phuntsog also marks the beginning of uprising from petty subsidiaries. Most important of such uprisings took place from the side of the Magars.[71] *Sikkim- A Concise Chronicle* states that, being subordinates of Sikkim King, the Magars asked permission from Sikkim Court to install the son of the deceased Chief. The Tibetan Regent, Rabden Sarpa, refused to fulfil leading the Magars to seek Bhutanese protection.[72] The dissenters were annoyed in such a manner that they even made a plan to conquer Sikkim and to bring it under Bhutan.[73] However, the plans of Magars could not materialise but, it is evident that owing to an unbending act of the Tibetan regent Sikkim had lost one of its faithful allies. Similarly, in or about 1752, a Tsong uprising took place under the leadership of Sing-sa-Gyal, but it was successfully tackled by *Chagzod* Karwang.[74]

Pleased with the services of *Chagzod* Karwang and his son *Chagzod* Chogthup Tibetan Government had rewarded with lands at Rhenock in Sikkim.[75] On the other hand, entire property of usurper *Chagzod* Tamding was confiscated and transferred to Dzogchen Lama and Khanchen Rolpai Dorji as their annual allowance.[76]Amidst these internal commotions, Bhutan invaded Sikkim in 1770. However, the Lepchas and the Bhutias put up a joint front and defeated Bhutanese in the battle of Teesta. After the defeat of Bhutanese, negotiations were made at Rhenock and both parties agreed to eschew war and finalised and accepted their present borders.[77]

The boundary tension did not end with Sikkim. Soon it started experiencing a new threat from Nepal borders. The rise of Gorkha Kingdom under the leadership of *Maharaja* Prithivi Narayan Shah was a new threat to Sikkim. In 1775 to after the Tibet-Nepal war, treaty between Tibet and Nepal was concluded in which Sikkim Nepal boundary was also determined. However, terms of the treaty were soon violated by the Gorkhas and in late 1775 they invaded Sikkim, however, due to the Tibetan assistance under Depon Patsal, they could not succeed in changing territorial limits.[78] This was followed by several minor skirmishes and the same were heroically defended by Sikkimese forces. It was during this course, Lepcha leader *Chagzod* Chogthup earned epithet of *Satrajeet* (Victor of Seventeen battles) from his Gorkha opponents. *Chogyal* Namgyal Phuntsog died in 1780 and was succeeded by his eleven year old son Tenzing Namgyal.[79]

The reign of *Chogyal* Namgyal Phuntsog can be considered as a period of tussle and scuffle between Lepcha and the Bhutia aristocrats in which the former had been able to maintain their supremacy with mediation of Lhasa. However, process of rewarding land grants to the pro-state and confiscation of estates of the antagonistic was still maintained by the State. The Bhutia aristocrats belonging to the Tamding faction who supported him against *Chagzod* Karwang were dispossessed of their landed estate that is evident from the elimination of Gelong Rinzing (supporter of *Chagzod* Tamding) from his estate.[80] In the administrative aspect, it appears that, Namgyal Phuntsog continued policy of his ancestors to interweave all other elements under his banner to avert any internal threats. A notification issued in 1779, states that *rDo mig pa* (a Limboo) was given the authority to collect taxes at a place called Da Lad by *Chogyal* Tensung Namgyal and according to it; the descendents of Limboo were still executing same charges conferred upon them by the *Chogyal.*[81]

The Gorkha Invasion

Chogyal Tenzing Namgyal (1780-1793) was born in 1769 and upon his father's death was coroneted as the sixth consecrated ruler of Sikkim in 1780. He married Anyo Gyalum, daughter of Lepcha aristocrat *Chagzod* Karwang and the royal couple had a son Tsugphud Namgyal in 1785.[82] Sikkim experienced sense of insecurity, instability, and invasions during the entire period of *Chogyal* Tenzing Namgyal. As stated, by the last quarter of the eighteenth century, Sikkim experienced Gorkha menace under the leadership of *Maharaja* Prithivi Narayan Shah who is also credited with the unification of Nepal. The Gorkha Empire was continuously extending towards East and was an emerging threat for the Sikkimese frontier. Through shrewd diplomacy and annexation, Prithivi Narayan Shah had been able to carve out an extensive empire in the west of Sikkim. Many tribes and shattered principalities were merged into the Gorkha Empire. Gorkha became a *synonym* for the peasantry which came under the Gorkha banner and Kathmandu emerged as the capital of the new Kingdom.[83] *Maharaja* Prithivi Narayan Shah died in 1775, leaving much of his projected mission unfinished. Upon his death he was succeeded by his son, *Maharaja* Simha Pratap Shah who continued the policy of his father and persuaded the unfinished agenda. He soon annexed the Limboo and the Khambu principalities of Eastern Nepal and was turning his attention towards Sikkim that boarders Limboowan in Eastern Nepal. As stated before, there had been many raids from Nepal, but, those attempts were foiled by the Sikkimese and the Gorkhas were unable to change the territorial limits.[84] In 1788-89, one more attempt from the part of Gorkhas was made. Under the leadership of General Jahar Singh they crossed Chiabhanjyang pass and made a shocking raid at Rhabdentse. The capital was captured without any resistance.[85] *Chogyal* Tenzing Namgyal and his family fled hurriedly and got asylum in Tibet.[86] In the mean time, another band of the Gorkhas under Purna Alley captured Southern Sikkim through Ilam.[87] Similarly, another Gorkha force, under Damodar Pandey, re-enforced the Gorkhas and made harassing raids throughout the country.[88]

After the raid at Rhabdentse, and seizure of the capital town, Gorkhas became the real masters of Sikkim beyond Teesta. Thus, until 1815, Pemiongchi and all the inhabitants of the south Teesta tract were obliged to pay tribute to Nepal.[89] In 1790, *Chogyal* Tenzing Namgyal went to Tibet seeking help from Tibetan Government against any future Gorkha invasion.[90] Within a year or so, Gorkha army invaded Tibet and sacked Tashilhunpo monastery that lead to Chinese intervention.[91] Consequently, Chinese instructed the Sikkimese General to coordinate with them during the Gorkha invasion of Tibet[92] and also instructed further to invade Nepal if the Gorkhas invaded Tibet.[93] Conversely, amidst such a tough Chinese protection Sikkim did not make any aggression against the Gorkhas although the latter were defeated by the Chinese and were forced to make an ignominious treaty in 1792.[94] The Gorkhas signed the Sino-Nepalese Treaty (1792), from which Sikkim got a small portion of her lost territories, however, was obliged to pay tributes to Nepal.[95] *Chogyal* Tenzing Namgyal died in Lhasa in 1793 and his minor son Tsugphud Namgyal was crowned as the Seventh consecrated *Chogyal* of Sikkim in 1793.[96]

Anglo-Sikkim Relations and the Kotapa Affair

Chogyal Tsugphud Namgyal (1793-1863) came to power when the seat was shaky with not much territory to rule or prestige to stand on. Effectively, the Sino-Nepal Treaty of 1792 had reduced the Kingdom to a small principality. Comprehending the feeble phase, few leading Sikkimese officials like Regional Heads and General Officer of Chumbi requested Sikkim Government not to increase taxes from their respective areas.[97] However, process of granting lands to the influential was maintained in the reign of Tsugphud Namgyal.[98] It was a period when Gorkhas were extending their Kingdom in the Eastern Himalayas whereas the British seemed busy in strengthening their position in the North Indian plains. The British East India Company wanted to extend their trade in the interior of Tibet, as the latter was supposed to be rich in gold and *Kasturi*.[99] To achieve their covetous dream of securing Tibetan trade, British were naturally interested in Sikkim, as one of the possible routes to Lhasa laid from there. The reign of *Chogyal* Tsugphud Namgyal witnessed Anglo-Gorkha war of 1814-1816 that took place due to the border disputes originated long back in 1801.[100] Exchange of letters between the East India Company and *Chogyal* Tsugphud Namgyal substantiates a squared planning against the Gorkhas by them. Such letters also suggest weaponry support from East India Company to Sikkim to paralyze Gorkha menace at the Eastern front of the Himalayas.[101] As almost half of her territories in the West were taken over by the Gorkhas, Sikkim at this juncture seemed enthusiastic in supporting East India Company. To actualise her long desire to chase away Gorkhas from her borders, Sikkim had also obtained armaments from the East India Company.[102] Amidst these strategies, it appears that, Sikkim had a diminutive role to play in the Anglo-Gorkha war as the war was mostly fought in the Western front. Thus, with an infinitesimal role of Sikkim, East India Company defeated the Gorkhas in the War due to their edge on superior weaponry and war strategies. Information from the Chinese officials to the *Chogyal* regarding withdrawal of the Gorkha troops from Sikkim after the War indicates an affable relation of Sikkim with both the northern and southern big giants.[103] After the war, *Chogyal* Tsugphud Namgyal was invited for a meeting by the Governor General to Calcutta. However, the meeting between Governor General and the *Chogyal* could not be made and it was attended by a representative of Sikkim.[104]

The Treaty of Titalia of 1817 restored Sikkim most of its traditional areas[105] and with its espousal, boundaries between Sikkim and Nepal were laid along Mahanadi and Mechi rivers and the Singalila range. A little later, however, some more territories were handed over to Sikkim these territories also included tract of Nepalese Morang which is evident from the tax receipt belonging to 1819.[106]

However, troubles of Tsugphud Namgyal were not yet over. A serious quarrel arose between the *Chogyal* and his maternal uncle *Chagzod* Bolek. The *Chagzod* or the Minister had allegedly used 'Red Seal' and misappropriated public money to satisfy his personal desires. The matter began to take a serious turn by the year 1819, and it needed intervention of the *Kazis* and the Lamas.[107] Amidst process of reconciliation, the *Chogyal* issued an order to kill *Chagzod* with his family members in 1826.[108] Bolek's cousin, Yug Dathup fearing a similar consequence, fled from Sikkim and took refuge at Unthoo in Nepal with some 800 followers.[109] Intended to a bloody revenge, the Kotapas (the relatives of *Chagzod* Bolek or the exile Lepchas) with the Nepalese aid, began insurrection, and committed several raids in Sikkim.[110]

Tsugphud Namgyal with no other option pleaded Tibetan Government to intervene and to settle the border issues between Sikkim and Nepal.[111] In an another instance, people of Gro gZhi made a petition in 1831 to the *Chogyal*, asking for replacement of their representative with one of the Kotapa brothers in order to regain peace between the two.[112] In addition to this, in a letter to the Tibetan Government, *Chogyal* alleged the Kotapas for preventing Tibetan representatives from travelling to Sikkim and also accused them for destroying the property of around 3000 Sikkimese.[113] On the other hand, Tibetan Government insisted Sikkim to make a decision to either declare a war against the insurgents or sue for peace.[114] The Kotapas were later extradited to Sikkim on Tibetan negotiation with the Nepalese Government and they were pardoned by the *Chogyal*. However, due to their dispute with Khangsa Dewan, who purportedly had threatened and persecuted them on their way to Ilam, did not retreat and continued harassing raids. The disillusioned Kotapas, actively supported by the Gorkhas of Eastern Nepal, made such incursions an everyday event. Once again,

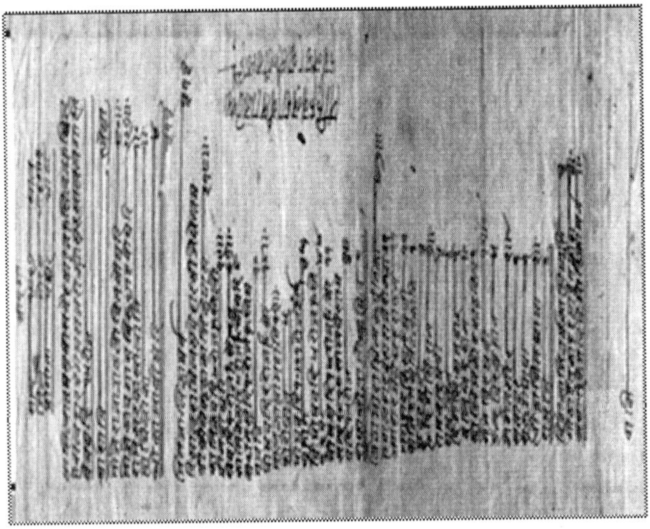

Figure 2.1: Details of the tax collected by the Sikkimese from Morang dated 1819. Namgyal Institute of Tibetology.

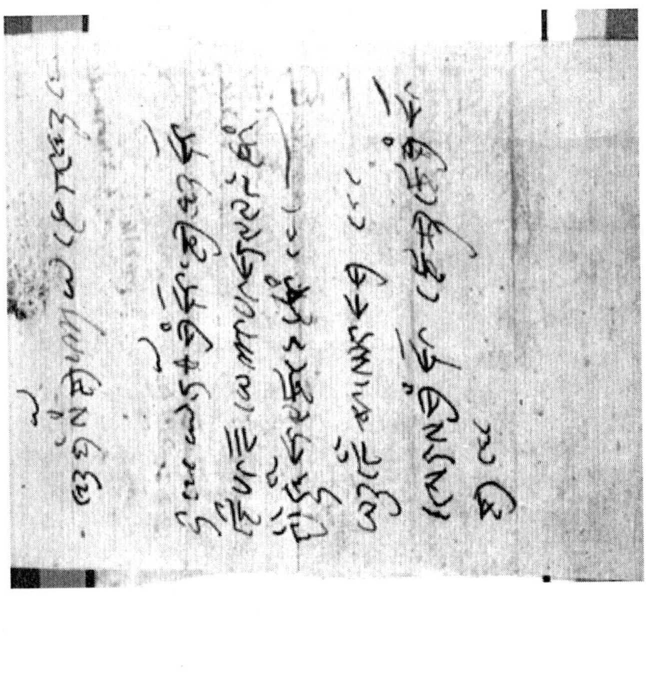

Figure 2.2: Noting related to the tax collected from Morong in Lepcha Language for further procedure. Dated 1819, Namgyal Institute of Tibetology.

to get rid of such raids and incursions, Sikkim Government notified Tibetan Government with an appeal to help Sikkim in establishing a pleasant relation with the Kotapas.[115] It is thus evident that the Kotapa episode intimidated *Chogyal* of Sikkim who was in a serious threat of being invaded by the Gorkhas. The frightened and perplexed King communicated Panchen Lama of Tibet apprising about chaos created by the rebellious Kotapas and had also ask him to protect against Gorkha invasion.[116] Conversely, amongst several notifications from Sikkim, the Tibetan Government maintained a deep silence to resolve the affair that led to an enlargement of prevailing antagonism for a longer yard.

On the other hand, Gorkhas were in high spirits to provide asylum to the rebellious Kotapas and consequently the rebels were given a pleasing treatment.[117] They were given a land grant by Nepal Government as an endowment from which they could collect land revenue and were also bestowed with the judicial rights.[118] It is necessary to mention here that, the regions of Ilam and Morang were paying their taxes to Sikkim until 1778 however, due to the Gorkha invasion in these parts there was a split in the payment.[119]

However, the affectionate attitude of Nepal Government towards the Kotapas led to disputes between Sikkim and Nepal in 1827 over Unthoo, a small hill situated on the east of river Mechi. Annoyed with the Tibetan response, *Chogyal* Tsugphud Namgyal on the other hand requested the Governor General Lord William Bentinck for arbitration. Accordingly, the Governor General sent Captain C.A. Lloyd and G.W. Grant in 1828, to investigate and settle the disputes. The deployment of these two officials for the investigation of Unthoo dispute marks the beginning of protective influence of British power in Sikkim.

Reign of Tsugphud Namgyal also noticed the loss of Darjeeling district by Sikkim to the British East India Company in 1835. Tsugphud Namgyal granted Captain Lloyd a deed, giving the hill of Darjeeling for a sanatorium to the East India Company out of friendship to the Governor General; but, with the condition that boundary dispute would be favourably resolved and that an equivalent land would be given in substitute.[120] However, taking a budge ahead, the Sikkimese King asked for revenue from Darjeeling area and even warned the British to leave the place if they were unwilling to pay.[121] This led to a misunderstanding between *Chogyal* and Deputy Commissioner of Darjeeling Mr Campbell. Adding fuel to the fire, Sikkimese authorities arrested a person Bhir Shing tsug rta ri from Morang upon which Mr Campbell had shown his dissatisfaction and opined that the prisoner should be released.[122] The matter got extra complex when

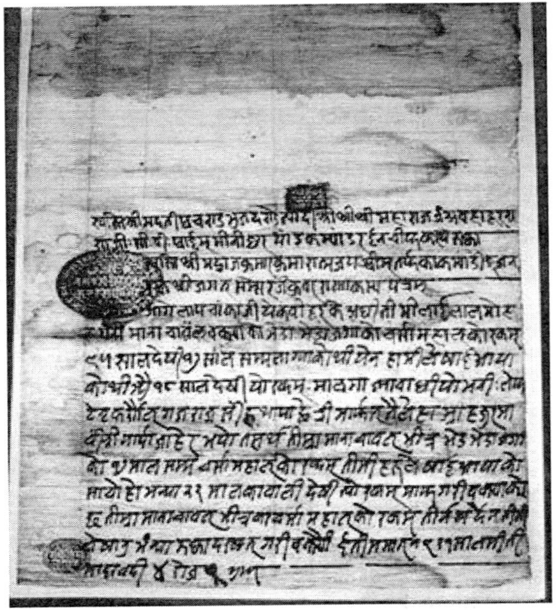

Figure 2.4: Letter of Maj.Gen. Janga Bahadur Rana the Prime Minister of Nepal to Lepcha Kazi *of Ilam confirming the exemption from the payment of revenues of his estate granted to him by the Nepal Government. Dated Maguh 9th 1921 Vikram Samvat (23rd January 1870 AD). Credit: Miss Jennifer Bentley.*

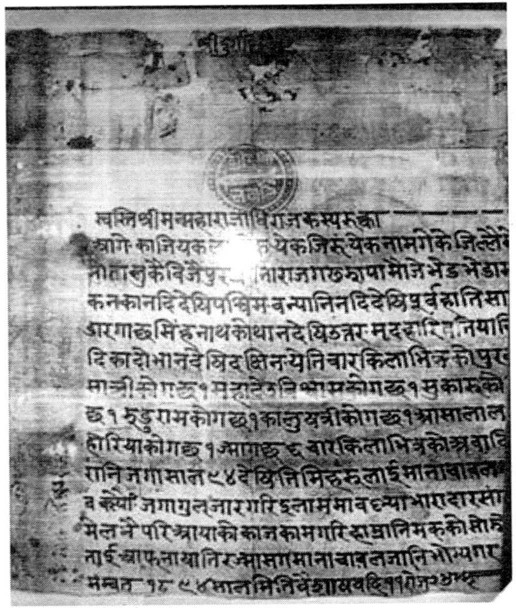

Figure 2.3: Letter from the Maharaja *of Nepal to the Kotapas with a grant of an area or* Mana-Chamal *that corresponds to East of Banyani till Hathisar Gach in Eastern Nepal. Year* Vikram Samvat *1884 (1827 AD) Credit: Miss Jennifer Bentley.*

Tsugphud Namgyal appointed a *Dewan* or Chief Minister, named Tokhang Namguay or Thokhang Namgyal alias *Pagla Dewan* in 1847, who was considered by the East India Company as a Tibetan of a strong anti-British feeling. The depressing Anglo-Sikkim relation was further depreciated with the arrest and imprisonment of Dr Campbell and Dr Hooker. The *Journal of Asiatic Society of Bengal* suggests that Dr J.D. Hooker, a distinguished British botanist, had obtained prior permission of the Governor General, Lord Dalhousie, and the *Chogyal* of Sikkim was supposed to felicitate his journey to Tibet. However, not complying with the permission of the Governor General, Sikkimese *Dewan* caused him excessive annoyances and obstructions.[123] Therefore, in order to assist Dr Hooker, Dr Campbell made his trip to Sikkim in September 1849 after obtaining permission of the President of the Council of India. Correspondence between the people of Lachung and Government Officials also suggests that a formal complaint was made by the natives of Lachung to the Sikkimese Officials objecting the visit of Europeans.[124] However, in spite their reluctance; the Sikkim Government had directed the people of Lachung to allow the duo to conduct their research without disturbances.[125] Conversely, after crossing Chola Pass on 7th November 1849, the duo was debarred from getting into interior of Tibet and retreated to Sikkim and got arrested at the hands of *Dewan* Thokhang Namgyal.[126] After the release of the botanists, in 1860, whole of Darjeeling and Morang were annexed. Another expedition followed next year, forcing Sikkim to get into a treaty in 1861 and with this treaty annexation of Darjeeling was confirmed. The treaty which consisted of 23 Articles was signed between Asley Eden on behalf of Earl Canning, Governor General in Council and His Highness Sidkeong Namgyal, the Crown Prince on behalf of the *Chogyal* of Sikkim on 28th March 1861 at Tumlong Palace.[127] According to the Treaty, Sikkim was opened for free trade with India. Sikkim also agreed to render all possible help to the British in their efforts to develop trade with Tibet. Likewise, *Dewan* Namgyal, the architect of all troubles was banished to Tibet. The *Chogyal* of Sikkim began to be addressed as the *Maharaja*.[128]

It has to be noted here that the Sikkimese had a strong resentment against such iniquitous treaty and hegemonic attitude of the British Government and they alleged that ₹ 46,000 annual revenue of Darjeeling was stolen by the British.[129] Similarly, Sikkim also had a grievance regarding the failure of Campbell to delimit the border between Sikkim and Darjeeling.[130] Likewise, after the Treaty of 1861, the Sikkimese Court seemed more concerned about the border security and considered casualness in the border as the main reason of the British expedition of Sikkim.[131] Tsugphud Namgyal died in 1863.

The long reign of almost seventy years made Tsugphud to come across a variety of adversaries. However, he had been able to tackle all of them with the Tibetan assistance. Tsugphud's enormous Tibetan expectation met a severe blow when the Tibetans refused to help him to settle the dispute arose in 1827 over Unthoo between Nepal and Sikkim. Therefore, he approached British Government for intervention leading to the opening of gates of Sikkimese administration for British interference. However, the practice of pleasing with land grant to the pro-state elements remained static paving way to the birth of several aristocratic families. The family of *Chagzod* Karwang who played a prominent part in subduing *Chagzod* Tamding and suppressing Kotapa rebellion was credited with a large land grant. His five sons were granted estates in their own name and further four estates were granted to his other descendents[132] escalating the significance of land both among the aristocrats and the peasants at the highest level.

Thus, it will not be an exaggeration to articulate that from the signing of *Lho Mon gTsong gsum*, (1663) till the treaty of Tumlong (1861) Sikkim was practically engineered, guided, and protected by Tibet. It is evident that, Kingdom of Sikkim was established by Tibet, with Tibetan assistance her boundaries were fixed, and at the whims of Tibet her policies were formulated. For almost two centuries, every affair, either bigger or smaller was formulated with the consent of Tibetan Government. From the very day of the establishment of Namgyal dynasty, it emerges that, Tibet had come forward to protect the interest of Sikkim. In the course of its establishment, the Limboos, without much tussle accepted their supremacy and came into terms. However, the Magars resisted, consequently they were subdued with the assistance of Tibet. Even the trivial threats like the threat of Mangal Gyelpa and *Chagzod* Tamding were averted with the help of Tibetans. The chaos created by the usurpation of *Chagzod* Tamding was eliminated with the appointment of Rabdan Sarpa, a Tibetan, as regent. Similarly, for the larger menace it is obvious that, Tibet had always played an imperative part to protect the Sikkimese interests in general and Namgyals in particular. The Bhutanese invasion was nullified with the mediation of Dalai Lama and the baby King Tenzing Namgyal got asylum in Tibet during Gorkha invasion. In fact, whenever the perilous situation arose, almost all the Sikkimese rulers had sought for asylum from Tibet and the latter had gladly facilitated Sikkim. Even during the Kotapa affairs, Sikkim sought Tibetan help for her defence and when Tibet did not pay attention she was compelled to knock the doors of East India Company. The involvement of British to settle Kotapa affair led to loss of Darjeeling that ultimately paved way to Sikkim to get closer to British. Apart from asylum and protection, Sikkimese Kings were allotted *Jagirs* by the Tibetan Government in Tibet.

Likewise, some instances refer to the allotment of such *Jagirs* to the Sikkimese officials in Sikkim by the Tibetan Government. Therefore, the period from the establishment of Namgyal dynasty till the conclusion of Treaty of Tumlong may be consider as the period of Tibetan patronage over Sikkim.

Notes

1. *Maharaja* Thotub Namgyal and *Maharani* Yeshey Dolma (un-published type script 1908, translated by *Kazi* Dousansup) *History of Sikkim*, p. 19.
2. Lepcha, Sonam Rinchen, (2002) *The wealth of Sikkim,* Mayal Muluk House of Treasure and Citi News, Gangtok, p. 58.
3. Dahal Dharnidhar, (1984) *Sikkimko Rajnaitik Itihaas*, (Political History of Sikkim), Subba Prakashan, Gangtok, p. 2. He has referred *Chunakh Aakhen* an ancient Lepcha text to substantiate his hypothesis.
4. According to Chemjong, the Kiratas were converted to Hinduism by Chanakya however, later on they abandoned their faith on Hinduism owing to the intrigues heaved upon them by the Mauryan Prime Minister. The adoption of Hinduism by the Kirats in this period is evident from the names of their Kings like Bajdev, Devasankh, Sankhdev, Deva Bhiksuk, Chemjong, pp. 24-27.
5. Chemjong, Iman Singh (3rd Edition, 1982) *Kirat Itihaas*, (History of the Kiratas) Prakash Printing Press, Vishwanath Gali, Banaras, pp. 25-26.
6. Singh, G.P. (2008) *Researches Into the History and Civilization of the Kirâtas*, Gyan Publishing House, New Delhi, p. 450.
7. Limboowan is derived from a Limboo word Li-bu-aan meaning a place captured with bow and arrow. It is believed that, the Limboos got their settlement in this area by defeating the Lhatso Mong, a group of Tibetan invaders, with bow and arrow and thus their principality got its name as Limboowan. Dahal, p. 13.
8. *Ibid*, p. 13, According to him the Limboos were granted Land deeds in 16th century through an agreement having 'Laal Mohor' or Red Seal by the Lepcha *Panu*.
9. Subba, J.R (2008) *History Culture and Customs of Sikkim*, Gyan Publishing House, New Delhi, p. 2.
10. According to the opinion of others, Bijayapur was a feudatory State of rulers of Palpa and were Thakuris by their birth.
11. A Laal Mohor (Red Seal) issued in Vikrama Samvat 1837 (1780 AD) in the name of Shah King mentions '*Aghi Hindupatile bakseko Subhangi saraha haamile pani nagara nishan maan maryada panchakhatbahek aafna ambal bhitrako Subhangi gari bakseu*' meaning we too have granted the *Subhangi* in our dominion as granted earlier by the Hindupati indicates the process of granting *Subhangi* was existed even during the reign of Sen Kings of Eastern Nepal, from the archival collection of Bharat Thunghang a descendent of erstwhile Subba of Chha Thar, Bancharey, Dhankuta Nepal.
12. In a letter to his commanders fighting against the Limboowan principality, King Prithvi Narayan Shah has used the word *Subba* to address the Limboos

as '*Limbu Shrengyaka Subbale Manna aayaako*' meaning We have come here to appreciate the Limbus of Shrengyaka as the Subbas. Year, Vikrama Samvat 1835 (1774 AD), from the archival collection of Bharat Thunghang a descendent of erstwhile Subba of Chha Thar, Bancharey, Dhankuta Nepal.

13. Chemjong, (1982) op cit, p. 30.
14. *bcu dpon gi lag 'dzin* a document issued to the sub village leader (*bcu dpon*) to have control over the tax collection in his region. Iron Monkey year, 7th Month 9th Day, PD/1.1/045, Namgyal Institute of Tibetology.
15. Land grants made to Samhang Thi at Nyosakambur above Sherdang with a condition to serve the country by abiding him with the convention and usages of the State. The grant also forbids the entry of the refugee of Solokhumbu (Sherpas?) to the allotted areas. Year 1665, Wangdu Phudang Palace, Rhabdentse (Dahal, p. 14).
16. Appointment Letter to Thopa Singh Dabyong Patuk as a courtesan with a condition to support and advice the Government, Year 1733, Wangdu Phudang Palace, Rhabdentse (Dahal, pp. 14-15).
17. Approval letter to Yupa Singh to use Chyabrung during religious and festive occasions, Year 1742, Wangdu Phudang Palace, Rhabdentse (Dahal, p. 15).
18. Dahal (1984) op cit, p. 16.
19. Namgyal and Dolma (1908) op cit, pp. 4, 5.
20. Rao, P.R. (1978) Sikkim-*The story of its integration with India,* Cosmo Publication, New Delhi, p. 3.
21. Basnett, Lal Bahadur, (1974) *Sikkim- A short Political History,* S. Chand and Co. (Pvt.) Ltd. New Delhi p. 13.
22. Risley H.H, *Gazetteer of Sikhim* (1894), Bengal Secretariat Press, Calcutta, p. 8.
23. White, John Claude (Printed in India 1971) *Sikhim and Bhutan- Twenty One years on the North East Frontier 1887-1908*, Vivek Publishing House, New Delhi, p. 16.
24. Risley, (1894) op cit, p. 8.
25. Basnett, (1974) op cit, p. 13.
26. White (1971) op cit, p. 16.
27. *Ibid.*
28. Risley, (1894) op cit, p. 8.
29. Namgyal and Dolma (1908) op cit, p. 9.
30. *Ibid,* p. 11.
31. Risley, (1894) op cit, p. 05.
32. *Ibid,* p. 8.
33. *Lho Mon sTsong gsum* Agreement, Year 1663, translation, Dr. Saul Mullard, and Hissey Wongchuck, PD/1.2/001, Namgyal Institute of Tibetology.
34. *Ibid.*
35. Risley, (1894) op cit, p. 10.
36. Namgyal and Dolma (1908) op cit, p. 20.

37. Mullard, Saul and Wongchuk Hissey (ed) (2010) *Royal Records: A Catalogue of the Sikkimese Palace Archive* IITBS GmbH, Andiast p. 7.
38. *Sikkim- A Concise Chronicle*, published by the Royal Wedding Committee, Printed by the Sikkim Durbar Press, Gangtok, March 20, 1963 p. 4.
39. Namgyal and Dolma,(1908) op cit, p. 20.
40. *Ibid,* p. 23.
41. Dhamala, Jai, (1983) *Sikkim Ko Itihas* (History of Sikkim), Darjeeling, Shyam Prakashan, p. 43.
42. Kotturan, George, (1983), *The Himalayan Gateway-History and Culture of Sikkim*, Sterling Publishers Pvt. Ltd. New Delhi, p. 35.
43. *Ibid.*
44. Mullard and Wongchuk (2010) op cit, p. 8.
45. Dhamala, (1983), p. 44.
46. Basnett, (1974) op cit, p. 18.
47. Mullard and Wongchuk (2010) op cit, p. 8.
48. Kotturan, (1983) op cit, p. 36.
49. Sikkim- A Concise Chronicle, op cit, p. 4.
50. Dhamala, (1983), op cit, p. 44.
51. Namgyal and Dolma, (1908) op cit, p. 26.
52. *Ibid.*
53. Dhamala, (1983), op cit, p. 45.
54. Basnett, (1974) op cit, p. 19.
55. The *Sanad* states: Whereas our aged Minister Karma Dargey has served us most loyally and satisfactorily in every capacity and especially distinguished himself during the Bhutanese invasion by the aged Minister taking the command of Sikkimese forces from Rhabdentse to Gangtok. In spite of his 75 years of age, and there succeeding in killing the Bhutanese leader of the middle camp, and bringing his head and right arm, beside rendering most useful services to the state prior to that, we are pleased to reward his faithful and loyal services to the state lands, mentioned in this document. Within Sikkim he has been given pasture lands as per boundaries which will be demarcated by the two agents (Kuchap) Wangdu and Tashi Phuntso in Barmiok Barthang and the Martam Lepcha Raiyats to ag-kar-pa brothers. Rhabdentse Palace, Dated 15th day of the 2nd Month of Shing-Durg Year (Wood Dragon)

    Source: Namgyal and Dolma (1908) op cit, p. 27.
56. *Ibid.,* p. 29.
57. Sikkim- A Concise Chronicle, op cit, p. 5.
58. Risley, (1894) op cit, p. 14.
59. Namgyal and Dolma, (1908) op cit, p. 34.
60. Risley, (1894) op cit, p. 14.
61. Kotturan, (1983) op cit, p. 38.
62. Namgyal and Dolma, (1908) op cit, p. 35.
63. *Ibid.*
64. *Ibid.,* p. 38.

65. *Ibid.*
66. *Ibid*, p. 39.
67. Memoir of *Chagzod* Karwang in Tibetan, translation Dr. Saul Mullard, and Hissey Wongchuck, PD/9.5/003, Date 10th Day 9th Month of Earth Rabbit Year (1759 AD), Namgyal Institute of Tibetology.
68. Dhamala, (1983), op cit, p. 49.
69. Namgyal and Dolma, (1908) op cit, p. 39.
70. Sikkim- A Concise Chronicle, op cit, p. 6.
71. *Ibid.*
72. *Ibid.*
73. Namgyal and Dolma, (1908) op cit, p. 41.
74. *Ibid.*
75. The letter of Tibetan Government reads thus: "Whereas Changzod Chongthup has loyally served the interest of Tibet and Bhutan Governments, and whereas Tibetan Government has rewarded him by conferring on him the Rhenock Lands…" Namgyal and Dolma (1908) op cit, p. 40.
76. Namgyal and Dolma, (1908) op cit, p. 43.
77. Kotturan, (1983) op cit, p. 41.
78. Namgyal and Dolma (1908) op cit, p. 45.
79. Risley, (1894) op cit, p. 16.
80. Mullard and Wongchuk (2010) op cit, p. 9.
81. *Da lad Tsong bha ra khel kyi lag khyer* Notification issued to the entire *blon po, rdzong sde pa*, Year, 1779. PD/1.1/002, Namgyal Institute of Tibetology.
82. Sikkim- A Concise Chronicle, op cit, p. 7.
83. Kotturan, (1983) op cit, p. 42.
84. Namgyal and Dolma, (1908) op cit, p. 46.
85. Basnett, (1974) op cit, p. 25.
86. Kotturan, (1983) op cit, p. 42.
87. Sikkim- A Concise Chronicle, op cit, p. 7.
88. Namgyal and Dolma, (1908) op cit, pp. 48-49.
89. Risley, op cit, (1894), p. 19.
90. Letter from Tsugphud Namgyal to a high ranking Tibetan Official (Date Unknown), translation Dr Saul Mullard, and Hissey Wongchuck, PD/6.6/015, Namgyal Institute of Tibetology.
91. Kotturan, (1983) op cit, p. 43.
92. Letter of Chinese Amban to the Sikkimese General Yug Phyogs thub in Tibetan, Year 1792, translation Dr. Saul Mullard, and Hissey Wongchuck, PD/6.1/004, Namgyal Institute of Tibetology.
93. Letter of Chinese Amban to the Sikkimese General Yug Phyogs thub in Tibetan, Year 1792, PD/6.1/006, Namgyal Institute of Tibetology.
94. White, (1971) op cit, p. 17.
95. Sino-Nepalese peace treaty concluded after the Gorkha invasion of Sikkim Year 1792. The Treaty was mediated by Tibet. PD/6.1/003, Namgyal Institute of Tibetology, Gangtok.

96. Namgyal and Dolma, (1908) op cit, p. 51.
97. A request made by *Spyi dpon* (General Officer of Chumbi) *lTum langs rgad po* (Regional Head of lTum langs and the rgad po Nyin ltos zhang phyug to the Sikkim Government in 1796, PD/1.1/004, Namgyal Institute of Tibetology.
98. Land Grant made to Karma Dargey and Debasang Ringzing, originally in Tibetan, Year 1796, translation by Dr Saul Mullard, and Hissey Wongchuck PD/1.2/003, Namgyal Institute of Tibetology.
99. Dhamala, (1983), op cit, p. 55.
100. Anglo-Nepalese War (British Asian History) Encyclopedia Britannica, www.britannica.com /anglo-Nepalese War, date of access 15th February 2014.
101. Letter of the Sikkimese Court to the East India Company Calcutta, Early19th Century, PD/7.1/001 Namgyal Institute of Tibetology.
102. Letter to the Governor General in Calcutta from Tsugphud Namgyal, Bangdustse palace Tumlong, Year 1815-1816, originally in Tibetan, translation Dr Saul Mullard, and Hissey Wongchuck, PD/9.5/009/Sec/ (b), Namgyal Institute of Tibetology.
103. Letter to the Sikkimese *Chogyal* from Chinese Officials Year 1816: originally in Tibetan, translation Dr Saul Mullard, and Hissey Wongchuck PD/7.1/003, Namgyal Institute of Tibetology.
104. Letter to the Governor General in Calcutta from Tsugphud Namgyal, Bangdustse palace Tumlong, Year 1815-1816, originally in Tibetan, translation Dr Saul Mullard, and Hissey Wongchuck, PD/9.5/009/Sec/ (b), Namgyal Institute of Tibetology.
105. Treaty of Titaliya (Reproduced Copy),10th February 1817, Article I.
106. Tax Receipt maintained by the rTa Sa (village official) of Morang (Nepal), year 1819: originally in Nepali, translation Dr Rajen Upadhyay, PD/1.1/001 Namgyal Institute of Tibetology.
107. Namgyal and Dolma,(1908) op cit, p. 55.
108. *Ibid*, p. 58.
109. Risley, (1972) op cit, p. 19.
110. Namgyal and Dolma, (1908) op cit, p. 58.
111. Petition of *Chogyal* Tsugphud Namgyal to the Tibetan Government asking to intervene for the settlement of the border issues between Sikkim and Nepal Year 1829: Originally in Tibetan; translation, Dr. Saul Mullard, and Hissey Wongchuck PD/4.2/003, Namgyal Institute of Tibetology.
112. Petition from the people of Gro gzhi to the Summer Palace in Chumbi, Year 1831: originally in Tibetan, translation Dr. Saul Mullard, and Hissey Wongchuck PD/4.2/004, Namgyal Institute of Tibetology.
113. Letter from Sikkim *Chogyal* Tsugphud Namgyal to the Tibetan Government in which Tsugphud had informed the Tibetan Government that from 1826 the Kotapas started a rebellion which was supported by the Gorkhas, Year 1832: originally in Tibetan, translation Dr Saul Mullard, and Hissey Wongchuck PD/4.2/013, Namgyal Institute of Tibetology.
114. Letter from the people of Tibet to the Sikkimese Summer Palace in Chumbi, Year 1831: originally in Tibetan, translation Dr Saul Mullard, and Hissey Wongchuck PD/4.2/007 Namgyal Institute of Tibetology.

115. Letter of the Sikkim Government to the Tibetan Government stating about the activities of the Kotapas, Year 1830's: PD/4.2/017, Namgyal Institute of Tibetology.
116. Letter of the *Chogyal* Tsugphud Namgyal to gTsang Panchen rin po che (Panchen Lama), Year 1831: PD/4.2/005, Namgyal Institute of Tibetology, Deorali, Gangtok.
117. Letter from the *Maharaja* of Nepal to the Kotapas with a grant of an area or *Mana-Chamal* that corresponds to East of Banyani till Hathisar Gach in Eastern Nepal, Year *Vikram Samvat* 1884 (1827 AD), Originally in Nepali, translation Dr Rajen Upadhyay, Credit: Miss Jeniffer Bentley, NIT Complex Gangtok.
118. *Ibid.*
119. List of Tax payers under Ilam rDzong, PD/3.3/001: Namgyal Institute of Tibetology.
120. Sikkim- A Concise Chronicle, op cit, p. 10.
121. Letter from the Sikkimese Government to the British Officials in Darjeeling, year 1843, PD/7.1/008, originally in Tibetan, translation Dr Saul Mullard, and Hissey Wongchuck, Namgyal Institute of Tibetology.
122. Letter of Dr Campbell, date pre 1849, originally in Tibetan, translation Dr Saul Mullard, and Hissey Wongchuck PD/3.3/002, Namgyal Institute of Tibetology.
123. Journals of Asiatic Society of Bengal (1852), (pub 1883) Edited by the Secretaries, Vol. XXI, No. I-VII, '*Diary of a Journey through Sikkim to the Frontiers of Thibet- By Dr. A. Campbell, Superintendent of Darjeeling- with a Map*' Baptist Mission Press, Calcutta, p. 407.
124. Complaint Letter of the People of Lachung to the Government Officials about the visit of Dr Hooker and Dr Campbell, originally in Tibetan, translation Dr Saul Mullard, and Hissey Wongchuck PD/3.1/004, Namgyal Institute of Tibetology, Deorali, Gangtok.
125. Reply to the Complaint Letter of the People of Lachung to the Government Officials about the visit of Dr. Hooker and Dr. Campbell, originally in Tibetan, translation by Dr Saul Mullard, and Hissey Wongchuck PD/3.1/004, Namgyal Institute of Tibetology.
126. Journals of Asiatic Society of Bengal (1852), (pub 1883) p. 409.
127. Tibetan text of the Treaty of 1861 signed by Ashley Eden on behalf of Earl Canning Governor General in Council and His Highness Sidkeong Namgyal, Date 28th March 1861, Tumlong Palace, translation Dr Saul Mullard, and Hissey Wongchuck PD/9.5/024.
128. *Ibid.*
129. PD/4.1/003, Section 1, Year of origin 1867 (?) originally in Tibetan, translation Dr Saul Mullard, and Hissey Wongchuck Namgyal Institute of Tibetology.
130. *Ibid.*
131. *Ibid.*
132. Mullard and Wongchuk (2010) op cit, p. 9.

Chapter 3

Sikkim under the Colonial Patronage and Thereafter

As examined in the previous chapter, deployment of two officials Captain C.A. Lloyd and G.W. Grant in 1828 for the investigation of Unthoo dispute marks the beginning of influence of British power in Sikkim. With British involvement it evolves that Sikkim was made closer to the East India Company than to her traditional ally, Tibet. It was during this period Sikkim granted East India Company a deed, giving the hill of Darjeeling for a sanatorium. However, the friendly atmosphere soon diluted as Tsugphud Namgyal began to work at his whims and fancies. The appointment of *Dewan* Namguay alias *Pagla Dewan* as Prime Minister was disliked by the British that later proved fatal to Sikkim. Allegedly, the *Pagla Dewan* is considered to be a chief architect for the arrest and imprisonment of the two Botanists Dr Campbell and Dr Hooker. The alleged act of Diwan Namguay proved to be a key factor for an alienation of Sikkim from her traditional ally. Arrest of the duo Botanists culminated into an expedition in 1860 that annexed the whole of Darjeeling and Morang. Similarly, another expedition, followed next year, compelled Sikkim to get into a treaty in 1861. With the signing of treaty, the British secured what they were awaiting since long. It not only provided a provision to carry out free trade with Sikkim but, had also equipped the British to ask for possible help from Sikkim to develop trade with Tibet. Similarly, the Tibetan title of *Chogyal* was done away with and now onwards, akin to all other Indian rulers, the *Chogyals* of Sikkim began to be addressed as the *Maharajas*.

Commencement of the Nepalese Settlement

Before the conclusion of Treaty of 1861, Sidkeong Namgyal (1863-1874) had received a royal order from *Chogyal* Tsugphud Namgyal that provided him the royal authorities of the *Maharaja*.[1] However, leading to his father's death, he was formally coroneted as a *Maharaja* in 1863. The new ruler was directed by Tsugphud, to continue his policies that included collection of taxes from Darjeeling and to maintain cordial relations with Nepal and Bhutan.[2] Establishing himself as a good and a strict administrator,[3] he appointed a new official *Zam gdong rdzong dpon* and ordered him to work for the Government and represent their interest by maintaining law and order.[4] Soon after the treaty of 1861, J.W. Edgar was appointed as Deputy Commissioner of Darjeeling and by virtue of his office; he came to be the in-charge of political relations with Sikkim. *Maharaja* Sidkeong Namgyal remained friendly with the British and he seemed to have developed a good relation with Edgar.[5] The period of his reign was perhaps the happiest period of Anglo-Sikkim relations.[6]

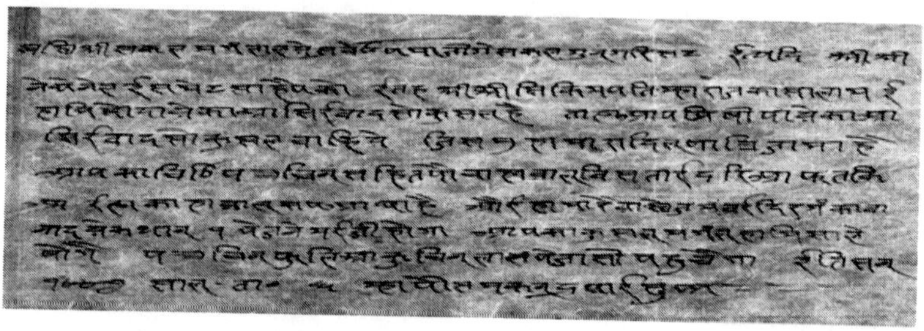

Figure 2.5: Letter of Sikkim* Maharaja *(Name and Date unknown) to one Nathaniel Smith* aka Rangapore Sahib *asking for his well being. The letter ascertains that many of such correspondence were being exchanged between them. However, the content seems to be written by* Maharaja *Sidkeong Namgyal as none of his predecessors had such a calm relations with the Imperial British India. Namgyal Institute of Tibetology.

It is because of such relations, the British increased Darjeeling subvention to nine thousand rupees in 1868 and to twelve thousand rupees in 1874. Further, he was entitled to receive 15 guns of salute from the Imperial Government. In March 1873, *Maharaja* Sidkeong Namgyal visited Darjeeling to meet Sir George Campbell, the Lieutenant Governor of Bengal. In the same year, he settled a dispute with the people of Lachen- Lachung regarding grazing tax, which according to the conventional laws was to be referred to Tashi Lama of Tibet.[7] Along with this, Sidkeong had also resolved two minor disputes with Bhutan.[8]

Immediately after the treaty of 1861, British Government began to encourage the Nepali settlement into Sikkim. However, majority of the councillors opposed British idea vigorously. The dissatisfaction of the councillors ended with the division of the Sikkimese aristocrats. In 1863, issues related to the settlement of the Newars led to a conflict between

Khangsarpa and the Pemayangtse Lamas.[9] It comes into light that, *Maharaja* Sidkeong Namgyal was not unenthusiastic to allow the Nepali settlers into Sikkim. However, in all probabilities, owing to the gloomy atmosphere he made a request to the British Government to allow settling the immigrants on waste and uninhabited lands.[10] It is important to mention that; prior to Nepali migration in Sikkim, the willing peasants could ask their respective landlords for permission to open new areas of forests for cultivation. Such requests happened to be lucrative to the landlords as that would multiply their income. Similarly, according to the Sikkimese law, peasants who cleared forest and cultivate had to pay a half amount of tax than the peasants who cultivate in the created lands and the half payment of taxes was in lieu of their service to clear the forest for cultivation.[11] In 1867, by eliminating this convention the Government of Sikkim, made a formal grant of lease to two *Newar* (Nepali) brothers Laxmi Dass Pradhan and Chandra Bir Maskey.[12] After securing the deed of grant, the traders began to bring a large number of Nepali peasants for cultivation in their allotted areas. Soon the process was followed by Sikkimese aristocrats as they too find it to be profitable that eventually led to widespread settlement of the Nepalese peasants in Sikkim. The Sikkimese aristocrats who were in favour of settlement of the Nepalese had strongly felt the importance of land, labour, and capital, and supported the British eradicating every other practices and convention.

Emboldened with his cordial relationship with the British, *Maharaja* Sidkeong Namgyal requested permission for the return of *Dewan* Namgyal, who was in exile in Tibet at the orders of British Government. However, the request was turned down. Thus, in a short period of eleven years *Maharaja* Sidkeong did some significant works in securing a peaceful relation with the British that was strongly deteriorated during his father's reign. He died in 1874.

An Uneasy Era (1874-1914)

Sidkeong Namgyal was succeeded by his 14 years old step brother *Maharaja* Thotub Namgyal. Thotub's long reign of 40 years had come across with many disturbances and commotions. The harmony and amity maintained by Sidkeong Namgyal, remained on the verge of disappearance after his ascendance. As the decision of Nepalese settlement was not appreciated by several Bhutia aristocrats the land issue seemed still to be a big problem.[13] Although, agreement between *Maharaja* Sidkeong Namgyal and British had a clear parameter concerning the settlement, the agreement was widely opposed by Sikkimese aristocrats.[14] As per the said agreement, if the signatories wanted to use Nepali labourers for construction of roads, bridges, houses etc. they first must seek permission from the King.[15] Probably, emboldened with support of the anti-settlement nobles, Thotub appeared unbending and continued enraging the British and nullified the exertions of Sidkeong Namgyal. A royal Decree was issued in 1876 that partially allowed the Gurung clan to come to Sikkim forbidding the rest of Nepalese.[16] This decision of *Maharaja* Thotub Namgyal led to the division of Sikkimese aristocrats into pro- and anti-immigration factions. The high sense of resentment of anti-immigrant aristocrats' got precipitated into an oath to prevent Nepalese settlement into Sikkim.[17] The pro-immigration faction was led by Khangsa *Dewan* likewise anti-immigration faction was led by Dala Athing Densapa and Tarching Lama of Pemiongchi. They held Khangsa *Dewan* and Phodang Lama responsible for giving lands to the Nepalese and alleged that the duo did not comply with the orders of Thotub Namgyal to stop Nepali settlement.[18] It is noteworthy that, these two aristocrats are considered as 'bad men' of Sikkimese history.[19] In the midst of opposition and dissatisfaction of a larger section, they settled a large number of Nepalese at Rhenock in East Sikkim. Such monopolistic approach of Khangsa *Dewan* and Phodang Lama infuriated other aristocrats leading to which a dispute arose.[20] The opposition of anti-migration section was obvious as they probably perceived it as a direct encroachment of British in the Sikkimese affairs. This dispute can be regarded as the outburst of a long-standing hidden transcript of the anti-immigrant faction. Exhibiting their age old anti-British concealed ideas they ordered the Nepalese of Rhenock to vacate the place and petitioned the ruler to approach to the Governor of Bengal. Abiding with the petition of anti-immigrant aristocrats, Thotub met Mr Ashley Eden, Governor of Bengal at Kalimpong and pleaded with him for the stoppage of Nepalese immigration. However, no positive response could be secured from the Governor that eventually dangled his endeavours to forbid Nepali settlement. On the other hand, the hidden transcripts of the aristocrats were still appearing with a trivial magnitude that was evident from minor skirmishes between the Nepalese settlers and the agents of anti-immigrant Bhutia laymen and the monks. In 1880, a major quarrel was started when the Bhutias attacked the Nepalese settlement areas at Rhenock with a motive to drive them out. Khangsa *Dewan* came to support the Nepali peasants with guns and attacked the natives of Rhenock killing two people and injuring number of others.[21] Similarly, Tarching Lama of Pemiongchi suffered some casualties and recoiled for the safety of Yang gang monastery but, that too, was captured by the supporters of Khangsa *Dewan*.[22] Later, with the intervention of British, the affair was settled in favour of the Nepalese and Khangsa *Dewan* and in annoyance Thotub Namgyal decided to retire to Tibet.

As it has been discussed, British were looking for trade facilities in Tibet ever since a century before the accession of Thotub Namgyal.[23] After the accession of Thotub, in 1884-85, they sent a mission for the same under Finance Secretary, Government of Bengal, Colman Macaulay. In October 1884, the mission reached Sikkim to investigate the reason causing the fall in trade. However, that had to be withdrawn in difference to the wishes of the Chinese.[24] After the failure of Macaulay mission, in all possibilities due to suspicion, Thotub Namgyal was asked to stay in Sikkim during summers by the British.[25] This was another important measure taken by the British to gain Sikkim towards their crease and to curb her from her customary attachment with Tibet.

The breach that was created by the settlement of Nepalese in Sikkim was further broadened by a misunderstanding between the *Maharaja* and Lt. Governor of Bengal in which the people of Chumbi had asked the British to stop collecting taxes in the Darjeeling area.[26] Auxiliary, in 1887, the *Maharaja* was invited to attend a meeting by the Superintendent of Darjeeling.[27] Though, due to some unknown reasons, Thotub Namgyal could not attend the same.[28] Probably, perceptive of its small extent, it appears that Sikkim wanted to outwit any sort of conflict against the British.[29] Least bothered of the Sikkimese idea of averting conflict, British sent Sikkim Expedition in 1888 in pretext of Tibetan encroachment at Lingtu.[30] It is also said that, Tibetans force numbering 300 had come to 13 miles inside the Sikkimese territory and blocked Darjeeling Tibet road. The *Maharaja* who was in Chumbi, on the other hand, neither remonstrated nor opposed; he did not even reported outrage to the British and supposedly acted as if he were a Tibetan feudatory.[31] It was in all probabilities on these grounds; the British officials at Darjeeling were obligated to take over the administration of Sikkim by empowering Phodong Lama and Khangsa *Dewan*.[32] Consequently, in June 1889, John Claude White was appointed as the first Political Officer of Sikkim with powers of *de-facto* ruler.[33] Thotub was removed to Kurseong in Darjeeling and was given a stipend of ₹ 1000 per month.[34] Further, the amount of ₹ 12,000 as tax from Darjeeling was also stopped since 1886.[35] Thotub was kept in solitary confinement for sometime in Ging and then for two years in Kurseong where only the *Maharani* Yeshe Dolma with few personal attendants were allowed to stay. Discouraged with the British actions, Thotub made complaint to the Chinese Amban through the Tibetan authorities regarding the due taxes of Darjeeling.[36] However, it appears that the Chinese made no response to his complaint and left Thotub at his own fortune.

During Anglo Chinese Convention of 1890,[37] John Claude White, the Political Officer, approached Thotub Namgyal with deeds of land grants by which new landlords were created. Since, these Grants were made at conjure of the British and it was also believed that several acts of injustice were perpetrated, Thotub refused to give ascent. One of such injustice as per the King was restoration of landed estates to the descendents of Gelong Rinzing, who supported Chagzod Tamding who usurped power from the baby King Namgyal Phuntsog back in 1738.[38] However, ignoring the opinion of *Maharaja*, John Claude White carried out the process of creating new landlords.

As a remedy to have a cordial relation, in 1894, Thotub wrote a petition to the Commissioner of Bengal apologizing for his past behaviour. Consequently, he was sent to Darjeeling, and finally he was allowed to enter into Sikkim.[39] This change of British attitude was conceivably due to the subsequent Young husband's expedition to Lhasa, for it a friendly Sikkim was essential for the success of the mission.[40] The success of Young husband Mission compelled Tibet to come into terms and out of which the Lhasa Convention was signed in September 7th 1904.[41]

Pleased with these developments, the *Maharaja* and *Maharani* were invited by Government of India to visit Calcutta on the occasion of the visit of Prince of Wales.[42] In 1906, control over Sikkim state affairs was transferred from Government of Bengal to Government of India.[43] After gaining a restricted power, Thotub Namgyal made his ministers to sign an oath confirming their loyalties to their King.[44] It has to be reiterated that, conflict between the King and his ministers (Khangsa *Dewan* and Phodang Lama) was an important factor for the growth of British interference in the Kingdom. In the political ground, in 1901, Lord Curzon decided to keep the internal administration of Sikkim under the Bengal Government while issues related to political and commercial questions the Foreign Department of Government of India was to be corresponded by the Political Officer.[45] Accordingly, as stated above, the transfer of political charge of Sikkim from the Government of Bengal to Government of India took place in April 1906. John Claude White left Sikkim in 1908 and on 11th February 1914, *Maharaja* Thotub Namgyal also passed away.[46] Sikkim continued to be in the cordial terms with the British Empire.[47]

Period of Reformation

It is usually believed that the era of reformation was initiated by HH *Maharaja* Sir Tashi Namgyal (1914-1963). However, the short yet dumpy reign of eleven months of HH *Maharaja* Sidkeong Tulku (February 1914-December 1914) appears to be the preliminary phase of the reformist zeal of Sikkimese monarchs. With the recognition of Government of India, *Maharaja* Sidkeong Tulku succeeded his father *Maharaja* Thotub Namgyal on 29th April 1914 as the tenth ruler of Sikkim.[48] He had the benefit of sound modern education and was an undergraduate at Pembroke College, in Oxford.[49] Alexandra David Neel, who met Sidkeong Tulku during her research, writes that the King would speak English more fluently than Tibetan and could also speak a fluent Hindi and a bit of Chinese.[50] During his stay in Oxford, he had been exposed to the revolutionary ideas of the West. With the Political Officer J.C. White, he had the privilege of travelling around India as well as in the neighbouring countries. In 1908, after his return from Oxford, Sidkeong had been entrusted with the charges of Forest, Monasteries, and Schools. Even before assuming the power of a *de facto* ruler, Sidkeong made some important transactions in 1913. Among them the important was abolition of imprisonment as a penalty for non-payment of debts. Similarly, the Council Proceedings were recorded on the ban of settlement of plain-men. Immediately after his accession, Sidkeong Tulku made negotiations with Messrs Burn and Company, Calcutta for concession to cut and sell timber, for manufacture of bamboo pulp, for hydro electric project and wire ropeways.[51] It was due to his affectionate relationship with the British,[52] even the Tibetan elites like Panchen Lama requested Sidkeong for the arrangement of a meeting with the British at Delhi.[53] This exhibits him as a brilliant diplomat apart from an excellent and placid ruler. *Maharaja* Sidkeong Tulku eliminated all the prior policies to be in good terms with British India.

Maharaja Sidkeong Tulku attempted to bring the monasteries towards their social obligation. However, the monks were hesitant with his radical ideas as that would make them to stand at a ridiculous position. This was a revolutionary sacrilege coming from the ruler who was supposed to preserve the interests of the clergies. It is interesting to note that, the clergies in terms of position were enjoying an upper status in the society while in economic terms their position was not better than the lot. The writings of Ms. Neel provide a testimonial that even the condition of the Clergies was not economically prosperous. She writes:

> "The peasant clergies of these forests are generally poor and ill fed, and it is difficult for them to suppress a thrill of delight when death of a rich villager promises them several days' feast".[54]

Moving further, Sidkeong had raised his voice of opposition, against the privileges enjoyed by the feudal aristocracy who had an imperative role in decision-making in the earlier period. The pathetic condition of the peasants, due to feudal encroachments, forced them to send several complaints to the *Durbar* regarding the harassment they met in their daily lives. The amount of assessment was relatively high than what they produce and the revenues were collected forcefully by their landlords. Similarly, there were also other cases of migration of the peasants to Bhutan and Darjeeling due to the lopsided and oppressive taxation system.[55] The hidden transcripts of Sikkimese peasantry now thus started to come out in the form of petition and prayers to the *Maharaja* against the injustice they were subjected to at the hands of their landlords. In order to curb the selfish interests of the landlords, Sidkeong Tulku abolished the discriminatory taxation rates among the Lepcha-Bhutia and Nepali peasants and reverted to the old system of *Koot* or *Kut.*[56] Possibly, by taking the matters of harassment and exploitation into consideration, Sidkeong Tulku proposed to liquidate landlordism that was indeed a matter of relief to the subjugated peasants of Sikkim.[57] However, the proposal of Sidkeong Talku could not get actualised due to his untimed demise. On the contrary, by his reformist zeal, he was exasperating both the ends i.e. the landlords, and the Political Officer, Charles Bell.

In a very short period of hardly ten months, Sidkeong did some remarkable tasks for the development of Sikkim. His reign witnessed opening of several schools for the propagation of western education. From the available administrative reports, it comes into light that there were two secondary schools at Gangtok, 25 primary and village schools, 16 missionary schools and 6 schools at the landlords' estates. Likewise, few other schools were in the process of opening in the remote villages.[58] Auxiliary, he made certain amendments in the prevailing laws and encouraged his subjects for plantation of trees in waste lands. Reserved forests were categorised into two ranges namely, Eastern and Western and they were kept in charge of the Foresters. It is worth to mention that, these forests were to be managed by the landlords as Forest Officers of their respective *Elakhas*. It is also revealed that strict rules and laws were adopted to abolish corruption from the forest resources and that if a Forest Officer failed to execute his responsibilities he would be dealt with a heavier hand. Eleven Landlords were fined by the Durbar due to their negligence and casualness towards their duties that also includes the Bermiok *Kazi* who was occupying a higher position in the State Council.[59] The evidence is ample enough to argue that Sidkeong Tulku was an austere, a devoted, and a peasant adoring *Maharaja* who was keen to eliminate corruption from every level of administration including monastery. Apart from these reformations, the *Maharaja* also encouraged his subjects to live a clean and hygienic life. Probably, considering the hardships of his subjects in attending medical help, he established a hospital and a dispensary at Gangtok.[60] On the contrary, his zeal and enthusiasm to provide a healthy administration in Sikkim did not last long as his heterodoxy and revolutionary ideas led him to death.

In December 1914, Sidkeong was taken ill and died soon. It is believed that the King died due to a heart failure caused by jaundice due to a severe chill.[61] However, it is also said that, a British physician from Bengal made a heavy transfusion of brandy, put him under a number of blankets, and burnt charcoal near his bed and the King died out of suffocation.

Peasant Resistance and Democratic Aspirations

The suspicious death of Sidkeong Tulku led to succession of Tashi Wangyal as the eleventh ruler of Sikkim. He assumed his office with the title of Tashi Namgyal.[62] Tashi Namgyal was born on 26th October 1893 at Kurseong from *Maharani* Yeshey Dolma, where his parents were under British surveillance.[63] He ascended the throne on 5th December 1914, at the age of 21 and began to rule under the tutelage of Charles Bell, the Political Officer. He was assigned with the charges of forest, education and monastic departments due to his naivety towards administration.[64] Complete administrative powers of the *Maharaja* were restored to him in 1918.

After his accession, the *Maharaja* took up the subject of social and economic reforms.[65] A Chief Court, consisting of three benches of four members each, selected from the State Councillors and foremost men were created to deal with judicial matters. However, the final court of appeal remained at the Court of Political Officer of Sikkim.[66] The important among those reforms was setting up of an independent judiciary in 1916. It was done to bring the judicial functions of the *Kazis* under the superior Court. Even though, their proceedings were supervised by the superior court, King remained unable to set himself free from their clutches in his daily affairs. Hence, the reforms made by *Maharaja* Tashi Namgyal were not implemented properly and it emerges that the common man's condition was at the same stage where it was before.[67]

The reign of *Maharaja* Sir Tashi Namgyal is important from the peasants' point of view as it witnessed a resistance which have been discussed in the forthcoming chapters. No doubt, the King had made a grand initiative to strengthen the condition of the peasants by snatching judicial and right of arbitration from the landlords. However, he had not been able to grasp threat and intimidation of landlords from the ignorant minds of the peasants that ultimately led to their resistance. It is important to state that, agrarian society of Sikkim after the Nepalese settlement had taken various curves in different stages of time. A major transformation of such agrarian changes can be noticed after the appointment of J C White as the First British Political Officer to Sikkim. Within a year or two of his service, the number of Nepali settlers doubled and their arrivals continued till the accession of Tashi Namgyal.[68] In all possibilities, to stop the Nepalese migration, in 1912-13, the State formulated varied rate of taxation as one fifth of the produce to the Nepalese and one eight of the produce to the Lepcha-Bhutia peasants.[69] As discussed above, this mode of assessment was suspended by Sidkeong Tulku and a temporary measure of *Koot* or *Kut* was adopted till the new mode would be introduced. According to a decision of a meeting of the State Council on 26th January 1915 a new mode of assessment was adopted. This new rate of the revenue had a disparate feature between the Lepcha-Bhutia and Nepali peasants.[70]

It is important to discuss that, the state did not collect any tax through its departmental agencies. The land revenue tax was collected from the peasants through middlemen known as *Elakhadars*.[71] These *Elakhadars* or Managers were appointed on commission by the state and were allowed 10 per cent commission on the gross revenue collected.[72] The prevalent discrepancy between the Lepcha-Bhutia peasants and the Nepali peasants was further broadened by Revenue Order No.1 of 17th May 1917. According to this Order, no Lepcha-Bhutia would be allowed to sell, mortgage or sublet any of their land to any person other than Lepcha and Bhutia without the express sanction of the *Durbar*, or officers empowered by the *Durbar* on its behalf.[73] These biased policies of the state had obviously raised the feeling of being discriminated among the Nepali peasants who also were putting all their efforts for the economic growth of the Kingdom. James C Scott justifies

> "At the top are those who give orders to virtually all and take none; at the bottom are those who take orders from virtually anyone and give orders to none".[74]

Thus, the majority of the peasants in Sikkim were forced to live a combatant's life by resisting the State and its prejudiced laws in the 'symbiosis of dependency and exploitation'.[75]

Along with the land tax, the peasants were severely harassed by their landlords known as *Kazis* and *Thikadars* and their subordinates namely *Mukhtiyars*, *Mandals,* and *Karbaris*. Apart from the peasantry, a peasant also had to carry governmental loads known as *Kalo Bhari* and also had to render free labour services like *Jharlangi*, *Theki-Bethi* and *Kuruwa*. Likewise, they too had to pay *Dhurikhajana* of ₹ 6 for their dwelling places.[76] To get rid of a brutal and unscrupulous system several acts of disobedience were devised by the resisters of Sikkim. The adoption of acts like poaching, stealing, trespassing, and tax evasion by the Sikkimese peasantry were nothing more than a measure to shield them against the State's oppression. The peasants whether Lepchas, Bhutias, or Nepalese, were the sufferers under the same yoke, there was a vague consciousness among them of their common interests.[77]

No important progress can be noticed in the daily lives of the Sikkimese peasantry till the conclusion of Second World War. However, even at this juncture, it seems that, the Sikkimese peasantry neither had any dream to have a colossal change in their lives, nor were they prepared to confront against a devastating consequence. They were happy with the small gains what they could make through poaching, stealing, trespassing, and tax evasion etc. In a modern sense of interpretation, such acts of the peasants as discussed above were not adequate enough to change a set up.[78] The sense of antagonism against the State machinery in a cohesive manner began to grow among the peasants from the early 40's. From this phase one can notice resentment of the peasant folks reaching its pinnacle. It has to be reiterated here that, peasants were petitioning Sikkim *Durbar* about discrepancy in taxation and injustice at the hands of landlords since the reign of *Maharaja* Sidkeong Tulku. Yet, it comes into surface that, nothing had been done by the State to settle the rural dissatisfaction, to overrule over taxation, and for the elimination of varied forced labours. The silent and hush attitude of the *Durbar* had definitely multiplied their discontentment and resentment against the exploitative mechanism. Howard Zinn believes

> "Change in public consciousness starts with low level discontent, at first vague, with no connection being made between the discontent and the policies of the government. And then the dots begin to connect, indignation increases, and people began to speak out, organise, and act".[79]

The low level discontentment of the peasants was now taking a severe curve during the Second World War. To get rid of the faulty administration, youths of Namthang, South Sikkim organised an underground movement against feudalism. They founded the first ever political association of Sikkim known as the Member Party in 1940.[80] Similarly, in the later half of the year 1946, the villagers of Temi Tarku gathered themselves and founded a peasant association called *Rajya Praja Sammelan*.[81] To end the autocratic policies of the *Kazi Thikadars*, yet another village level meeting was held at Chakhung paving the way for the foundation of another peasant association known as *Rajya Praja Mandal*.[82] Amid these activities, Sikkim witnessed the opening of another peasants' association *Praja Sudhar Samaj* at Gangtok.[83] Finding its authoritarian set up in a shaky position, some hasty measures were taken up by the *Durbar* to curtail various forced labours from the state. In 1947, just before the independence of India, the

Government of Sikkim put a ban on the notorious *Kuruwa* labour which had a deep antipathy among the subjects.[84] On the other hand, after the Indian independence, the peasants of Sikkim were getting restive at the impact of fast developments in the neighbourhood. Just like in other native states, the independence movement in British India had given inspiration to similar movements in Sikkim. The Indian independence greatly encouraged these 'petty' or 'confined' organisations founded before the independence to come together with a solid political aim. Thus, on 7th December 1947, the Sikkim State Congress was formed under the Presidentship of Tashi Tshering.[85] Howard Zinn observes,

> "The uneasiness grows and grows and the citizenry gathers in resistance in larger and larger numbers, which becomes too many to control; one day the top-heavy empires collapse".[86]

The foundation of the State Congress in Sikkim as a very replica of the Indian National Congress, heralded a new era in the political and democratic horizon of the Kingdom. The Sikkim State Congress made several political demands to the *Durbar* after its foundation and accordingly the three Secretaries to the *Maharaja* of Sikkim from the State Congress Party were appointed.[87] Goyal states that, a series of deputations were sent to the *Durbar* for the abolition of slavery, protection against forced labour and demanded that the people be allowed to pay their taxes direct to the state instead of the landlords who had often cheated them in recording the payments.[88] Hence, after the foundation of the Sikkim State Congress, the Kingdom was clamoured with many political agitations demanding equality and democracy. The cohesive resistance of the Sikkimese peasantry included the No Rent -No Tax Campaign of 1949, demonstration of February 11th 1949, and demonstration of 1st May 1949. These agitations led to the formation of a 'Popular Ministry'. This ministry was formed on 9th May 1949 and was headed by Tashi Tshering as Prime Minister.[89] However, it could not function well and was dissolved after the 29 days of its formation. After the dismissal of ministry, the *Maharaja* Sir Tashi Namgyal issued a proclamation also called 'Constitutional Proclamation' on 23rd March 1953. However, the electoral process, the voting procedure, counting system and even Election Tribunal were maintained in the Proclamation in such a way that the Nepalese in general and the democratic forces in particular were at a great disadvantage.[90] Under this unbalanced electoral law, *Maharaja* Tashi Namgyal conducted two elections during his tenure. The election result was a clear indication that still there was a long way to go for the peasants of Sikkim to attend democracy. The wedge was firmly and effectively driven between the Lepchas-Bhutia and the Nepalese in Sikkim. However, the lone outcome of these elections was that the peasants of the Kingdom were at least marching from the stage of nonentity to a little.

Last Phase of Peasant Agitation and the Take Over

The Sikkimese throne was ascended by *Maharaja* Palden Thondup Namgyal on the death of his father HH Maharaja Sir Tashi Namgyal. After six years from the death of Sangay Diki, his first wife, *Maharaja* Palden Thotub Namgyal married Miss Hope Cooke, an American.[91] He and his American bride were crowned as King and Queen of Sikkim at a colourful ceremony at the palace chapel, on 4th April 1965, on the 42nd birthday of the *Maharaja*.[92]After assuming power, Palden Thotub Namgyal discarded the Indian title of '*Maharaja*' and went back to the old Tibetan title of his forefathers- *Chogyal*.[93]

His reign marks the era of politicisation of the peasants' aspiration of democracy. The introduction of 'parity formula' in 1951-52 was a great setback for democratic forces by which about 25 per cent Lepcha-Bhutia seats were equated with 75 per cent of the Nepali seats.[94] This very formula later on became the major cause of confrontation between the peasant supported political parties and the *Durbar*. The reign of *Chogyal* Palden Thondup Namgyal also witnessed, democratic aspirations reaching its highest watermark. Further, the growth of Sikkimese sense of nationalism was escalated during his tenure. The birth of a forum known as 'Study Forum' and the popularity of Sikkimese national flag and anthem, which were alleged to be anti-Indian, are some of the important inputs to strangle his relationship with India.[95] On the other hand, the Sikkim National Congress headed by *Kazi* Lhendup Dorjee repeatedly clamoured for the political reforms but, the *Chogyal* went on ignoring the demands.[96] However, a proclamation known as *Gram Panchayat Act of 1965* was issued granting representation to the *Tsongs* and the Scheduled Castes and also increasing the Bhutia Lepcha and the Nepali seats.[97] The *Chogyal* at this point, seemed to have played a game of divide and rule to make further division among the three major ethnic communities. Under the new proclamation Sikkim went for the Third General Election but, due to the parity formula none of the parties could secure majority. In contrast, revision of the treaty of 1950, which was termed as unequal by the Sikkimese, became the talk of the Capital town. The resentments of the Sikkimese intelligentsia reached its pinnacle on the 21st Indian Independence Day on 15th August 1968. It is said that the Sikkimese Government Officers boycotted the celebration to show their anguish against India. On the same day, Gangtok, the Capital, witnessed its first demonstration clamouring with anti-Indian slogans.[98] These acts of the Sikkimese naturally enraged the Indians who termed it as Quit Sikkim Movement.[99]

On the contrary, the Third Sikkim Council, which was functioning as an alliance, was simply working to please the *Durbar* and was not paying much attention for the development of the peasants.[100] The major issues of land reforms and citizenship to a vast majority of its subjects was not yet solved. Though, the Sikkimese peasants were now not obligated to carry forced labour and also their grievances of unequal taxation was done away with, they were yet a mile away from having their active participation in the State Council due to the parity system. Further, the peasantry was definitely a deciding factor in the Council Elections of Sikkim, none of the political parties had ever attempted to raise their voices for their betterment. Keeping these issues of the peasants awaiting, the Sikkim *Durbar* issued a Proclamation scheduling the Fourth General Elections of Sikkim in 1970 on 31st December 1969.[101] The Proclamation has not mentioned anything about the dissolution of parity formula and therefore it is obvious that the elections were held according to the prevailing biased laws. [102] The National Party, which was regarded as the extreme royalist and anti-Indian party both by India and the leaders of the democratic forces, came out as the largest party in the Council.[103] In September 1970, Sikkim witnessed the birth of another anti-Indian association known as Sikkim United Front.[104] Prominent posters were displayed all over, asking Indians to quit Sikkim and grant full independence to her.[105]

However, amid these events Sikkim went on polls for its Fifth General Election in February 1973 under the same asymmetrical electoral laws. The Sikkim National Party had been able to gain majority in the Sikkim Council. Nevertheless, the parity formula and its vices brought the *Chogyal* into conflict with the majority of his people and India. Depriving the vast majority of his Nepali subjects of equal rights of opportunities, led the masses to go against the existing system. The agitation of 4th April 1973, which remained successful due to the active participation of the peasants seeking equality, was followed by an Agreement signed on 8th May 1973 also known as Tripartite Agreement.[106] The Agreement was signed to provide a democratic set up for Sikkim and to maintain a closer links with India. Accordingly, a poll was conducted in April 1974. Sikkim Congress a political party, born with the merger of Sikkim National Congress and Janata Congress, swept the poll. The new Assembly was headed by the Chief Minister, *Kazi* Lhendup Dorjee Khangsarpa, had 31 seats in 32 members Assembly. On 10th May 1974, Mr B.S. Das, the newly appointed Chief Administrator according to the 8th May Agreement, was sworn in as President of the Assembly[107] and on the next day *Kazi* Lhendup Dorjee, the leader of the House made a formal resolution seeking for Sikkim's participation in the political and economic institutions of India.[108] The resolution passed by the Sikkim Assembly was forwarded to the *Chogyal* and after his observation, it was sent to Delhi. Without much delay, Delhi sent a constitutional expert with a draft constitution to be presented to the Assembly and to the *Chogyal*. However, the draft of the constitution did not satisfy any side.[109] This was followed by Anti-Constitutional Bill protest in the Capital on 20th June 1974. However, the protest was suppressed with the help of CRPF by the Indian diplomats housed themselves at India House, Gangtok.[110] Thus, in the midst of reluctance of the people, the *Chogyal*, and the Sikkimese leaders, the Government of Sikkim Act was passed in the midnight of 20th of June 1974.[111] On 24th June, the Chief Executive forwarded the resolutions of Sikkim Assembly to the *Chogyal* for his assent. However, the *Chogyal* with a view to meet the Indian Prime Minister Mrs Gandhi left for Delhi.[112] In the absence of the Head of the Government of Sikkim the Chief Administrator Mr Das called an Assembly session on 28th June1974.[113] The *Chogyal* sent his draft of speech to be read in the House and after hearing his views, the Sikkim Assembly unanimously adopted the Bill. On 4th July 1974, the *Chogyal* gave his assent to the Bill.[114]

Emboldened with the administration of Mr Das, the members of Sikkim Assembly now began to request the Indian Government to allow them to send a representative in each of the houses. Accordingly, the Lok Sabha voted the constitution's 35th Amendment Bill to associate Sikkim with the Indian Union on the 4th of September 1974.[115] On the other side, the *Chogyal* was dissatisfied with his status as a constitutional head and tried to wreck the new arrangement by initiating an attitude of confrontation with the Assembly headed by *Kazi* Lhendup Dorjee.[116] The ruling party there upon began a campaign for the removal of *Chogyal*. The State Assembly met on 10th of April 1975 and a resolution demanding the abolition of the office of the *Chogyal* and the merger of the state with the Indian Union was adopted unanimously.[117]

In an unopposed atmosphere, the Indian diplomats supported by most of the Sikkimese leaders, conducted a special opinion poll on 14th of April 1975.[118] The pink ballot papers with the resolution "A" of 10th April 1975 were introduced for the special poll.[119] Within the 72 hours of the referendum, the results were out and it was declared in support of the resolution.[120] On the other hand the Union parliament adopted a resolution on the 19th April 1975 proposing to include Sikkim as a full-fledged State in the First Schedule to the Constitution and to allot one seat according to the resolution made by the Sikkim Assembly on 10th April 1975.[121]

Thus, India with its shrewd diplomacy was not only been able to topple the *Chogyal* but also save herself from the criticism of having ominous design towards Sikkim.

Notes

1. Royal Order giving Royal authority to Sidkeong Namgyal by his father *Chogyal* Tsugphud Namgyal Year 1861, originally in Tibetan, translation Dr Saul Mullard, and Hissey Wongchuck PD/1.2/010, Namgyal Institute of Tibetology.
2. *Ibid.*
3. PD/1.1/023, PD/1.1/024, PD/1.1/025 are the letters related to the collection of taxes. PD/1.1/025 is an agreement between the defaulters of trade profit tax of 8 *srang* and Sikkim Government, originally in Tibetan, translation Dr Saul Mullard, and Hissey Wongchuck Namgyal Institute of Tibetology.
4. Letter of *Maharaja* Sidkeong Namgyal to the *Zam gdong rdzong dpon*, Year 1863, written in Devanagari, translation Dr Rajen Upadhyay, PD/1.1.022, Namgyal Institute of Tibetology.
5. Letter from the Sikkim Government to the Sikkimese representative in Darjeeling in which the Sikkim Government has made a request for ₹ 1000 from the British in the Year 1871: originally in Tibetan, translation Dr Saul Mullard, and Hissey Wongchuck PD/1.3/008, Namgyal Institute of Tibetology.
6. Kotturan, George (1983), *The Himalayan Gateway- History and Culture of Sikkim*, Sterling Publishers Pvt. Ltd. New Delhi, p. 68.
7. Notice to the monks and public of Lachen and Lachung by the *Chogyal* in which the *Chogyal* had ordered the people of Lachen and Lachung to pay a tax on pasture lands and only send their animals periodically and if they failed to do so they would be punished. The Document also states that the people of Lachen had to pay a yearly tax of three *dngul srang*: originally in Tibetan, translation Dr Saul Mullard, and Hissey Wongchuck PD/3.1/007, Namgyal Institute of Tibetology.
8. *Maharaja* Thotub Namgyal and *Maharani* Yeshey Dolma (un-published type script 1908, translated by *Kazi* Dousansup) *History of Sikkim*, p. 68.
9. Royal Decree from Bangdutse Palace Year 1880, originally in Tibetan, translation Dr Saul Mullard, and Hissey Wongchuck PD/1.7/002: Namgyal Institute of Tibetology.
10. Lepcha, (2002) op cit, p. 68.
11. Mullard, Saul and Wongchuk Hissey (ed) (2010), *Royal Records: A Catalogue of the Sikkimese Palace Archive* IITBS GmbH, Andiast, p. 12.
12. Basnett, Lal Bahadur, (1974) *Sikkim- A short Political History,* S. Chand and Co. (Pvt.) Ltd. New Delhi, p. 44.
13. Dhamala, Jai, (1983) *Sikkim Ko Itihas* (History of Sikkim), Darjeeling, Shyam Prakashan, p. 62.
14. Agreement regarding the use of Nepali labourers between a leader of the Nepali community and Bermiok and Sang *Kazis* in which the agreement between Sir Asley Eden and His Highness Sidkeong Namgyal has been stated: originally in

Tibetan, translation Dr Saul Mullard, and Hissey Wongchuck PD/9.5/050, Date 12th Month of the Water Horse Year (in Tibetan), Namgyal Institute of Tibetology.

15. *Ibid.*
16. Legal Code of Government of Sikkim Year 1876: originally in Tibetan, translation Dr Saul Mullard, and Hissey Wongchuck PD/9.5/027, Clause No 15, Namgyal Institute of Tibetology.
17. Oath Agreement between the lHo Po (Bhutias) and Lepchas signed by representatives of Chu mig, sPa lding, gSang mo and Ling mogs: originally in Tibetan, translation Dr Saul Mullard, and Hissey Wongchuck PD/9.5/070, Namgyal Institute of Tibetology.
18. Letter from Tsugphud Namgyal to the Lt. Governor of Bengal John Woodburn dated 20th day of 9th month of Iron Ox year (1901 AD): Originally in Tibetan, translation Dr Saul Mullard, and Hissey Wongchuck PD/7.4/003: Namgyal Institute of Tibetology.
19. Mullard and Wongchuk (2010), op cit, p. 9.
20. Document related to the Nepali Settlement in Sikkim, originally in Tibetan, translation Dr Saul Mullard, and Hissey Wongchuck PD/9.5/041: Namgyal Institute of Tibetology.
21. Letter of a Sikkimese Minister to the *Chogyal* Year 1880: originally in Tibetan, translation Dr Saul Mullard, and Hissey Wongchuck PD/9.5/075, Namgyal Institute of Tibetology.
22. *Ibid.*
23. Sarkar, S.C., (1930) Some Notes on the Intercourse of Bengal with the Northern Countries in the Second Half of the Eighteenth Century, in proceedings of the Indian History Records Commission, Vol. XIII, p. 99. It was in 1767, the East India Company sent its first unsuccessful mission to Tibet under Kinlock with a desire to secure Tibetan gold.
24. Bhattacharya, Pranab Kumar (1984), *Aspect of cultural History of Sikkim-Studies in coinage*, K.P. Bagniet of Company, New Delhi, p. 17.
25. Letter to the Superintendent of Darjeeling from the Sikkim *Chogyal*, Year 1885: originally in Tibetan, translation Dr Saul Mullard, and Hissey Wongchuck PD/7.4/006 (a), Namgyal Institute of Tibetology. Note: Before 1885, the Sikkimese Kings used to reside in Chumbi Valley in Tibet during summers.
26. Letter from Edgar to the Sikkimese Year 1887: PD/7.3/003, Namgyal Institute of Tibetology.
27. Letter from Sikkim *Chogyal* to the Superintendent of Darjeeling Year 1887: originally in Tibetan, translation Dr Saul Mullard, and Hissey Wongchuck PD/7.2/029, Namgyal Institute of Tibetology.
28. Letter from Sikkim *Chogyal* to the Superintendent of Darjeeling Year 1887: originally in Tibetan, translation Dr Saul Mullard, and Hissey Wongchuck PD/7.2/030, Namgyal Institute of Tibetology.
29. Letter from *Chogyal* Thotub Namgyal to the Secretary to the Lt. Governor of Bengal J.W. Edgar Year 1887: PD/7.3/002, Namgyal Institute of Tibetology.
30. Captain, Iggulden H.A. (1900), *The Derbyshire Campaign Series, No.4, Sikkim Expedition of 1888*, Swan Sonnenschein and Co, London, p. V.

31. *Ibid.,* p. IX.
32. Letter to the Secretary of the Lt. Governor of Bengal and it refers about a decision that if the *Chogyal* would not come to meet him by 9th month the Lt. Governor would take control of Sikkim and empower the Phodang Lama and (Khang gsar pa) with the administration of Sikkim, Year 1887: PD/7.2/030, Namgyal Institute of Tibetology.
33. White, John Claude (Printed in India 1971), *Sikhim and Bhutan- Twenty One years on the North East Frontier 1887-1908*, Vivek Publishing House, New Delhi, p. 16.
34. Letter from *Chogyal* Thotub Namgyal to the Lt. Governor of Bengal John Woodburn Year 1901: PD/7.4/003, Namgyal Institute of Tibetology.
35. Letter from the Queen and Prince of Sikkim to the *Chogyal* and Tibetan Government, Year 1890: PD/7.3/006, Namgyal Institute of Tibetology.
36. Correspondence between Sikkim and Tibet regarding the Anglo-Sikkimese conflict of 1889-90, Year 1890: PD/7.3/005, Namgyal Institute of Tibetology.
37. The Anglo-Chinese convention of 1890 confirms Sikkim as a protectorate of British India.
38. Mullard and Wongchuk (2010), op cit, p. 9.
39. Dhamala, (1983), op cit, p. 65.
40. Bhattacharya, (1984) op cit, p. 19.
41. Rao, P.R. (1978), *Sikkim-The story of its integration with India,* Cosmo Publication, New Delhi, p. 144.
42. Kotturan, (1983) op cit, p. 77.
43. Bhattacharya, (1984) op cit, p. 19.
44. Oath signed by the Sikkimese Ministers confirming their loyalties to their King in which the signatories have vowed to act with loyalty and if they fail they would pay a fine, Year 1907: PD/9.5/044, Namgyal Institute of Tibetology.
45. Grover, B.S.K (1974), *Sikkim and India storm and consolidation*, Jain Brothers, New Delhi, p. 28.
46. Administration Report 1913-14, I, 2.
47. A rough book belonging to Prince Tashi Namgyal used in between 20th September 1911 to 27th August 1914, PD/9.4/002: Namgyal Institute of Tibetology.
48. Administration Report 1913-14, I, 2.
49. *Ibid.*
50. Neel, Alexandra David (1931), *With Mystics and Magicians in Tibet*, Penguin Books, London, p. 17.
51. Administration Report, 1913-14, I, 4.
52. Unnamed Document, Year 1914, PD/7.3/010, Namgyal Institute of Tibetology.
53. Letter to Sidkeong Namgyal from Panchen Lama dated 1909-1913, PD/6.2/003, Namgyal Institute of Tibetology.
54. Neel (1931) op cit, p. 19.
55. Administration Report 1913-14, I, 5.
56. Administration Report 1914-15, II, 2.

57. Sikkim- A Concise Chronicle, op cit, p. 20.
58. Administration Report 1913-14, I, 5.
59. *Ibid.*
60. Administration Report 1913-14, I, 4.
61. Administration Report 1914-15, I, 1.
62. *Ibid.*
63. Sikkim- A Concise Chronicle, op cit, p. 22.
64. Administration Report 1914-15, I, 1.
65. Sikkim- A Concise Chronicle, op cit, p. 22.
66. Administration Report 1914-15, I, 1.
67. Basnett, (1974) op cit, p. 65.
68. Administration Report 1914-15, VI, 8.
69. *Ibid.*, II, 2.
70. *Ibid.*, II, 3.
71. Administration Report 1930-31, IV, 11-12.
72. Administration Report 1926-27, II 5.
73. Central Department, 17th of May 1917.
74. Scott, James C (1990), *Domination and Arts of Resistance Hidden Transcripts*, Yale University Press, p. 23.
75. Scott, James C (1985), *Weapons of the Weak everyday forms of peasant resistance*, Yale University Press, p. 180.
76. *Dhurikhajana* receipt of ₹ 6 paid to the *Mandal* Dhanapati Upadhyay by the Late Ravilal Pyakurel, 26th August 1945, Tareythang, East Sikkim.
77. Basnett, (1974) op cit, p. 65.
78. Scott, James C (July 1987), '*Resistance without Protest and without Organisation: Peasant Opposition to the Islamic Zakat and the Christian Tithe*' Comparative Study in Society and History, Vol. 29 Issue 3, p. 421.
79. Zinn, Howard, (2007), A Power Government Cannot Suppress, City Lights Books, San Francisco, p. 15.
80. Gaunley Gopal, (2002), *History of Democratic movement*, (Translation Dr A.B Chettri and Mukunda Giri), Published by Department of IPR, Government of Sikkim, Gangtok 20.
81. *Ibid.*
82. *Ibid.*
83. Basnett, (1974) op cit, p. 76.
84. Notice for the abolition of Kuruwa, 31 January 1947, Ram Gauri Sangrahalaya Rhenock.
85. Grover, (1974), op cit, p. 34.
86. Zinn, (2007) op cit, p. 15.
87. Parsai, Brihaspati (Unpublished Notes), Publicity Secretary, Sikkim State Congress.
88. Goyal, Narendra (Second Edition 1966) *Political History of Himalayan States- Tibet, Nepal, Bhutan, Sikkim and Nagaland since* 1947, Cambridge Book and Stationary Store, New Delhi, p. 141.

89. Gaunley, (2002) op cit, p. 32.
90. Proclamation of His Highness *Maharaja* Tashi Namgyal, 23rd March 1953, Clause 3, p. 2.
91. Cooke Hope, (1980), *Time Change-An Autobiography*, Simon and Schuster, New York, p. 84.
92. *Ibid.*
93. Kotturan, (1983) op cit, p. 102.
94. Basnett, (1973) op cit, p. 95.
95. Basnett (1974) op cit, p. 141.
96. *Kanchenjunga*, Vol. 6, No. 26, 15th November 1965 Editorial of the Journal.
97. *Kanchenjunga* Vol. 6, No. 9, 15th January 1966, pp. 120-121.
98. Cooke, (1980) op cit, p. 196.
99. Datta Ray, Sunanda K. (1984), Smash and Grab-Annexation of Sikkim, Vikash Publishing House, New Delhi, p. 145.
100. Sharma, Tulshi Ram (1996), *Sikkim Hijo Dekhi Aaja Samma* (Sikkim from yesterday till Today) Aankura Prakashan Gangtok, p. 154.
101. Elections Proclamation of 1970, Dated 31st December 1969 (Nepali Translation of English Proclamation) Section 4, clause 1 (b).
102. *Ibid.*
103. Sharma (1996) op cit, p. 159.
104 *Ibid.*, p. 158.
105. Sharma (1996) op cit, pp. 159-160, Basnett (1974) op cit, p. 162.
106. Tripartite Agreement signed between the political parties, Indian Government and the *Chogyal,* May 8th 1973 Article I.
107. Das, B.S (1983), The Sikkim Saga, Vikash Publishing House Pvt. Ltd, New Delhi, p. 45.
108. Proceedings of the Sikkim Assembly dated 10th May 1974.
109. Das, (1983) op cit, p. 49.
110. *Ibid.,* p. 50.
111. Datta Ray, (1984) op cit, p. 220.
112. Das, (1983) op cit, p. 51.
113. Proceedings of the Sikkim Assembly, Friday, June 28th 1974.
114. Datta Ray (1984) op cit, p. 234.
115. The Constitution (THIRTY FIFTH AMENDMENT ACT) 1974, Dated 22nd February 1975 Article 2A. Source: http://indiacode.nic.in/coiweb/amend/amend35 date of access 21 December 2013.
116. Kotturan, (1983) op cit, p. 108.
117. Resolution passed by the Sikkim Assembly Dated 10th April 1975, pp. 1-2.
118. Cooke 1980 op cit, p. 278.
119. Resolution passed by the Sikkim Assembly, Section 'A', p. 2.
120. Datta Ray (1984) op cit, p. 311.
121. The Constitution (THIRTY SIXTH AMENDMENT ACT 1975) Statement of Objects and Reasons Source: www.indiacode.nic.in/coiweb/amend Date of access 23rd December 2013.

Chapter 4

A New Agrarian Arrangement after the British

In all human societies, patterns of land ownership have shaped the pattern of human relations. This has also helped in determining the prospect and pace of economic expansion of a country. However, almost in all histories, the landownership stands on the foundation of theocracy that usually patronizes the notion of prominence of State over farmlands. It is due to such landscape; the peasants, who are the nubs of human growth, have always resisted the un-proportionate distribution of land between them and the state. The lop-sided pattern of landownership usually keeps peasants in a lesser position amidst their larger and generously proportioned contribution to the State. Instead of recognition, peasants are harassed, suppressed, exploited, and in many occasions even embarrassed by the State taking advantage of their constrained circumstances and scaring temperament.

We do not have much information about the pattern of land ownership of Sikkim before the establishment of Namgyal Dynasty. However, after the Namgyals, as in any monarchy, the Sikkimese theory of landholding was established on the principles of pre-eminence of State. The King of the Kingdom was regarded as the *de-facto* owner of entire lands belonging to the territory of Sikkim.[1] Thus, it is obvious that, land grants with ownership rights to the celebrated families for their services to the State were introduced after the accession of Namgyals in Sikkim. Although, the method and procedure of revenue assessment from such land grants till the advent of British are obscure. However, after the British, Sikkim began to extract revenue through various sources in a diminutive manner. If we have to believe on the account of Richard Temple, even during the reign of Thotub Namgyal (1874-1914), the State was assessing revenue in kind that consisted of agricultural produce and transit duties. It is said that, hardly the King could collect $ 1,000 per annum as revenue from his subjects.[2]

Similarly, Balikci writes about a significant role of the Lamas in the revenue collection before the British intervention.[3]

The British Idée Fixe

After the takeover of administration by the British, feudalism appeared in Sikkim in a modern sense of interpretation. A seigniorial[4] from of tenure was devised by the whimsical Imperial Government and encouraged the Nepalese peasants to get settled in Sikkim leading to a substantial demographic change. Ignoring all the prevalent consent, a massive migration of the Nepalese was favoured by the British that even led to some violent consequences.[5] It was immediately after the conclusion of Treaty of 1861; the British engaged themselves for the settlement of the Nepalese in Sikkim. Hence, in 1867, a formal grant of lease was accorded to two Newar brothers, the traders Laxmi Dass Pradhan and Chandra Bir Maskey. With the grant of lease, the bottom class of agrarian sector of Sikkim began to be dominated by the Nepali peasants. The process of their migration continued till the accession of Tashi Namgyal.[6] Such unrestricted and interminable process of migration from the nearby Kingdom of Nepal had ultimately sidelined the native Lepcha-Bhutia peasants.

A wholesale transformation in agrarian sphere emerges after the formal appointment of J C White as the first British Political Officer to Sikkim. As per the new land reforms initiated by him, thirty five monasteries of Sikkim lost their land holdings with the exception of five important monasteries. Similarly, large number confiscation of the land holding of erstwhile *Kazis* was initiated by the Political Officer owing to their allegiance with the *Maharaja* Sir Thutob Namgyal.[7] Likewise, several other estates were created in South, West, and East Sikkim and handed over to the local *Kazis* and *Thikadars*. Such newly created estates were begun to be filled up by the Nepali peasants, who had come to Sikkim probably for a better livelihood. White began to rule as a *de facto* President of the Council composed of few pro-British Lamas. Within a year or two of his service, the number of Nepali settlers doubled. The main purpose of such a heavy Nepali settlement according to White was to bring more land under cultivation on favourable terms to the Nepalese.[8]

In all probabilities, to protect the native interests, the Political Officer through a notice, forbade the vending and subletting any land of the Lepcha-Bhutia community without the express sanction of the council.[9] The policy was further broadened by Revenue Order No.1 of 17th May 1917. According to this Order, no Lepcha-Bhutia would be allowed to sell, mortgage or sublet any of their land to any person other than their community without the express sanction of the *Durbar*, or Officers empowered by the *Durbar* on its behalf.[10] Likewise, it was also decided that no immigrant Nepalese would be appointed as the head (*Mandal*) of a village.[11] However, it seemed to be a temporary measure as in the later years the Nepali dominated villages were kept under the Nepali *Mandals*. It is important to state that in any agrarian society, control over farmland is regarded as a major apparatus to acquire prosperity, permanence, and power and this very idea seemed to have been well understood by the Sikkimese aristocrats who were in favour of settling the Nepalese. Thus, in all likelihoods, the Nepali settlers who set their feet in Sikkim in the first decade of twentieth Century had probably come to Sikkim as it might have served as a better option than what they had in their native land.

Many other issues related to agriculture and farming was streamlined by the British with the consent of local elites. As intended by the State, for a continuous collection of the revenues, new policies and measures were adopted. Strict rules and regulations for revenue assessment were framed after the departure of J.C. White. C.A. Bell, who succeeded White in the office of Political Officer made alterations and adjustments in the dates and times for the tax payments. According to his notice, dated 20th April 1916, 30th of November every year was fixed as the due date of payment to the tenants and 31st of December to the *Zamindars*.[12] The said notice of Mr Bell was later on rectified in 1926 that made the time of tax payment from 1st of Aug till 31st December each year.[13] Shifting cultivation was forbidden in 1925 and it was also fixed to keep 10 per cent of the total land of a landlord as home farm.[14] Further, it was allowed to have minimum 100 acres of land to a landlord and considering merit of a landlord that could be extended up to 200 acres.[15]

New Mode of Revenue Assessment

As stated, after the appointment of J.C. White, many new estates were created and were handed over to the lessee holders. Creation of such large scale estates had not only changed the very face of rural Sikkim but, had also paved way for the evolution of a new revenue system. Before the British, there were twelve *Kazis* who exercised jurisdiction over specific tracts of lands. These officers collected revenue from the peasants settled in their jurisdiction and paid a certain fixed contribution to the *Raja*. Further, a cultivator did not have a claim to the soil he trilled, but, he could settle down on the unoccupied areas without any formality and no one could uproot him except the King.[16] The system of collection of taxes in this form was adopted long back in 1747 with the appointment of Rabden Sarpa as a regent of baby King Namgyal Phuntsog and the system was then known as *Bisa Panja*.[17]

A systematic change appears in the revenue system after the advent of the British Political Officer. His appointment heralded a new epoch in the revenue history of Sikkim as all the taxes now began to be collected in cash.[18] Conversely, still there were few neglected and ignored aspects associated with the haphazard mode of revenue assessment. The available Administration Reports of Sikkim reveals no scientific survey of the land was made for the purpose of revenue settlement and preparing records.[19] Thus, in absence of a scientific measurement, various traditional methods like *Nazar Janch*[20] were applied for the revenue extraction that never goes unbiased. It is worth to mention that, the state did not collect any of its taxes through its departmental agencies. The land revenue was collected from the *Raiyats* through middlemen known as *Elakhadars*.[21] These *Elakhadars* or Managers were appointed on commission of 10 per cent on the gross revenue collected from the various estates.[22] The provisions for the assessment of revenues to the *Elakhadars* were laid down in the various Administration Reports of the Sikkim State.

> "These *Thikadars* or lessees pay to the *Sirkar* a fixed sum calculated at the rate per acre which varies according to the conditions of the Elakhas leased. They are authorised by virtue of the terms of the lease (which are identical) to realise land revenue tax from the Raiyats of the Elakah on a fixed and certain assessment the expenses for realising are incurred by the lessees themselves".[23]

The rate of lease varied from the productivity of lands and keeping this very fact in mind rates were fixed on the leaseholders. From the available sources it is evident that, while collecting revenues from the peasants similar approach of assessment had been maintained. However, the mode of revenue assessment of one-fifth of the total produce to the Nepalese and one-eight of the total produced to a Lepcha-Bhutia peasant was removed. This mode of assessment of land revenue which was implemented in 1912-13 was eliminated in 1914. It emerges that, the then *Maharaja* Sidkeong Tulku had realised the problems of peasantry as he believed that the rates were quite heavy for his *Raiyats*. Therefore, he proposed that the assessment should be made on the *Pathi*[24] of the seed sown and not on according to the total produce.[25] After the accession of Sir Tashi Namgyal, lands were classified according to their arability and a new rate of assessment was fixed at a meeting of the State Council on 26th January 1915. Unlike the rates of *Maharaja* Sidekong, the rates introduced by Sir Tashi Namgyal were bit incongruent between the Lepcha-Bhutia and Nepali peasants.[26] The new rates of assessment were as under:

Table 4.1: Showing the new rate of assessment of the rice fields at the meeting of the Council held on 26th January 1915

	Rates per Pathi of seeds sown								
	1st Class Land (Land that could produce 1 Murhi of rice from 4 Manas of seed)			*2nd Class Land (Land that could produce 1 Murhi of rice from 4-6 Manas of seeds)*			*3rd Class Land (Land that could produce 1 Murhi of rice from more than 6 Manas of seeds)*		
For	**Rs**	**Anna**	**Paisa**	**Rs**	**Anna**	**Paisa**	**Rs**	**Anna**	**Paisa**
Nepalese	2	0	0	1	8	0	1	0	0
For Bhutia and Lepcha	1	8	0		2	0	0	12	0

Source: Administration Report of the Sikkim State for 1914-15, Chapter II, p. 3.

Classification of Land and Ownership

As stated elsewhere, the Sikkimese theory of landholding was also based on the principles of pre eminence of State. The King of the Kingdom was regarded as the *de-facto* owner of the entire land belonging to the territory of Sikkim.[27] Therefore, in all probabilities by taking the King in confidence, few alterations were made in the existing convention that led to the classification of terraced rice land in December 1915.[28] It is not fair enough to assume that the terraced cultivation in Sikkim was an unknown phenomenon before the arrival of the Nepalese. The process of terrace cultivation appears to be in vogue in the Kingdom as Waddell suggests that few Lepchas possessed a little terraced land for rice cultivation.[29] O'Malley also indicates the existence of a terrace fields in the rural areas of Sikkim.[30] Diverse to these, for the first time, the Government itself had classified terraced lands that covered approximately 10,000 acres and that could produce estimated 80,000 mounds of rice.[31]

After the classification, the earlier concept of the ownership of land had been vividly transformed. Provisions were made to allow the Nepali peasants to acquire a tract in lease for 10 to 30 years. The lands were leased at varying rates from one *Anna* to eight *Anna* per acre for the period of 15 years to Lepcha-Bhutia landlords and for 10 years to Nepali landlords. However, the rates were liable to revision at the end of each period.[32] On the contrary, few of the Lepcha and Bhutia landlords were granted leases for 30 years, and their rent was liable to revision after every ten years.[33] This new lease process to a few Lepcha-Bhutia landlords was an amendment to the lease system created at a meeting of the Council on 16th August 1909.[34]

It is to be noted that the procedure of granting a lease in Sikkim was made in an organised manner. A form had to be filled up by the person aspiring to be an *Elakhadar* stating the area of the estate along with the sum to be deposited in the royal exchequer agreeing upon the terms and conditions. Term No. 6 of the form makes a clear stand about the collection of rents from the peasants fixed by the *Durbar*. It states:

> "The lessees shall issue leases to the *Bustiwallas* in such form and on such rentals as may be approved by the *Durbar* and he shall not raise the rents thus fixed without obtaining in writing, the previous consent of the *Durbar* nor must he eject any *Bustiwallas* without the sanction of the *Durbar*".[35]

It seems that the State was concerned enough about the prevailing rural indebtedness; hence, through condition No. 7 of the lessee form, it directed the leaseholders not to overtax its subjects.[36] The terms and conditions meant for the Leaseholders had all together 28 provisions that were basically implied for the betterment of the Kingdom as a whole. However, it is evident that, the *Elakhadars* had never complied with the terms and conditions maintained by the *Durbar* leading to rural indebtedness and also forced the peasants to resist the State.

Although, the lands were classified according to its fertility and a new rate of assessment was made compulsory among the peasants, the State seemed unenthusiastic to enforce common laws against the landed aristocrats. It is also evident that the non-transparency of leased estates was an important column of land ownership in the territory of Sikkim. However, it evolves that, none of the lands leased to the *Elakhadars* or the *Kazis* were ever been confiscated by the State upon their deaths. Owing to the death of such *Elakhadars*, without much opponent from the part of State, their properties were inherited by their surviving family members. In actuality, as per the terms of the lease, such *Elakhas* were to be taken over by the State. For an instance, in 1920, In 1920, Pinchu *Thikadar* of Rinchenpong and he died and his estate was transferred to his son SLD Sharab.[37] Even if a *Kazi* or an *Elakhadar* died without a proper heir to succeed, the leased lands of the deceased *Kazi* were transferred to his surviving wife. In another instance, a *Kazi* named Dallam died without a male heir at Daramdin however, eliminating all the prevailing laws, the State allowed his wife to manage the estate.[38] The non-transparency of lessee thus simply remained in theory; but, practically, almost all the *Elakhas* were transferred in the name of the children or wives of the former *Elakhadar*.

Unlike the lessee estates, a *Bustiwalla* who secured the cultivation right by paying *Chaar Daam*[39] could transfer his land in the name of his children. The task of *Banda* as it was known had to be made before the village *Mandal* and elder people.[40] The earlier system of *Banda* or division is still prevalent in Sikkim. As per Administrative Report of 1926-27, the estate managers in respect of private estate and *Kazis* and *Thikadars* in the leased areas were allowed to exercise powers of registration in their respective *Elakhas*. Nevertheless, they were required to obtain the sanction of *Durbar* before registering any document in their names or in favour of their *Mandals*.[41] The Report further ascertains one per cent of the market value of property to be accessed as the registration fee of a newly purchased land. The entire amount thus collected was to be credited to the *Durbar*.[42]

The grant of lease of 1867, to Lakshmi Das Pradhan and Chandra Bir Maskey, two Nepali contractors had heralded an era of *Thikadari* system in Sikkim.[43] They secured estates known as *Elakhas* in contract or *Thika* hence they were known as the *Thikadars*. By 1925-26, the number of such *Thikadars* and *Elakhadars* or estates had gone up to 70. However, 13 of such *Elakhas* were under the direct control of the State; 16 under the managers of Private Estates of His Highness; and five under different monasteries. Other 36 *Elakhas* were divided among various Landlords of which 21 were *Kazis*, 6 Bhutias, 8 Lepchas, 10 Nepalese and 1 plainsman.[44]

The Intermediaries

The estates possessed by the *Kazis* and *Thikadars* or the *Elakhadars* had several sub-divisions. The land at the block level was distributed among some people who became intermediaries between the *Kazis* and the *Raiyats* or peasants. These intermediaries were called *Bustiwallas* and *Mandals* according to the amount of land they possessed. It appears that till 1930-31, the State had not followed the policy of the sale of State lands instead the State was allotting them in a lease. A free grant of such land was allowed to all *Paharia*[45] who wanted to settle in the Kingdom. A nominal sum of ₹ ¼ called '*Chaar Daam*' was usually paid to the *Mandal* of the block in which new land was reclaimed by the intending settlers.[46] Sinha suggests that the process of paying *Chaar Daam* existed only in the private estates of the *Kazis* who were the regional lords and as such were in charge of their territories.[47] The collection of taxes of the land secured through '*Chaar Daam*' was made through a *Nazar Janch* by a *Mandal* to fix the amount of revenue. In some villages like Tashiding, Lasso, Chongrang, Gerethang, and Nesha of West Sikkim, there used to be an official called *Bichari* who would fix the taxation amount to a *Raiyat*.[48] Field survey reveals that majority of the Nepali peasants did not pay the prevalent *Chaar Daam* to clear up the waste lands for a permanent settlement and cultivation; relatively they preferred to be the tenants of the *Kazi*/*Thikadars*.[49] Even the *Chaar Daam* peasants who were also known as *Bustiwallas* also did not have a right of vast possession of land. The provision reflected in the Administration Report of 1930-31 had forbidden *Bustiwallas* from acquiring a vast tract of lands.

Ordinarily, a *Raiyat* was not permitted to acquire more than twenty acres of cultivable land. In a case of *Mandals* of the various blocks of an *Elakha*, maximum could go up to thirty acres, whilst, the 'Lessees' could not acquire more than one hundred acres.[50] The *Raiyats* who could afford to pay *Chaar Daam* got a plot of land for self cultivation. They had to pay their land tax along with house tax to their *Mandals* in cash fixed by the latter through *Nazar Janch* yearly.[51] They were known as the *Bustiwallas* and hence, being the owners of the land, the *Bustiwallas* became direct tax payer to the State. The *Raiyats* who could not afford to pay the *Chaar Daam* created a new tenancy system in Sikkim.

Types of Tenancy in Sikkim during Early Twentieth Century

The official records maintained in the form of Administrative Reports mention only two forms of tenancy in the Kingdom namely *Adhiadars* and *Kutdars*. Such tenancy tenures may be classified into two parts (i) those who pay rent in the shape of a division of produce (locally known as *Adhiya*) or (ii) those tenants who pay fixed rent as may be determined by contract in the form of "kind" or "cash" (locally known as *Kutias*).[52] It is evident from these orientations that the State was unfamiliar with the prevalence of other forms of the tenancy in its domain. Apart from these, the erstwhile Himalayan Kingdom had many other forms of tenancy which did not have a direct dealing with the State. Probably, due to the very nature of such tenancies the State was less enthusiastic to hassle much about other forms of tenancy in the Kingdom. The various forms of tenancy were as under:

Adhiadars/Adhiars

The *Adhiadars* had to pay 50 per cent of the total produce to his landlord. Further, he had to take a prior permission from his owner for the tilling up of land and for raising the next crop. If he raised paddy in the land of his landlord, he had to pay 50 per cent of the total produce as per the prevalent practice along with 50 per cent of total paddy straw gathered during harvest for the cattle.[53] The same process of share was applicable in any of the crops an *Adhiadar* raised. In case of failure of crop, the *Adhiadars* had to pay the share of his landlord. According to Sinha, the *Adhiar* or *Adhyadar* in most of the cases was allowed to raise subsidiary crops. However, this contract was given only when the tenant accepts his total subordination to the landlord.[54]

Kutdar/ Kutiyars

The origination of *Kutiyari* or *Kootiya* or *Koot* form of land arrangement is in obscurity. Baļkci believes the system was adopted in Sikkim with the settlement of the first Nepalese tenants in the South Western part in 1870's.[55]

However, it comes into surface that the tenancy pattern of *Kutdar* or *Kutiyar* varied from village to village and landlord to landlord. It depended on the tract of a land a *Kutdar/Kutiyar* had taken for a lease. According to Subba, it was determined according to the stipulated amount of a particular grain that had to be taken by the tenant as a rent irrespective of the amount of production.[56]As there were no fixed lease terms, the arrangements were determined arbitrarily by the land owner at his own convenience. It is revealed from the field survey that the *Kut* leases were generally made verbally. However, few family papers like that of some *Mandals* trace the prevalence of written agreements between a *Kutiyar* and a *Bustiwalla* who is sometimes also known as a *Pattadar*.[57] Although this is a rare instance as far as the written lease terms between a landlord and a *Kutiyar* is concerned. The *Mandals*, being the elites of feudal Sikkim, used to make such written documents for their convenience. Excluding such rare case, the majority of rural population followed the traditional methods of granting a lease in an unwritten manner. Apart from such arrangements of the *Kutdars/Kutiyars*, the system of a middleman was also prevalent in some remote places. Hence, due to the lack of a proper lease terms and monopoly of the landlords, the plight of *Kutiadar* tenants seemed very deplorable.

Chakhureys and Pakhureys

Unlike the *Adhiars* and *Kutdars,* the *Chakhureys* and *Pakhureys* used to exist in the Monastery Estates. The five monastery estates of Sikkim were further divided into 38 Revenue Blocks and were distributed among the tenants. The tenants of such estates, *Chakhurey* and *Pakhurey* were given land for their cultivation by the monastery and individual Lama Private Landholders. The *Chakhurey* and *Pakhurey* would receive plots in those estates in lieu of their services of manual labour rendered by them to the monastery and the Lamas.[58] Analogous to *Kutiyar* land lease terms, the process of lease in these estates was also made in a verbal manner. Since there were no terms and conditions laid down for this compulsory labour, normally the tenants had to send one member of their family for such labours daily or as and when required by the monastery. Within the monastery the Lamas as primary holders, hold large areas. They settled these lands with the tenants under various repressive and unsatisfactory conditions.[59]

Apart from these three forms of tenancy, feudal Sikkim had also witnessed another form of tenancy which was not much popular as compared to the other three forms discussed above. This less trendy tenancy was then known as *Massikatta* system.[60] The family papers[61] of some semi-landlords of erstwhile Sikkim provides a clear sketch about the functioning of the *Massikatta* form of tenancy in Sikkim. A tenant had to deposit a fixed amount to a concerned landlord to secure a plot of land for cultivation in *Massikatta* system. As per the conditions mentioned in the family papers the tenant used to get a plot of land for a fixed period of five to ten years. The tenure of his cultivation rights would depend on the amount he deposited to the landlord. The important feature of the *Massikatta* method of tenancy is that it was done through a written agreement.[62] In the midst of all these diversities prevalent among the tenancy forms, we can categorise them in two significant agrarian classes: the *Bustiwallas* those who owned lands and the *Pakhureys* who were landless. Though, they were different in their dealings with the state and its functionaries, both these sections of the peasants were the one who had resisted their State for its whimsical approach towards them.

Thus, it is evident that after the upper hand of British in Sikkimese administration, a fully matured structure of feudalism appeared in the territory of Sikkim. The allocation of estates to various private holders inaugurated a new chapter of coarseness in the silky and serene history of the tiny Himalayan Kingdom. The Sikkimese villages now began to feel the pressure upon them from the estate holders who were assisted by their subordinates with several names like *Kazi*, *Thikadars*, *Mukhtiyars*, *Mandals*, and *Karbaris*. The only motives of private estate holders' appears to be earning and to get their pockets full and to gain these they often cheated meagre peasants. Every human society, since evolutionary period, has to some extent resisted the existing norms to protect it from the elite's domination. While struggling for its survival in an unbalanced world created by the dominant class, the subordinates sometimes adopt some techniques to shield it. Such acts of protection from the part of peasants are usually known as resistance. A full sense of devotion from the part of peasants towards their masters and a neglected attitude of the masters towards peasantry paved way for peasant resistance in Sikkim.

Notes

1. Administration Report 1930-31, IV.
2. Temple Richard (1887), *Journals kept in Hyderabad, Kashmir, Sikkim and Nepal*, Vol. II, W.H. Allen and Co. Waterloo Palace, Pall Mall, London, p. 164.
3. Balikci, Anna (2008), *Lamas, Shamans and Ancestors- Village Religion in Sikkim*, Brill, Leiden, The Netherlands, p. 49.
4. The seigneur rented most of the land to tenants, known as *censitaires* or *habitants*, who cleared the land, built a house and other buildings, and farmed the land. It was introduced to New France in 1627 by Cardinal Richelieu. Harris, Richard Colebrook (1966), *The Seigneurial System in Early Canada. A Geographical Study.* Madison: University of Wisconsin Press.

5. Royal Decree from Bangdutse Palace Year 1880: PD/1.7/002, Namgyal Institute of Tibetology.
6. Administration Report 1914-15, VI, 8.
7. Balikci, (2008), op cit, p. 49.
8. White, John Claude (1909), *Sikkim, and Bhutan 21 years on the North East Frontier 1887- 1908*, Cosmo Publication, New Delhi, p. 25.
9. Political Officer's Notification, 2nd of January 1897, 1.
10. Central Department, 17th of May 1917, 1.
11. Sinha, A C (2008), *Sikkim- Feudal and Democratic,* Indus Publishing Company, New Delhi, p. 77.
12. Circular No.1 in Nepali, from the Office the Political Officer of Sikkim, 20th April 1916, Ram Gauri Sangrahalaya Rhenock, East Sikkim.
13. General Department 8146-08/G, 19th June 1926.
14. General Department, 8545/G, 16th October 1924.
15. *Ibid.*
16. Temple (1887) op cit, p. 164.
17. Administration Report 1930-31, IV, 11-12.
18. *Ibid.*
19. *Ibid.*
20. *Nazar Janch* was a method to measure the newly acquired land by village headmen known as *Mandal*. He used to climb on a tallest tree of the locality to make an assessment of the land and to fix the amount of revenue to be levied. *Source:* Field Report.
21. Administration Report 1930-31, IV, 11-12.
22. Administration Report 1926-27, II, 5.
23. Administration Report 1930-31, IV, 12.
24. *Pathi* is a copper utensil used by the Nepalese peasants to weigh grains. The earlier weighing process of cereals by the Nepalese includes *Muthi, Mana, Pathi,* and *Muri*. The lowest unit of weighing system was *Muthi* or fist, likewise 8 fists was equivalent to 1 *Mana* and 8 *Manas* of grains were equivalent to 1 *Pathi* and 20 *Pathis* (60 Kgs approximately) of grain was considered as 1 *Muri*. The process was known as *Muti, Mana, Pathi, Muri* in the Nepali inhabited areas of the Himalayas. *Source:* Field Report.
25. Administration Report 1914-15, II, 2.
26. *Ibid.,* p. 3.
27. Administration Report 1930-31, IV.
28. Administration Report 1915-16, II, 24th June 1916.
29. Waddell, L.A. (1899), *Among the Himalayas*, Bibiliotheca Himalayica Series I, Vol. 18, p. 95.
30. O'Malley, L.S.S. (1917), *Provincial Geographies of India, Bengal, Bihar, Orissa, and Sikkim*, Cambridge University Press, London, pp. 14-16.
31. Administration Report 1915-16, II, 24th June 1916.
32. Administration Report 1916-17, II, 24th June 1916.
33. *Ibid.*

34. Administration Report 1909-10, II.
35. Lessee form with Terms and conditions issued to the lessees by Sikkim *Durbar* in 1931.
36. *Ibid.*
37. Administration Report, 1920-21, 4.
38. Administration Report, 1909-10, 2.
39. Administrative Report,1930-31, IV, 13.
40. Field Report 2011-2012: Information collected through personal interview from the erstwhile Mandal of Tarku village, South Sikkim.
41. Administrative Report 1926-27, II, 8.
42. *Ibid.*
43. Agreement regarding the use of Nepali labourers between a leader of the Nepali community and Bermiok and Sang Kazis in which the agreement between Sir Asley Eden and His Highness Sidkeong Namgyal has been stated, PD/9.5/050, Date 12th Month of the Water Horse Year (in Tibetan), Namgyal Institute of Tibetology.
44. Administration Report 1925-26, V.
45. *Paharia* was an administrative term used by the Government of Sikkim to classify the peasants of Nepali origin.
46. Administrative Report 1930-31, IV, 13.
47. Sinha, (2008), op.cit, p. 56.
48. Field Report, 2011-2012.
49. Field Report 2011-2012: Information collected through personal interview from the erstwhile Mandal of Namli village, East Sikkim.
50. Administration Report 1930-31, IV, 13.
51. Field Report: 2011-2012: Information collected through personal interview from erstwhile *Mandals* of Sikkim.
52. Administration Report 1930-31, IV, 11.
53. Field Report: 2011-2012: Information collected from the related peasants of Soreng, Pakki Gaon, Suntaley villages West Sikkim.
54. Sinha, (2008) op cit, p. 56.
55. Balikci, (2008) op cit, p. 50.
56. Subba, Tanka B. (1988), '*Agrarian relations and Development in Sikkim*' Rural Development in Eastern and North- Eastern India', Calcutta I.I.M, p. 325.
57. Family Papers of erstwhile *Mandal* collected during field survey.
58. Subba, (1988), op.cit, p. 325.
59. *Ibid.*
60. Field Report: 2011-2012: Information collected from the peasants of Soreng, Pakki Gaon, Suntaley villages West Sikkim.
61. Family papers collected from Suntaley village, West Sikkim.
62. *Ibid.*

Chapter 5

Hidden Transcripts, Resentment, and Resistance-The provoking issues

Adoption of new agrarian policy had naturally brought new dimensions to prosper along with some new challenges. The advent of a new system had not only affected the rural ways of life but, had also made far reaching changes in the existing set up. The newly established chain of command had a different feature that had extraterrestrial aspects that seemed to be a direct consequence of the British hegemony. The only motive of the British to open up Sikkim was to elaborate their trading avenues in Tibet for which they needed a cheap labour supply. Owing to its difficult terrain, a smooth trade with Tibet was indeed a challenging task for the British capitalist interest. Therefore, in the consent of the Sikkimese aristocrats, they devised such a bureaucracy that would not only serve their interest but, could also help the State to collect its revenues systematically. The entire State was bifurcated into several estates and was given to the estate holders and it was further given in charges to the other officials. It is worth to mention that, the feudal set up of Sikkim resembles many similarities with the neighbouring Kingdom of Nepal. The new officials in Sikkim like *Kazi*, *Mukhtiyars*, and *Mandals* already had their existence in Nepal though; in terms of their roles they differ from their Sikkimese counterparts. Similarly, forced labours with several names had deepened their roots in the villages to overcome the British design for a silky trade with Tibet. Undoubtedly, the larger cargos were transported by means of the mules but, for the smaller ones they asked for the porters from among the rural lots. Similarly, the rate of taxation, forced labours, and feudal laws, in which one could hardly think of justice were some of the pivotal factors that ignited the idea of resistance among the ignorant minds of the rural populace.

It is obvious that, the origin of peasant resistance in Sikkim was basically due to the encroachment of an economy with a capitalist mindset against the conventional economy. It also appears that, the traditional economic structure that stood on the principle of self sufficiency was greatly shaken by the creation of estates. Such estates, after the lapse of time, had broken the ethical standard of traditional economy that not only had separated the peasants from land but, as it indicates, had even converted land, labour, and resources into simple commodities. Therefore, to regain their lost security against the estate holders the peasants often engage themselves in quarrel against their landowners. Scott elucidates over taxation, forced labour, warfare, and revolt, as the major mechanism for the origin of peasant resistance.[1] When they were forced to knell before the unbending feudal structure, the Sikkimese peasants also adopted some techniques for their survival in the world created by the dominant for acquisitive gain.

Feudal Chain of Command

To reiterate, according to the Sikkimese convention, the sole owner of all the lands belonged to the territory was the *Chogyal.* Therefore, his position was on the top and he possessed unlimited and unquestioned powers. However, with the appointment of the first Political Officer J.C. White, position of the Sikkimese *Chogyal* was greatly reduced to his subordinate. Being equipped with an unimaginable power, at least from the Sikkimese perspectives, initial task of the Political Officer was to set up a council in which he himself had to be the President.[2] In a brief, the Political Officer now became the ruler of Sikkim to all intents and purposes and the King was granted ₹ 1000 as retinue and allowances.[3] As being squeezed in between the Political Officer and the *Kazis*, it seems, the Kings could not function according to the peoples' aspiration even if they desired. In spite of reluctance of the King, the lands were lacerated in several spheres in the forms of *Elakhas* and distributed among the faithful and the loyal. Such policy from the part of State made several masters in the profile of *Kazis* and *Thikadars*, who were assisted by their subordinates like *Mukhtiyars*, *Mandals*, and *Karbaris*.

Kazi

The word *Kazi*, seemed to be borrowed through the Nepalese from the Mohammadan rulers of India, and it might have been distroted from Persian word *Kazi* or *Kadi*, that correspond to Magistrate.[4] With the arrival of British, these *Kazis*, because of their proximity to the paramount power, became the most influential part of the Sikkimese administration. There is no doubt that the earlier *Blon Pos* (Ministers) were now attributed with the new soubriquet of *Kazis*[5] however, they vary in the terms of their functions with the earlier ones. Their new contacts with the British seemed a blessing to them as they now could own vast estates, enjoyed enormous powers, and were privileged of being the elites of Sikkim. Adding more feathers to their caps, the Council Meeting of 23rd April 1919 provided license free guns to all the *Kazis*.[6] Thus, even a landlord for the name sake could carry a gun without license which later proved to be a best tool of peasant exploitation. It is said that, tax evaders were threatened at gun points before they were sent to rigorous torture.[7] Having both lands and capital at their spheres, the *Kazis* had a very comfortable life. *A Few Facts about Sikkim*, a pamphlet has highlighted their position in the following manner:-

> "The *Kazis*, who are the landlords, claim to belong to the old nobility and compare themselves with the barons of the feudal system. By long usage they have accustomed to oppress the people and to expect the utmost subservience from them. They form the exclusive and influential coterie around the ruling family and are able to impose their will on all and sundry. The rest of the landlords called '*Thikadars*', are content to play second fiddle to the *Kazis* and thus share in the loaves and fishes of office and other privileges. Bound by a common policy to oppress the ryots, the '*Thikadars*' especially the more influential among them, have proved as bad as any of the *Kazis*. Landlordism as obtaining in Sikkim has proved the curse of the ryots. It has enabled the landlords through coercion and intimidation, to acquire for themselves the best holdings of the ryots. The landlords pay no taxes, which consequently fall with greater severity upon the ryots. On the other hand, the landlords receive large unearned commission from the state as reward for carrying on a thoroughly corrupt system of government".[8]

The pamphlet further states:

> "The landlords are vested with magisterial powers in both civil and criminal matters. They are also empowered to register documents for the sale or transferred of landed properties. There are no effective checks on these powers and the landlords are free to abuse them for their own gains. The more fine a landlord can impose, the larger his share of spoils, for he receives one half of the collection as his fees and the other halves goes to the state. When as has happened many times, a landlord 'forgets' to enter a fine in his books, nobody is wiser, and he appropriates the whole amount to himself. A grabbing landlord has no difficulties in disposing an uncompromising ryot of his cherished possession, be it a paddy field or a herd of cattle. The slightest delay in the payment of taxes, a matter of common occurrence, enables a landlord to seize the very property of he has set his eyes upon, to the exclusion of any other, and thus transfer is affected speedily and very

profitably to the landlord. Numerous ryots have thus been reduced to penury and practical slavery. Landlords are invested with different classes of legal powers with due regard to their merits and qualifications. But, most of the landlords live away from their estates and their powers are exercised by ignorant and rapacious underlings who have no scruples about filling their own pockets besides extracting as much as they can for their masters".[9]

The *Kazis* exploited peasantry in a greater manner by promoting forced labours like *Kalo Bhari*, *Jharlangi*, *Kuruwa*, *Theki Bheti* and to stockpile a lot of wealth. As landlords they monopolised control over farms where most of the people simply worked as their tenants. Unable to bear the suppression of the *Kazis*, many Sikkimese families left Sikkim and took refuge in Nepal, Assam, Darjeeling, and Siliguri.[10] It is said that there was a 'trend' of migration from Sikkim to other neighbouring states. During the entire feudal era Sikkimese peasant was made to pay ₹ 6 as the rent for their dwelling space known as *Dhurikhajana* which was unreasonable to the peasants who usually had a poor income.[11] It is said that, for an ordinary peasant, the amount of *Dhurikhajana* was equal to a pair of oxen.

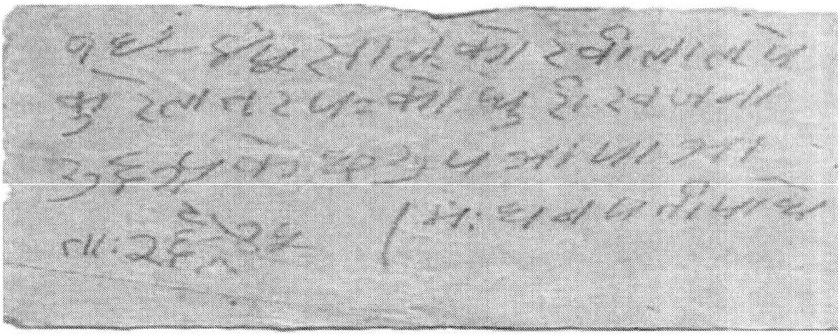

Figure 5.1: A receipt of* Dhurikhajana *of ₹ 6 paid to the* Mandal *Dhanapati Upadhyay by the Late Ravilal Pyakurel of Tareythang Busty East Sikkim. Date of payment of tax 26th August 1945. Credit: Mr Krishna Prasad Pyakurel of Tareythang Busty East Sikkim.

Besides such exorbitant rate of taxation, the farmers had to carry *Kalo Bhari* or Black Load at the orders of the *Kazis* and also had to render wage less services like *Jharlangi*. If they failed to do so, even on account of their health, they were severely dealt with by the *Kazis* and in some cases the peasants were put into *Thinguro*.[12] In the course of time, the Nepalese *Thikadars* too began to imitate their Bhutia counterparts and acted as same as the *Kazis*.[13]

Thikadars

As discussed in the previous chapter, commencement of the *Thikadari* or contract system was made in 1867 after the two Nepali contractors, Laxmi Das Pradhan and Chandra Bir Maskey secured a grant for a period of 20 years. According to the terms of the contract, the duo had to pay ₹ 500 to the King and ₹ 700 to Phodang Lama and Khangsa *Dewan* as annual rent.[14] In all probabilities, with a commercial motive, they began to encourage the Nepali settlers to get settle in their estates. The new Nepali settlers were asked to clear up forest for the creation of cultivable lands. Thus, once a forested area, considered to be wasted lands by the State, began to flourish. The terrace cultivation, in which the Nepalese seemed champions, and the fresh and the virgin soil, led to a boom in agriculture leading to a huge profit to the contractors. Soon this process of taking the Nepalese cultivators got popular and even the Lepcha-Bhutia aristocrats began to follow the practice. Consequently, with the increased number of Nepali population the *Thikadari* system had deepened its roots in the soil of Sikkim. In the social hierarchy, *Thikadars* enjoyed a position just below to the *Zamindars* or the *Kazis*. In the later years, many *Thikadars* due to their propinquity with the *Kazis*, acted like *Zamindars* and monopolised their estates. Along with the *Dhurikhajana* of ₹ 6, stated above, peasants were also made to pay other taxes like *Khet Khajana*[15], *Bari Khajana*[16], *Madati*[17], *Gaddi*[18] to their concerned *Thikadar* or *Zamindar*. Similarly, some unusual taxes like *Satsukey* and *Roadses* had also been introduced by the *Thikadars*.[19] The available sources of information associated with the State have not mention anything related to the issue, and therefore, it can be assessed that such unusual taxes were collected without the consent of the *Durbar*. While, in the succeeding years the assessment of *Satsukey* and *Roadses* tax were stopped.[20] The sudden stoppage of a form of tax indicates about the interference of State against monopolistic approach of the *Thikadars*. However, lack of supportive evidence forbids us to ascertain State's nosiness in the matter. Similarly, it is evident that, the assessment of ₹ 1 as *Madati* tax was still maintained by the State in the succeeding years.[21]

Being an important pillar of the feudal structure the *Thikadars* led extraordinary and exclusive lifestyles. It is said that, a *Thikadar* named Bal Krishna Kasaju *alias* Baburam Pradhan of Namthang in south Sikkim possessed an Arabic horse for his ride. Further, imitating the Nepalese aristocrats of Nepal, he also had kept a band party that would play music while he was riding.[22] A prevalent folksong of the valley '*Kasko Baaja Kasko Baaja Baburamko Baaja*' reveals his costly lifestyle and lavish existence.[23] The study reveals that, *Thikadars* had a sufficient autonomy to bring the Nepalese settlers, to allot them lands for cultivation, to levy taxes upon them, to eject them from their holdings, and so on. It is interesting to note that, some of the *Thikadars* would even use their personal seals to acknowledge payment of the revenues by a peasant. A tax receipt, placed below, dating 1973 Vikrama Samvat (1916 AD) of Dalbir Limbu bears a seal of *Zamindar/ Thikadar*. Written in Nepali, the seal mentions a name Hiralal, probably the *Thikadar* of the Rateypani estate that shares many similarities with the seals of the *Zamindars* in Nepal. Ignoring all other convention and usages of the Kingdom, the use of such autonomous seals by the *Thikadars* makes us to understand their acclaimed and applauded position in the State.

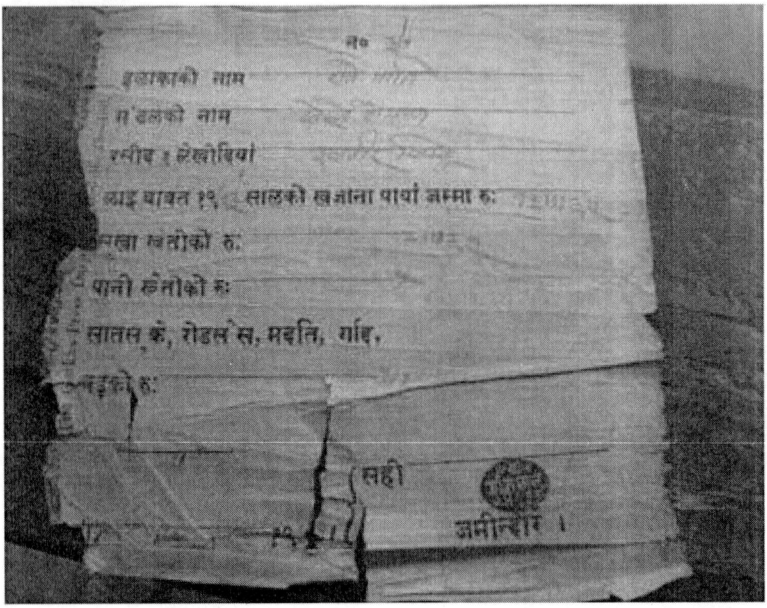
इलाकाको नाम
मंडलको नाम
पानी खेतीको रु:
सही
जमीन्दार

Figure 5.1: Tax receipt bearing a personal seal of a Thikadar/Zamindar of Rateypani Estate in South Sikkim. Year 1973, Vikrama Samvat that corresponds to 1916 AD. Source: Field Survey.

Their main role in the State mechanism was to deposit the collected revenues from their respective *Elakhas* to the government. However, being the elites of their respective *Elakhas*, some additional function like labour supply was also entrusted upon them by the *Kazis*. Such supplies of labours were basically meant for the construction of roads or bungalows to capitalise the trading zeal of the British Government with Tibet. Similarly, the supply of labourers was also needed in carrying belongings of the British Officials during their postings in far off places. In the name of service to the State, these *Thikadars* often compelled peasantry to carry *Kalo Bhari*, and to provide free labour for *Jharlangi* and *Kuruwa*. While doing so, they made extensive profit by taking advantage of the innocence and scaring attitude of the labourers.[24] Though, they were paid handsomely by the British, but, with a motive to gain more profit, *Thikadars* forcefully employed peasants to carry *Kalo Bhari* and *Jharlangi* with a very nominal amount. With the fear of confiscation of their property and livestock the ryots were bound to follow the orders of their *Thikadars*.[25]

Apart from such exploitations, the *Thikadars* who possessed vast land, distributed among their tenants (*Chakhurey* and *Pakhurey*) in *Koot* or *Adhiya* agreement. The peasants put their every effort to extract a bit of profit from those lands which they got after an agreement from their *Thikadars*. However, due to heavy tax, both land and house taxes, and free service they paid, very little gain could be secured by the peasants. Forced labour without any compensation was usually extracted by the *Thikadars* from the browbeaten peasants while cultivating and harvesting their crops. It reveals that, the peasants had reluctantly tolerated to this kind of exaction due to the fear of punishment. Under such set up, it is obvious that a peasant had to live his life always under threats of *Thinguro* and other intimidations.[26]

Mukhtiyars

In the administrative hierarchy of Sikkim, the *Mukhtiyars* enjoyed position next to the *Thikadars*. Balikci presumes that, the term got its origination from Ottoman Empire as the village Chiefs in Ottoman were known as *Mukhtar*.[27] Undoubtedly, the office of the *Mukhtiyars* evolved in Sikkim after the commencement of new agrarian system initiated by the British. The available source of information indicates about the appointment of such officials by both the State and the Estate holders. An appointment letter of "Uehung" Dawa Gyaltsen as a *Mukhtiyar* to Phensang Monastery Estate provides testimonial that such appointments were made at the consent of the State.[28] Similarly, documents belonging to *Rai Saheb* Durga Sumsher Pradhan of Rhenock also indicate that the *Mukhtiyars* were appointed by the *Kazis* and by other lessee holders.[29]

The *Mukhtiyars* were given charge of a whole *Elakah* of a lessee holder or a *Kazi*/*Thikadar*. He was also granted the charge of litigation under his jurisdiction. Their duty was akin to today's District Magistrate and was with a few hereditary exceptions, appointed on merit.[30] The photographs collected from the erstwhile *Mukhtiyar* family of Namchi in South Sikkim, discloses their comfortable and a reverential life.

Figure 5.2: Photograph of* Mukhtiyar *San Man Tamang of Namchi South Sikkim. The person sitting on a chair in the middle was the* Mukhtiyar. *The golden ornaments of the women and the dress they clad in shows that they had a very comfortable way of life. The people standing behind were the peasants of his estate in Namchi. Pic. Courtesy Late Rup Maya Tamang, Namchi Bazaar, South Sikkim.

Being a local of the Estate owned by the *Kazis*, the *Mukhtiyars* had detail knowledge about the settlers. The *Kazis* and *Thikadars*, being the 'high born' elites hardly visited their holdings in the far flung villages instead they gave charges to trusted persons of their respective estates. Therefore, the *Mukhtiyars* were to serve the *Kazis* as a link between the peasants and their Landlords.[31] They had to make necessary arrangements in their *Elakhas* during King's visits and other high ranking native and British Officials.[32] Further, they also had to maintain the land records of peasants of their respective *Elakhas*. Imitating their Masters, *Mukhtiyars* too divided their vast landholdings to the *Pakhureys* for cultivation. During *Dasain*,[33] these bulks of exploited and skimpy lot of people were asked to pay their visit to the house of *Mukhtiyars* with gifts and presents and presence of every household was highly expected. In lieu of this, while offering *Tika*, the *Mukhtiyars* blessed peasants with a long life and prosperity. Luscious dishes like boiled rice, pulses, meat, and pickles were offered to the half-starved peasants by the tubby *Mukhtiyars* on the cheerful day of *Dasain*. However, it is interesting to note, the same 'blessed' peasants were exploited by them through money lending business they carried out in their periphery.[34]

It is thus evident that, being a key official of the *Kazis*, the *Mukhtiyars* too had a very comfortable life. Mostly, the children of tax defaulters were kept as servants by the *Mukhtiyars* in their big houses.[35] They had constructed beautiful mansions, rode on the Arabic horses, and possessed enormous wealth. The *Kothi* of Namchi *Mukhtiyar* which was constructed nearly a century ago still steals a glimpse or two of every visitor. However, these officials were not prevalent in every estate hold by the lessee holders like the *Kazis* and *Thikadars*. It comes into light that, the estates in the proximity of the Kingdom's capital did not have any office related to the *Mukhtiyars*.[36]

Mandal

The *Mandals* played a vital role in igniting the idea of resistance among the slumbered conscience of the Sikkimese peasantry. They were appointed by the *Kazis* or in some cases by the *Mukhtiyars*. Their machinery role was to work as a village headman and to collect taxes from the peasants of their respective villages.[37] A peasant had to deposit his taxes in time, which included house tax and land tax known as *Dhurikhajana* and *Zamin Khajana*.[38] If he fails to pay his taxes on time, he would be given a chance to pay his taxes the following year. Undoubtebly, during his next payment the peasant had to pay his tax with a huge interest.[39] However, some provisions were maintained by the Kingdom to rebate interests of the past year's dues if a peasant made a full payment to his landlord. According to the Provision, Twenty-five per cent of reimbursements were to be made by the landlords to the peasants.[40] On the other hand, the reality seems to be very far, as it is known that the feudal officials never implemented these provisions in a devoted manner.

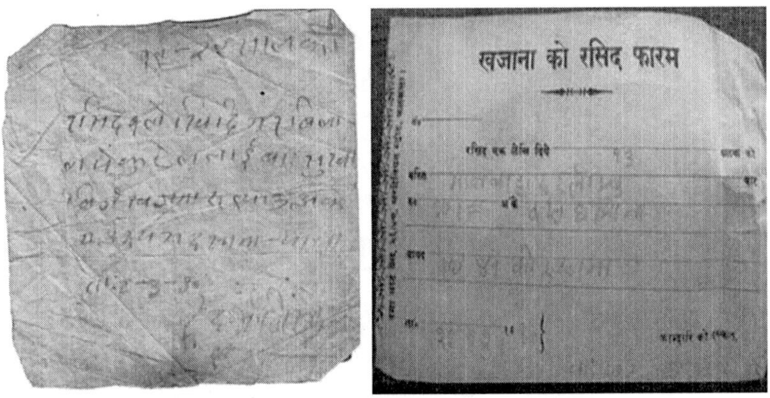

Figure 5.3: Document written with pen is a tax receipt of the year 1929 of Late Ravilal Pyakurel of Tareythang Busty East Sikkim, Date of payment of Zamin khazana 8th March 1930. Document written with pencil is tax receipt of Late Man Bahadur Limboo of Rabitar Namchi, Date of payment of Zamin Khajana 29th December 1941. Both the documents bear signatures of their respective Mandals.

The *Mandals* had to issue a receipt confirming the payment of land tax and house tax to the peasant.[41] Counterfoils of such receipts would be recorded in a register of demand and collection.[42]

Such receipts were mostly written in pencils which bore the *Mandal's* signature. In some cases, if the *Mandal* had any grudge against the peasants, they would issue a wrong receipt taking advantage of the illiteracy of the peasants.[43] This would lead to a big trouble for the peasants as whatever they earned had to be deposited as land tax. More pathetically, if the amount of tax happened to be registered wrongly, they had no option to appeal. However, some had shown their audacity to exhibit their resentments against the official concerned. A *Mandal* named Chatur Singh Rai of Assam Lingzey had made such false entry against one Dal Dhoj Rai of his village. The victim made an appeal to Gyaltsen *Kazi*,[44] the landlord of his village and it is said that his appeal went unheard. In frustration, the victim openly challenged his *Mandal*, and had even thrashed him out during a feast at the village. This was indeed a humiliating situation for the said *Mandal* and to avenge Dal Dhoj for the act of "disobedience" asked to pay ₹ 25 as fine.[45] Though, this incident lacks chronology yet, it is now evident that the hidden transcript of the Sikkimese peasantry was taking a shape of a full throated expression.[46]

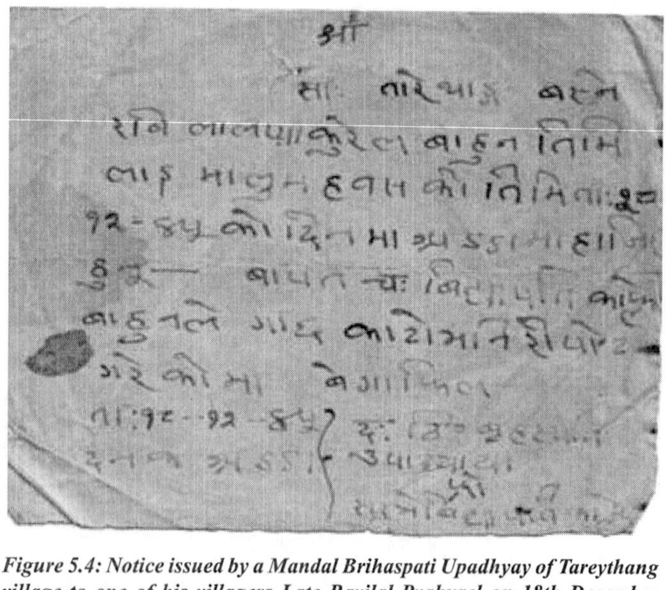

Figure 5.4: Notice issued by a Mandal Brihaspati Upadhyay of Tareythang village to one of his villagers Late Ravilal Pyakurel on 18th December 1945 against a report made by another villager Sarvey Bidhyapati Kafley stating that the accused had chopped off a tree at his land.

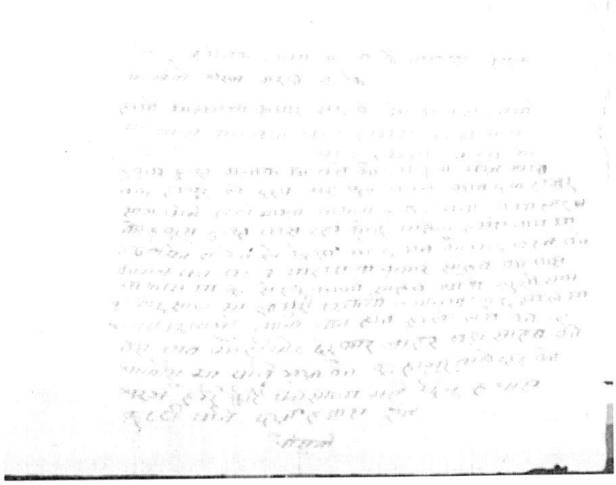

Figure 5.5: A written complaint made by Chungsungni Mandalni of Rumtek village, East Sikkim, to the Maharajkumar Sahib in 1907. The unsettled case of the complainer was related to land and paddy cultivation. Namgyal Institute of Tibetology, Deorali, Gangtok.

Along with the collection of revenues the *Mandals* were further entrusted with the rights of litigation as well. Despite the fact that their verdict was not pleasing, the peasants reluctantly had to accept and obey. For a trial, the *Mandals* would correspond with both the disgruntle parties through a notice. A notice issued by a *Mandal* Brihaspati Upadhyay of Tareythang village in East Sikkim to one peasant Late Ravilal Pyakurel substantiates this. Written in an intimidating language, the notice asks the latter to be present on 20th December 1945 at Danak *Adda* court without fail.[47]

In contradiction with the petty issues, major cases related to land and taxation of the villagers was forwarded to the Durbar by the *Mandals* through written complaints.

Due to their immediacy to power, these *Mandals* also exploited the Sikkimese peasants in the same manner as the *Kazis*, *Thikadars*, and *Mukhtiyars*. It has been revealed by the sufferers that commoners were heavily exploited by the *Mandals* during special occasions in the palace like the birthdays of Kings and the Princes, and on the occasion of the royal marriages. During such events, *Mandals* ordered the peasants to offer gifts which they would further present to the *Kazis* as a memento from the peasants of their respective villages.[48] The *Mandals*, during the process of collection, used to keep a portion out of the collected gifts leaving nearly

85 per cent to the palace. Again, those gifts were deducted by the *Mukhtiyars* and *Kazis* leaving hardly 25 per cent for the royal occasion. The justification of keeping such gifts seems very remarkable, as they say, "*Maha Kadnele Haat ta chatcha nai*" meaning 'a person who takes out honey from the hives certainly licks his hands'.[49] Apart from such collection, the peasant also had to gift rice, maize, butter, curd, wine and in some cases meat, fish, and other valuable edibles to the *Mandals*. Yearly collection of such gifts was made during *Meshu Purnima* in the month of *Bhadra* (July-August) also known as *Bhadau Purnima* in Nepali.[50] In addition to these, the peasants had to send a member of his household to assist the *Mandal* during farming as a *Bethi Khetala*. This *Bethi Khetala* was a free service to be rendered by a villager to the *Mandals*. The sufferers remind their dark phase in these words:

"We had to go to the fields of the *Kazi Thikadars* and *Mandals* for the harvest or for farming; they gave fistful of roasted maize to work for the whole day".[51]

Auxiliary, to resolve social obligations like marriage, death, illness and the like, as in any other feudal society, the Sikkimese peasants too had to depend on the *Mandals* for debts at a very high rate of interest. It is said that, if a peasant takes loan of ₹ 100 he had to pay interest of 1 *Muri*[52] of rice to the *Mandal* from whom he had taken the loan.[53] Considering their authority at the villages, it may be accessed that, the *Mandals* had designated themselves as *Kazi* or other higher officials among the peasants. Through their idiosyncratic decrees and eccentric regulations, they proved themselves to be the one who were directly responsible for the exploitation. Unarguably, these petty officials were highly responsible for the escalating troubles among the peasant commune which ultimately gave birth to the peasant resistance in the secluded Kingdom of Sikkim.

Karbari

The term *Karbari* is probably derived from a Nepali word *Karobar* which basically means dealing. They were appointed by the *Kazis* or *Thikadars* on the recommendation of the local *Mandals* to work as a dealer between the peasants and the higher authority. Their appointment was made through an official order of appointment by the *Kazis* or *Thikadars*.[54] The nature of appointment varies from one to other *Karbaris*. In some cases, they were appointed on hereditary basis and in others; they were replaced by the new ones.[55]

The major duty of the appointed *Karbaris* was to deliver messages to the peasants from the higher authorities about the schedule of tax payments.

They pre-informed the villagers about the visit of *Kazi* or other higher ranking officers to their respective villages or the *Elakhas*. However, in Western Sikkim, there existed a low ranking official called *Katuwal* to mete out such messages among the peasants. It is said that, he would climb to the tallest hummock of the village and blew whistle and pass the message to the peasants in a louder voice. There were some *Katuwals* in West Sikkim who used to beat drums for the said purpose.[56] It is to be noted here that, Brahmins and the Kshatriyas of Nepali origin do have a clan named *Katuwal*. Field reports suggest, these very clan members were entrusted with the charges of passing information by the State at Gayzing and the clan name eventually got a position of an Office. We are not sure about the process of appointment, termination, and inheriting the father's office by a son of a *Katuwal*. However, it appears that the office bearers were to be abided with the norms and regulations framed by the feudal set up. Similarly, illustrations from Namchi indicate that the peasants had to feed the horses and bulls of Royal caravan, at the orders of *Karbari*, during their visit to the town.[57] Being the nucleus of the feudal set up, the *Karbaris* too harassed peasants in their own ways. In order to escape from the superfluous persecute, peasants had no other alternative than to serve the *Karbaris* as free labourer.

The Sikkimese administration had branded all these lower level administrators as *Kamdaris*. As per the Administration Report of 1926-27, the *Kamdaris* were exempted from the payment of House Tax. Further, they were also exempted from carrying any sort of load like *Kalo Bhari, Jharlangi* and the Like. Apart from them, the other peasants who were exempted from this carriage were the family members of the army men. The Administration Report of 1926-27 provides testimonial of the exemption of *Jharlangi*. It states-

> "Four ex-soldiers, who had served in the Great War, were exempted from supplying *Jharlangi* labour to the State".[58]

The same Administration Report has also stated about the sparing the destitute villagers from the payment of House Tax.[59] However, the resolutions and norms of the Kingdom seemed to have been confined into the pages of the Administrative Reports as they were never been executed by the lower level administrators with a sense of duty.

Spaces for the Breeding of Hidden Transcript in Sikkim

The social norms of a feudalistic society, in the modern sense of understanding, were impositions upon the subordinates that had obligated them to show respect to their officials. The peasants were expected to bow their heads before the Landlords and were also asked to use respectable languages. Exhibiting their pleasing quality, the submissive lots would never resent and could tolerate every humiliation and embarrassments considering it to be an established order. However, the ferocious lots, with an utter sense of abhorrence would find this norm peculiar and tries to get rid of the nuisance. An Ethiopian proverb says 'when the great lord passes the wise peasant bows deeply and silently farts'.[60] This proverb illustrates a serious rancour amongst peasants against the feudal system in general and to their master in particular. Similarly, his eagerness to sabotage the existing norms and to live a life of equality and respect is also demonstrated in it. However, he was forced to suppress his repulsive ideas due to the fear of lawless laws promoted by his landlord. Akin to Ethiopian peasantry, the Sikkimese peasants too had to behave like subordinates and trusted slaves of the State and its feudal bureaucracy. The feudal bureaucracy of Sikkim, like any others, asked respect and reverence from its subordinates and dependents. Humbleness and modesty were expected from the peasants along with etiquettes and manners while they presented themselves before the authorities. Respectful words like *Kazi Sahib, Thikadar Sahib, Mandal Sahib, Karbari Sahib, Hajur, Jyu, Rai Sahib, Yapla, Ating*[61] etc. were to be used to make the authorities feel superior. As if the peasants were children of lesser god, had to stand aside, even if they were walking on the narrow streets, bowing their heads, or in some cases had to hide behind bushes, until their 'Great Lord' passes. Field report informs some of the 'Great Lords' would get disgusted seeing these lots of people using the same street for their passage. Probably, for these high elites poverty and its soreness were the things that would bring ill luck to them. These subservient acts were to be followed by everyone as they were considered as respectable acts to their Lords. The compelled or constrained lot of peasantry accepted such haughtiness due to the fear of losing what they had acquired so far.

Keeping aside the submissive acts and propriety in language, the peasants were not even allowed to wear good quality of clothes and shoes while visiting their lords. If they defy, they were out-and-out asked to pay a high amount of fine.[62] Apart from such grubby acts, the *Kazis* had even forced a Brahmin peasant of Aho village to spend a night at the pig shed. According to the information, the only offence of the Brahmin peasant was to visit the *Kazi* with his youngest son in a good cloth that was brought to them by his eldest son who was in the Imperial Army.[63] It is worth to mention that, Brahmins were regarded as the teaching and priestly caste and for them to touch a pig was a social taboo. Ignoring the social status and priestly duties of the said Brahmin, which was at the top most position in caste ridden Nepali society, was forced to spend a night at a reeking pig shed. It is also said that, to avenge the wicked act of Gyaltsen *Kazi*, the aggrieved Brahmin peasant had named his son as *Kazi*, (which was again a disobeying act) who passed away a few years back.[64] A part from such hauteur, occasionally the peasants had to pay their visit to the *Kazi Kothi* for free labour. Such free labours may include, making of cowshed, trilling of land, chopping of trees, and the like. These visits were compulsory during *Dasain* for receiving '*Tika*'[65] and blessings from the *Kazis*.[66] Ironically, the same "blessed" peasants were unnecessarily harassed, exploited, and tortured by the *Kazis* in their pursuit to happiness.

Apart from the big fishes in the shape of *Kazis* and *Thikadars*, small fishes like the *Mandals* and *Karbaris* were also to be fed by the peasants in the lake of feudalism that had spread all over Sikkim. These junior bureaucrats too were to be feed with linguistic decorum, obedience, and free services. If they failed to obliged, the matter was considered as disobedience and insubordination and were dealt with strong hands. Similarly, the *Arhdalis* or the royal guards and *Lal Fetey*, the guards of the *Kazis* seek similar respect from the villagers. Considering the ignorance of peasants, they also exploited them with the threat of the Royal House and the *Kazis*.[67] It is thus evident that, the existing social system had always compelled the meagre peasants to live a combatant's life. In the battle of survival against hegemony, the Sikkimese peasantry was always the looser and had always come ahead for compromises. The amount of compromise multiplied among these neglected lots that finally resulted in the mound of odium against discriminatory set up they were living in.

The prevalent facts cited above were some of the important spaces where the hidden transcripts of Sikkimese peasantry got germinated. In Sikkim, these embryos of transcripts later began to take shape of a full throttled resistance due to the continued discriminatory policies of the State. Keeping these facts in mind, one cannot eliminate umbrage against the feudal bureaucracy in the psyches of Sikkimese peasantry.

Germination of the Ideas of Resistance among the Sikkimese Peasantry

As discussed elsewhere, the peasants had to pay their taxes out of the money which they earned with a great toil to the feudal lords and were cheated in parallel by their masters from time to time. Undoubtedly, they had their grievances and complaints against the manipulative mechanism but, they lacked officials to listen to their problems and to approach for an agreeable settlement. Further, even if they attempted to make their complaints to the higher officials, or in some cases, even to the King, they had to travel a long way from the village officials till palace. Therefore, very few of such grievances had been able to reach to the King's table and remaining others disappeared in the dust, mud, and muck of rural Sikkim. It is evident that, their lives were miserable; but, neither the authorities nor any organisation prevalent in Sikkim initiated deeds to heal their wounds. Auxiliary, the prevalent forced labour had made the lives of a commoner much shoddier. At this stage, the Sikkimese peasants, as it appears, were used by the landlords as a full time farmer and a part time porter to fill up their bags. Both the ways were lucrative to the landlords and therefore, they did not want to lose any of these. The various forms of forced labours prevalent in feudal Sikkim were as under:

Kalo Bhari

The literary meaning of the term *Kalo Bhari* in Nepali is Black Load. The paucity of documents, refrain us from asserting the period of its commencement and institutionalisation among the Sikkimese peasants. However, it can be assumed that the system of *Kalo Bhari* evolved after the advent of British and adoption of new agrarian system in Sikkimese villages. The Anglo-Chinese Convention of 1890 kept the British in advantageous position and gave a full access to lucrative Tibetan trade. Exploring the secured privilege of trade with Tibet, an outcome of many disastrous missions, the British during Wars sold arms and ammunitions. For the safety and protection from rain and snow, the exported arms were wrapped in card boards and put inside gunny bags bedaubed with tar. In all probabilities, the black colour of tar applied to seal the bag gave the cargo its local name *Kalo Bhari* or black load.[68] It later became an institution of *Kalo Bhari*, an easy and effortless way to amass wealth for the landed aristocrats. The Sikkimese peasants had to carry huge sacks of British goods or *Kalo Bhari* in the fully snow clad areas of Tibet. These places were situated 7 Miles north to Jalep-La Pass on the elevation of 9,980 ft. above the sea level. The Chumbi Valley in Tibet had an International Trading Station established under the Treaty of 1894.[69] The Sikkimese peasants were reluctantly sent as porters at the orders of their village officials like *Mandals* and *Karbaris*, who were once again directed by their above officials like *Kazi* and *Thikadars* for the supply of porters from their villages. After the delivery of British goods, on their way back, the porters were loaded with other goods and materials that were to be brought to Sikkim. People who served as *Kalo Bhari* porters during the trembling period of Second World War believe that apart from the arms and ammunitions, they also had to carry items of daily use. Being sealed in the tight parcel, the porters could not assume what all they were carrying. However, they presupposed, they had carried merchandise like shoes, jackets, woollen blankets etc for the British officials at the Sikkim-Tibet border.

Sometimes, the load would come in a large quantity and the peasants of three or four villages had to carry them from the centres where they were ordered to go.[70] The peasants of East, West, and South districts of the Kingdom greatly suffered by the *Kalo Bhari* due to their immediacy to the border. The peasants of the surveyed villages of North Sikkim were not known to this form of forced labour.[71] Probably, being at the Dzongu belt, which was somewhat like autonomous Rong area, the people of these villages were not so harassed by their officials. However, Balikci indicates that the peasants of villages of North Sikkim like Tingchim, Namok and Seyam were not entirely free from the clutches of forced labours.[72] To get rid of the gluttonous attitude of Kunga Gyaltsen, who happened to be a monk and a *Mukhtiyar* of Phodong Monastery, the peasants of these villages had even made a written complaint to the *Durbar* in 1929.[73] Accordingly, a case was filed against the said *Mukhtiyar* and the verdict was given in favour of the peasants after a prolonged debate of three years.[74] The observation of Balikci bears ample testimony that the peasants were granted justice if their cases had reached *Durbar* for hearings. However, most of the Sikkimese peasants were busy dealing with bread and butter issues therefore, in probability; they preferred to bear the feudal jolt than to object to it. Apart from Balikci's observation, the compulsion of *Kalo Bhari* upon the peasants in other parts of the Kingdom shares a different picture.

A peasant who had a good relation with the *Kazi-Thikadar* and few other 'yes-men', in some cases, got exempted from carrying the load. Excluding such few, for others, the orders of their *Kazi* were something not less than a Decree of God. The people of West Sikkim had to go up to Darjeeling to carry their loads.[75] Similarly, the peasants of South Sikkim had to go up to Teesta and sometimes to Geil Khola to collect loads from a small railway station existed there.[76] Likewise, the people of East Sikkim had to come down up to Rangpo, a bordering town in British India. From there, they had to carry the loads to Gangtok and with the peasants of periphery of Gangtok; the loads were taken up to Segatshe in Tibet. Still few peasants are alive like Batomuni Saila of Bering and Nandalal Bhattarai of Namli in East Sikkim who carried such loads up to Tibet during Second World War. It is said that, the former reached Segatshe barefoot with *Kalo Bhari* on his back. Due to his journey on the fully snow clad mountainous roads for more than four days, his toes and fingers were bended.[77] The bent feet that he was cursed with as horror of *Kalo Bhari* is still visible.

Depending on the labour supplied by the *Kazi Thikadars*, porters were fixed by the British at the rate of ₹ 2 per person for a day. Allegedly, the *Kazis* and *Thikadars* would only pay 6 Annas per day to the labourers siphoning all other amount they obtained from British.[78] Thus, it can be accepted that the institution of *Kalo Bhari* had served as a best apparatus of peasant exploitation and for their abating condition. To reiterate, the institution of *Kalo Bhari* was associated to the whole peasantry and there was no specific ethnic group which was intentionally targeted by the State. In reality, in the name of State, the whole course of action was engineered by the Landlords (*Kazi Thikadars*) and for them it did not matter what community a peasant belonged to. The Bhutias, excluding the ruling clique and its tassel, and the Lepchas also equally suffered due to the system.[79] The important factor for the greater involvement of the Nepali peasants as *Kalo Bhari* porters appears to be their population. They constituted three-fourth of the total population therefore, naturally, they had a larger involvement. However, in such a messy demographic set up guided and funnelled by the *Kazis*, we even cannot ignore some unjust cases against the Nepalese. Therefore, apart from such cases, the others seemed non-intentional as justified by few others. Nevertheless, it was a regulation of the *Kazi-Thikadars* which was to be followed by everyone.

The exploitation of the peasants in the form of *Kalo Bhari* reached its highest level during the Second World War. At this juncture, huge quantities of such loads were transported to China *via* Tibet. It is said that, the deployment of peasants as the porters became lucrative to the landlords and they put all their efforts in spinning money towards their folds and they even falsely requisitioned forced labour to transport their private loads to Tibet.[80]

Jharlangi

As the real interest was laid on the Tibetan trade, Sikkim never had a magnetic attraction to the British. The enchanting factor that encouraged British to establish a cordial relation with the secluded Kingdom was to attain the easy and shortest route to Tibetan plateau that passes through Sikkim. To secure a peaceful Tibetan trade, British needed a peaceful Sikkim; therefore, alienating Sikkim from her natural ally, British converted her as their protectorate. After securing an easy access via Sikkim they began to construct roads and trade routes to get their trade flourish in the mainland of Tibet. For the construction of roads and routes, they required labourers and for this they had to depend on the *Kazi-Thikadars* and *Mukhtiyars*. Covetous in their dreams, the feudal officials asked their *Mandals* for the supply of labour from the villages. The fare of the labourers was paid by the imperialists to the local *Kazis* and *Thikadars* but, these officials forced their peasants to work without any wages.[81] Such forceful works done with disinclination is known as *Jharlangi* in Nepali. As a *Jharlangi* labour the peasant had to leave his home at least for a week and had to proceed for an unknown venture. He himself had to arrange warm clothing for his night stay along with food and all other necessary items. The striving family on the one hand and the orders of his landlord on the other, the peasants always had to stand on edge. If his family was his world his landlord was his universe. Therefore, negligence to any ends meant a disaster for him. Least bothered to these bewildering situations of a peasant, a greedy landlord on his part often took his chance of making further easy money and double the number of men actually required.[82]

The social norms of the Nepalese were overlooked especially by the *Kazis* and people belonging to the *Chettri-Bahun*[83] category were asked to carry the load of beef and pork as a *Jharlangi* labourer. Though peasants they were, they had their own social status in the caste based society. As stated, to touch a pig and beef was a taboo for the Brahmins and Kshatriyas and they could have been ousted from their commune, as for them, it was a gruesome act.[84] However, ignoring all their social responsibilities and duties they were asked to carry 'untouchable' items for the children of *Kazis* who were studying in Darjeeling or Kalimpong. A small number of the *Chettri- Bahun* peasants living in South Sikkim today claim that their forefathers had been compelled to carry the 'outlawed' at least once in their lifetime.[85]

There was no fixed time or place for *Jharlangi* labour. Any time the peasants were called by the *Kazis* and the obligated lot had to reach the ordered location in time. If they failed, it was regarded as an act of dishonesty and was asked for a rigorous penalty that may include punishment and confiscation of property and livestock.[86] Besides these, the Landlords and their officials had demanded *Jharlangi* from the peasants to carry the beddings of Government officials and English *Sahibs* during their transfers.[87]

It has come to the surface that, the Sikkimese peasants were sometimes called by the *Kazis* and *Thikadars* to render free services for their private construction. A house popularly known as 'Settlement House' at Assam Lingzey in East Sikkim was constructed by the peasants of Assam Lingzey as *Jharlangi* labourers. The peasants of the village and periphery were called by the *Kazi* to render their free service for the construction of the said House. The narration of the villagers indicates that the Settlement House was constructed for the trial and prosecution of the villagers and was established in the early 20's of last century.[88] In another instance, a bungalow for the British Postal Services known as *Dak Bungalow* was constructed at 32 No. in the vicinity of Singtam with the help of *Jharlangi* labourers. It is also said that even the children were not spared from this yoke as children belonging to 8-10 years were also engaged for its construction. Similarly, a

Maney[89] at Yoksam in West Sikkim was also constructed by the villagers of Tashiding, Chongrang, Gerethang and Nesha as *Jharlangi* labourers.[90] It is also said that the same peasants of these villages were called by Lasso *Kazi* for the construction of Namchi Bazaar in South Sikkim. The *Jharlangi* labourers of Tashiding area had cut off a hillock to establish a hart at Namchi and due to their engagement as free labourers they had missed their cultivation.[91] Few of such *Jharlangi* labourers of Tashiding area are still alive to tell the stories of their mistreatment and harassments by their *Kazis*. Likewise, the peasants of Chongrang and Gerethang had to go to Dentam to provide their *Jharlangi* services as ploughmen in the field of their *Thikadars*. It appears that, almost all the peasants of the surveyed villages had rendered their services to their *Kazis* or *Thikadars* or *Mandals* as *Jharlangi* labourers. In another instance, the Bhutia peasants of North Sikkim too were harassed by the system of *Jharlangi*. Peasants of Tingchim, Namok, and Seyam villages had to provide compulsorily for eighteen days a year to the State, to their landlord and *Mandal* and were regularly called for porter duty by the officials.[92] In addition to these, the peasants of Namphok in South Sikkim were asked to carry granite and *Sakhuwa*[93] planks from Namphok to Kalimpong. It is said that the Lingmoo *Kazi* had engaged himself in the construction of a mansion at Kalimpong, a sub-division of British India, and he asked his peasants to provide a free service as *Jharlangi* labourers.[94] It is interesting to note that, the same peasants had to work as both *Kalo Bhari* and *Jharlangi* labourers without any concession. However, during emergencies, they could send a substitute with a payment of 50 *Paise* (*AaTh Anna*) to the hired person per day.[95]

Theki-Bethi

Theki-Bethi was another form of forced labour existed during the feudal phase of Sikkim. The nature and features of this form of forced labour shares some similarities with the forms of labours discussed above. However, it differs in the context that *Theki Bethi* was related to agriculture and cultivation and mostly the free services from the peasants were expected during the time of cultivation. It is so far noticed that, below the *Kazi-Thikadars*, there was a class of officials called *Mandals* or *Karbaris*. From the available sources it can be assumed that, their appointments were made by the *Kazis* or by the *Thikadars* of their respective estate and they would be the trusted men of the landlords.[96] However, they, too, as middlemen exploited the farmers to the fullest. On festive occasions, they were supposed to be welcomed by gifts packed in special receptacle called *Theki*.[97] *Theki* is a wooden utensil specially used by the Nepalese to keep and preserve curd. The *Theki* was to be filled up with meat, curd, bananas, beaten rice, maize, local beer known as *Chhang* and other items. As discussed, besides the festive occasions, on the birthdays of the *Maharaja*, during the birth of princes, during marriages at the palaçe, these *Mandals* and *Karbaris* would ask for such gifts in a *Theki*.[98] Few erstwhile *Mandals* still believe that it was a convention to appraise respect by the peasants to their officials. If someone would not follow the existing norms was regarded as an act of dishonesty and insubordination.[99] Therefore, in a fear of losing what they had the peasants would show their respect with gifts in the *Thekis*. It is thus evident that even this cadre of feudal officials were ready to ask for the last ounce of blood from the browbeaten peasants. Along with the *Theki*, the peasants also had to offer the *Mandals* and the *Kazi-Thikadars*, their wage less labour called *Bethi*. Probably, both the *Theki* and *Bethi*, being associated with the villages and village level officials had come to be known as *Theki-Bethi*. The *Bethi* form of forced labour includes ploughing, terracing of lands, and hollow out the agrarian fields, construction of channels, and other field works. Another interesting feature of this form of labour was that even a woman could be sent as an assistant if she could work at her capacity. Therefore, mostly the women were sent to the *Mandals* and *Karbaris* as helper during paddy cultivation. A family of the peasants had to provide five assistants or the *Khetalas*[100] to a *Mandal* or *Thikadar*. At least one member of a household was obligatory and therefore, sometimes *Bethi* was also known as *Gharlauri Khetala*.[101]

It is worth to mention that under such ridiculous circumstances the only suffer would be the peasants. It was not only a physical exploitation but, the half stomached peasants were even exploited psychologically. It was simply because of their psychosomatic subordination the peasants were looted from every sphere. It seems that the entire set up was created after evaluating the minds of these lots of rural populace. Unconditional subordination of the peasantry was the basic norm of the then Sikkimese rural set up. Therefore, for a longer period, the peasants allowed their authorities to exploit them both physically and mentally without any resistance. It is very contradictory to assume that the peasants had to plough the fields, without any wages, of those people, who never paid tax to the government. Even during the hectic paddy season of *Ashar –Sawan* (June-July), they had to work for their *Thikadars* adjourning their very own cultivation. Out of their free services, they would not even obtain the smiles of gratitude from their masters. On the other hand, the tax payers or the peasants had to make a delay for cultivation owing to their engagement at the fields of their masters. No compensation could be secured if their crops failed due to their engagements in serving their masters.[102]

Kuruwa

Literally '*Kuruwa*' means a long wait in Nepali. Sometimes, on account of the road condition and other natural issues, people sent to transport the *Kalo Bhari* had to wait for several days for the arrival of the commodities.[103] The process of serving as a *Kuruwa* labour was very much similar with the process of *Jharlangi*. For this labour also, the British Officials offered contracts to the local *Kazis* and *Thikadars* for the supply of the porters. For such contracts, the *Kazi- Thikadars* were handsomely paid. During the entire wait for the *Kalo Bhari*, the peasant himself had to manage his resources. People who witnessed the tedious visage of *Kuruwa* state thus:

> "As Kuruwa labourers, rice, pulses, and *sattu*[104] were to be carried by the porters themselves.[105] My brother had worked as a *Kuruwa*; on their way from Geil Khola to Namchi, they would take their lunch at Melli. No excuses of a *Kuruwa* were entertained by the *Kazi-Thikadars*".[106]

There were few cases in Western Sikkim when the *Kazi-Thikadars* had forced the peasants to work as *Kuruwa* when they were performing the death rites of their deceased family members.[107] The reference suggests that, sense of humanism and compassion were at the fading stage and the only matter the *Kazis* and *Thikadars* were aspiring for was wealth. They were very observant with the fact that the peasants were the minters who could fill up their pockets with enormous wealth. Being easy earning in matter, the *Kazi-Thikadars* put all their efforts to extract more money from the British by taking a full advantage of baffling situation of the peasants. It could not be predicted for how long a *Kuruwa* labour had to engage him in carrying the government loads. From the study it evolves that, the only pulling factor to be a *Kuruwa* for a peasant was his adverse situation and rickety feudal laws. The *Kuruwas*, after receiving their orders had to reach their respective centres where they had been ordered to go. After a long wait, upon the arrival of the goods, the peasants had to carry them to Sikkim. Some of the important *Kuruwa* centres were, Geil Khola, 27th mile, Rangpo, Melli, Teesta etc. Geil Khola happened to be the nearest railway station in Darjeeling district of modern West Bengal. This place is nearly 70 kilo meters away from Gangtok, the Kingdom's capital. The *Kuruwa* had to carry their load for such a long distance and that too at their own expense.[108]

If we compare British Imperialism in India with the native feudalism of Sikkim, then, one can notice Sikkimese feudal system was much tougher and crueller. The Indians in the plains were directly exploited by the British imperialists, who were foreigners and were concentrated upon a profit making process. Of course, the pricks and pains which the Indian masses received from the colonial rule were also incomparable. However, it is evident that, the Sikkimese peasants were exploited by their very own masters in a much harsher manner than what the British did in the Indian plains. Nevertheless, in every resistance, some signs, some symbols, come to occupy a pre-eminent position and those signs or symbols become the watchword for the masses. In Sikkim, people's sufferings, their woes, trials, and tribulations came to be symbolised by the feudal chain of command and the forced labours stated above. When exploitation reached beyond their tolerance these silent, hushed and muted rural commune began to resist the system paving a way for confrontation against the system.

Notes

1. Scott, James C. (2010), *The Art of Not Being Governed-An Anarchist History of Upland South-East Asia*, Orient Black Swan Private Limited, Hyderabad India, p. 142.
2. White, John Claude (1909), *Sikkim, and Bhutan 21 years on the North East Frontier 1887- 1908*, Cosmo Publication, New Delhi, p. 25.
3. Letter from Chogyal Thotub Namgyal to the Lt. Governor of Bengal John Woodburn, Year 1901, PD/7.4/003, Namgyal Institute of Tibetology.
4. Waddell, L.A. (1899), *Among the Himalayas*, Bibiliotheca Himalayica Series I, Vol. 18, p. 433.
5. Mullard, Saul and Wongchuk Hissey (ed) (2010), *Royal Records: A Catalogue of the Sikkimese Palace Archive* IITBS GmbH, p. 7.
6. Administrative Report 1919-1920, I, 2.
7. Field Report - 2011-2012 - this respondent in an erst-while Mandal of Namli village.
8. Tshering, Tashi, "*A few facts about Sikkim*" a pamphlet issued by the Sikkim State Congress on 7th December 1947, p. 3.
9. *Ibid.*, p. 3.
10. Subba, (1988) op.cit, p. 64.
11. Field Report 2011-2012. This respondent is among the migrated people who left Sikkim due to the unnecessary harassment of the feudal officials.
12. The *Thinguros* were made up of wooden planks, the culprit had to put his legs inside the hole made at the middle of the plank, then the mouth of the *Thinguro* was to be tighten by a rod or an iron, thus, leaving the culprit standing in utter pain. *Source:* Field Report.
13. Subba, Tanka B. (1988), '*Agrarian relations and Development in Sikkim*' Rural Development in Eastern and North- Eastern India', Calcutta I.I.M, p. 64.
14. Sinha, A.C., "*Sikkim of Yesterday*", The Sikkim Times, Gangtok, Saturday June 9, 2007.
15. *Khet Khajana* was a tax paid by a peasant for the cultivation of wet lands.
16. *Bari Khajana* was to be paid according to the area possessed for the cultivation in dry lands.

17. *Madati* is derived from a Nepali word *Madat* meaning help or support to the State (?) that was accessed in the form of tax from the peasants. The tax receipt of Bar Dhoj Limbu of Sadam *Elakah* to a Mandal named Wangdu Lapchey makes reference of annual assessment of ₹ 1 as *Madati.*
18. *Gaddhi* is a Nepali word meaning throne and according to the respondents it was collected on behalf of the King or monarch.
19. Tax receipt of Dalbir Limbu paid to Mandal Dorjey Bomjan of Rateypani village in 1916. The receipt indicates that ₹ 5 was collected from the said peasant in the form of *Satsukey, Roadsey, Madati* and *Gaddi.*
20. Tax receipts of Dalbir Limbu paid to Mandal Dorjey Bomjan of Rateypani village in 1920's and receipts paid by Nar Dhoj Limboo of Sadam Elakha to Mandal Wangdu Lepcha. These receipts indicate only about the payment of *Madati* and *Gaddi* taxes excluding the *Satsukey* and *Roadsey.*
21. Tax Receipt of Dal Bahadur Limbu paid to a Mandal Wangdu Lepcha of Turuk Village South Sikkim dated 31 December 1934.
22. Dahal, Dharnidhar (1998), *Sikkim ko Rajnaitik Itihas Part II* (Political History of Sikkim) Nirman Publication, Namchi, p. 10.
23. *Kasko Baaja Kasko Baaja* is a popular folksong at Namthang village in South Sikkim. The song highlights expensive lifestyles of *Thikadar* Baburam Kasaju. *Source:* Field Survey.
24. Field Report: 2011-2012: Information collected through personal interview from the related peasants of East, West and South Sikkim.
25. Field Report: 2011-2012: Information collected through personal interview from the related peasants of Nandu Gaon, village of South Sikkim.
26. Field Report 2011-2012, Pakki Gaon, Soreng, West Sikkim.
27. Balikci, Anna (2008), *Lamas, Shamans and Ancestors- Village Religion in Sikkim*, Brill, Leiden, The Netherlands, p. 47.
28. Appointment Letter of "Uehung" Dawa Gyaltsen as *Mukhtiyar* of Phensang Monastery, 23rd Day of the 2nd Month of Iron Dragon Year of Tibetan (1940 AD), Kalimpong Durbar, the letter states: In due recognition of the long and faithful service rendered by Geydol Tsewang Gyatso for the benefit of Phensang Monastery, his nephew "Uehung" Dawa Gyaltsen is hereby appointed as Mukhtear of the Phensang Monastery Estate and to grant him exemption from the payment of rent and taxes and also from rendering Jharlangi labours. Be it known by all the Lamas, Mandals, and Raiyats and to respect the Mukhtear accordingly as before. Kalimpong Durbar, the 23rd Day of the 2nd Month of Iron Dragon Year of Tibetan.
29. Appointment letter of 1932 of a *Mukhtiyar* by Rai Saheb Durga Sumsher Pradhan of Rhenock East Sikkim, Ramgauri Sangrahalaya.
30. Field Report 2011-2012. This respondent is a granddaughter of erstwhile *Mukhtiyar* of Namchi Late San Man Tamang.
31. Field Report 2011-2012. This respondent was an erstwhile Bhutia *Mukhtiyar* of Tashiding area.
32. Field Report 2011-2012. This respondent is a granddaughter of erstwhile *Mukhtiyar* of Namchi Late San Man Tamang.

33. *Dasain* is Nepali *synonym* of Hindi word *Dasahara*, in this occasion the Nepalese seek blessings from their elders receiving *Tika*.
34. Field Report: 2011-2012: Personal interview from the related peasants of Tashiding village in West Sikkim.
35. Field Report 2011-2012.
36. Field Report: 2011-2012: Information collected from the related peasants of villages of Assam Lingzey, Kadamtam, Aho, Namin, Marchak and Samdur which are in proximity to Gangtok.
37. Tax receipts collected from Harka Bahadur Limboo of Chota Singtam East Sikkim on 21st January 2012.
38. Field Report: 2011-2012: Information collected through personal interview from erstwhile *Mandals* of feudal Sikkim.
39. *Ibid*, Interviews.
40. Revenue Administration, Order No. 4, 19th August 1949.
41. Most of the receipts were issued written with pencils and one cannot deny the cases of fraud and cheating against the peasants by their *Mandals*.
42. Revenue Administration, Order No. 4, 19th August 1949.
43. Field Report: 2011-2012: Information collected through personal interview from the related peasants of the study area of East, West and South Sikkim.
44. Gyaltsen Kazi had served the King's Council headed by Political Officer during World War I (Administrative Report 1915-16, II, 2) He had his estates at Assam Lingzey, Aho Yangtam and a part of Bhusuk area.
45. Field Report 2011-2012, Assam Lingzey, East Sikkim.
46. The Dal Dhoj incident of Assam Lingzey roughly corresponds to the 20's of the last century. (Field Survey).
47. Notice issued on 18th December 1945 by *Mandal* Brihaspati Upadhyay to Ravilal Pyakurel of Tareythang village, East Sikkim. The document is an important credential to understand the judicial rights enjoyed by the village *Mandals*.
48. Field Report: 2011-2012: Information collected through personal interview from erstwhile *Mandals* of Feudal Sikkim.
49. Field Report 2011-2012, This respondent is an erstwhile Mandal of Namin village. Field Report 2001-2012: Assam Lingzey, East Sikkim.
50. Field Report 2011-2012, Assam Lingzey, East Sikkim.
51. Field Report 2011-2012, Namchi, South Sikkim.
52. The weighing of rice was done with Pathi, 20 Pathi of Rice was considered as one *Muri*.
53. Field Report 2011-2012.
54. Appointment letter of a *Karbari* issued in 1931 by Rai Saheb Durga Sumsher Pradhan of Rhenock, Ram Gauri Sangrahalaya Rhenock.
55. Field Report 2011-2012, Tarku village South Sikkim.
56. Field Report 2011-2012, Middle Gyalshing West Sikkim.
57. Field Report: 2011-2012: Information collected through personal interview from the elders of Namchi South Sikkim.

58. Administration Report 1926-27, I, 2.
59. *Ibid.*
60. Ethiopian Proverb quoted by James C Scott in domination and arts of resistance.
61. Field Report: 2011-2012: Information collected from the related peasants of Tashiding West Sikkim.
62. Upreti, T.R. Personal Interview, Age 86, Assam Lingzey, East Sikkim, 24th January 2012. Informer says his father had to pay ₹ 5 as fine for wearing a pair of leather shoe while visiting the *Kazi* of his *Elakah*.
63. Field Report: 2011-2012: Information collected through personal interview from the elders of Namin, Saureni and Aho villages, East Sikkim.
64. At the request of the family members, the real name of the said Brahmin peasant is kept anonymous.
65. The custom of putting *Tika* among the Nepalese during Dussera is prevalent since time immemorial. On the occasion the Head of a family puts Rice Tika mixed with Red colour and curd to all other member of his family.
66. Field Report: 2011-2012: Assam Lingzey, East Sikkim.
67. Field Report: 2011-2012: Information collected through personal interview from erstwhile *Mandals* of Sikkim.
68. Gaunley Gopal, (2002), *History of Democratic movement*, (Translated by Dr A.B Chettri and Mukunda Giri), Published by Department of IPR, Government of Sikkim, Gangtok, p. 7.
69. Sandberg, Graham (1901), *An Itinerary of the route from Sikkim to Lhasa*, Baptist Mission Press, Calcutta, p. 7.
70. Field Report: 2011-2012.
71. Field Report: 2011-2012: Information collected from the respondents of Bey, Lingzya, Dzongu and Passingdang villages of North Sikkim.
72. Balikci, (2008) op cit, pp. 50-51.
73. *Ibid.*
74. *Ibid.*
75. Father of this respondent Late Bhotu Bir Karki had once opened the seal of *Kalo Bhari* out of his curiosity on his way back to Sikkim from Darjeeling. He found shoes inside the load and tried a pair of them on his foot. Later he threw off his load from a hilltop and pretended that he fell down from the narrow path that he was travelling through. He thus, escaped prosecution as there was no evidence against him. (*Source:* Field report 2011-2012, Middle Gyalsing).
76. Field Report: 2011-2012: Information collected through personal interview from the related peasants of Nandu Gaon, village South Sikkim.
77. Field Report: 2011-2012: Information collected from the related peasants of Angkuchen, Bering, and Manpur villages.
78. ` Subba, J.R.(2008), *History Culture and Customs of Sikkim*, Gyan Publishing House New Delhi, pp. 64-65, Gaunley, (2002) op cit., p. 18.
79. Field Report: 2011-2012: Information collected through personal interview from the related Lepcha-Bhutia peasants.

80. Basnett, Lal Bahadur, (1974), *Sikkim- A short Political History,* S. Chand and Co. (Pvt.) Ltd. New Delhi, p. 75.
81. Gaunley, (2002) op cit., p. 18.
82. Basnett, (1974) op.cit., p. 74.
83. Chettri is a Nepali synonym to the Sanskrit word Kshatriya is a high class warrior caste likewise Bahun is a Nepali synonym to Sanskrit word Brahmin.
84. Dahal, Dharnidhar (1998), *Sikkim ko Rajnaitik Itihas, Part II* (Political History of Sikkim) Nirman Publication Namchi, p. 10.
85. Field Report: 2011-2012: Information collected from the related peasants of Nandugaon, Tinzir and Temi Tarku villages in South Sikkim.
86. Field Report: 2011-2012: Information collected from the related peasants of East, West and South Sikkim who rendered their services as *Kalo Bhari* and *Jharlangi* labourers during feudalism.
87. *Ibid*, interview.
88. Field Report 2011-2012: Assam Lingzey, East Sikkim.
89. *Maney* is a wall constructed in the periphery of a Buddhist monastery where the Mantras are engraved on the stones.
90. Field Report: 2011-2012: Information collected through personal interview from the Peasants of Tashiding Lasso West Sikkim.
91. Field Report: 2011-2012: Information collected through personal interview from the peasants of Tashiding Lasso West Sikkim.
92. Balikci (2008), op cit, pp. 50-51.
93. In the earlier times Sikkimese people used to construct their houses using *Sakhuwa* planks which are the strongest planks found in the region.
94. Field Report: 2011-2012:, Ranipool Bazaar, East Sikkim.
95. Field Report: 2011-2012: Information collected through personal interview from the peasants of Sikkim who rendered their services as *Kalo Bhari* and *Jharlangi* labours during feudalism.
96. Field Report: 2011-2012: Information collected through personal interview from erstwhile *Mandals* of feudal Sikkim.
97. Gaunley, (2002) op.cit, p. 18.
98. Field Report: 2011-2012: Information collected through personal interview from erstwhile *Mandals* of feudal Sikkim.
99. Field Report: 2011-2012: Information collected through personal interview from erstwhile *Mandals* of feudal Sikkim.
100. *Khetala* is a Nepali synonym for the wage labourers or substitute labourers working in the agricultural field.
101. Field Report: 2011-2012: Tashiding, Arithang Chongrang, West Sikkim.
102. Field Report: 2011-2012: Assam Lingzey, East Sikkim. This respondent and his family was exempted from carrying State Loads owing to his service in the Imperial Army.
103. Gaunley, (2002) op.cit., p. 19.
104. Corn powder in Nepali.

105. Field Report: 2011-2012: Assam Lingzey, East Sikkim, 27th January 2012.
106. Field Report: 2011-2012: Dambu Dara Namchi, South Sikkim. The informer's brother had served as a Kuruwa porter and the respondent had grown up listening to such incidents associated with her brother.
107. Field Report: 2011-2012: Information collected through personal interview from the peasants of Tashiding Lasso West Sikkim.
108. Field Report: 2011-2012: Information collected through personal interview from the related peasants of East, West and South Sikkim whose ancestors had carried *Kalo Bhari* as *Kuruwa* labourers.

Chapter 6

Hidden Transcripts and its Varied Forms during Feudal Sikkim

The unspoken and tacit reactions of the subordinates or particularly the peasants can be considered as their hidden transcripts. The resentment of the peasantry and working class against the unjust and a self centred rule based on the 'money minting' principles began to take shape with the hidden transcripts.[1] The practices of domination and exploitation typically generate the insults and slights to human dignity that in turn foster a hidden transcript of indignation. James C. Scott has compared society with a theatre to elucidate how the wishes of dominant groups prevail to have things appear.[2] He opines, the dominant never control the stage absolutely, but their wishes normally prevail. Conversely, the hidden transcript generally takes place "offstage" beyond instant inspection of the authority. It is derivative and it may appear in various forms like spirit possession, rumour, gestures, plays, folksongs, code language, and gossips. To exhibit their abhorrence against the system or their superiors they compose songs, make mimicry of their masters, spread rumour, make plays showing the subordinates as heroes, develop code language to criticise the superiors or to make strategies to topple them, and create anonymous threats to their masters. The folk songs they composed have a curse against the mechanism and their ostentatious smugness. The outbursts of emotional expressions of the villagers were, sarcastic, witty, and sardonic and carry within it the sparks of hidden transcripts. There are many songs of the bygone days of feudalism which are still alive in the peasant society of Sikkim.

Hidden Transcripts in the Nepali Folksongs

As stated, the folksongs play an important role in exhibiting the wrath and frustration of the peasants. These marginalised folks usually composed such songs anonymously and collectively sing the same during their unpaid state works, in the absence of their masters to exhibit exasperation. It is to be noted that in spite of illiteracy and ignorance, the peasants, too profess a dream to live in a utopian system. However, usually their aspirations are recurrently disregarded by the authority leading to an utter disappointment in their livelihood. Subsequently, such sarcastic and witty songs serve as 'weapon of the weak' in the idiom of James C. Scott. The peasants vehemently performed the anonymous songs in occasions like village feasts, fests, village rituals, and so on. The only motives of the folksongs are to amuse the village community as well as to demonstrate their distress against their landlords or other concerned. It is interesting to observe that, peasants throughout the world have chosen folksongs as an easy and a safe mode to expose their bitterness against the asymmetrical social relations. Therefore, while studying the hidden transcripts of peasantry, the importance of folksongs cannot be miscalculated. Due to its inscrutability, one can notice the enormity of revulsion, resentment, and repugnance of the peasantry against state mechanism.

Analogous to all other peasant societies, Sikkim too had adopted folksongs to get rid of their boredom during working hours and moderately, to manifest their resentment against the theocratic feudal edifice. Field survey provides ample evidences from where one can peep inside the times of yore of the Sikkimese peasants which was in all respects, not better than any other peasant societies of the globe. The symphony of Sikkimese peasantry was an assortment of three ethnic groups namely, the Lepchas, the Bhutias, and the Nepalese. With the increase increased Nepali population, their language had become an unofficial *lingua-franca* of these peasant communes. The Nepalese, who are also accredited with the introduction of terrace cultivation in Sikkim, had constituted nearly 75 per cent of total Sikkimese population. In spite of the hurdles of Revenue Order No.1[3] and the discriminatory rate of revenue assessment[4] the number of Nepalese continued to swell and became an obligatory piece of Sikkimese feudal fabric. Thus, ignoring all stumbling blocks, in all probabilities, the Nepali settlers who set their feet in Sikkim had come to get a better life than what they had in their native country Nepal. Consequently, being a major ethnic group of erstwhile Himalayan Kingdom one can find several Nepali *Lok Geet* against the vices of feudalism which was sung by the three ethnic groups stated above.

The North District of Sikkim had a very little participation in composing satirical and witty folksongs. Being secluded from the rest, as it appears, North district had played a very little role against the feudal set up. Further, the villages of the study area are mostly inhabited by the Lepchas who had a great sense of affiliation towards the established feudal set up. Moreover, even today the Lepchas of Sikkim are honest, humble, and gentle in their social lives. Therefore, due to their very nature, they did not have anything much to go against the system in their rural lores. Their folksongs were composed in *Rong*[5] language, were mostly confined within the local problems confronted by them. Similarly, such songs were predominantly composed for the ways and means to survive from the natural catastrophe and in praise of nature for a better harvest. Correspondingly, the Bhutia peasants too were acquainted with the composition of folksongs and most of them happened to be nature oriented and lacked the spark of resentments. Hence, their songs did not have any bile sense; rather, they were submissive and defensive in their aspect. However, folksongs composed by the Nepali peasants of East, West, and South Sikkim were more rational and judicious. Those songs had a deep impact upon the villagers to set up their minds against daily feudal exploitation. Few such forgotten songs were collected through field survey to understand the level of peasants' frustration and hidden transcripts.

The seditious folksongs in Nepali appear in many forms like *Jhyaurey*,[6] *Sawai*,[7] *Chutkey*,[8] *Saṅgini*,[9] and *Selo*.[10] The composers were branded as *Kathakey* (writer), who were usually unknown, and the singer who arranged such jumbled words in the melody were known as *Gitangey*. In those songs, the anonymous composers have highlighted the issues of dissatisfaction of peasantry against the State. Though being illiterates, the composers had left no stone unturned to include the burning issues a peasant had to come across. It is also evident that the *Kathakey* had attempted to send a message of their repulsion to the authorities to get their attention in resolving social nuisance. On the contrary, the authorities never paid their attention to deal with the rural problems that had ultimately broadened the sense of antagonism between the State and the village for a longer yard. It is also said that, sometimes the *Jharlangi/Kalo Bhari/ Kuruwa* labourers themselves had composed such satirical verses while working as unpaid state labourers. Therefore, they had an easy access to look inside the genuine problems of their lot which had been reflected in the songs.

Some of the important and popular songs assembled are as follows:

"आन्द्रा लागे छुत्ती खेल्न
तिघ्रा लागे काम्न
सकिदैन महाराज
कालो भारी थाम्न
हात गोड़ा बसी सके
फुल्ली सक्यों जिउ
अब त हे महाराज
हामीलाई मुक्ती देउ।"

English Translation (Theme)

Maharaja!! It is just impossible to carry *Kalo Bhari*
with empty stomach and shivering thighs.
Body is swollen and feet exhausted
Oh! Maharaja now set us free.

This song having *Sawai* symphony had a great popularity among the peasants of Pakyong and its peripheries of East Sikkim. The *Kalo Bhari* porters had mostly sung this during their works at the orders of their *Kazis* and *Thikadars*. Through this song, the meagre have tried to apprise the King about their existing condition with acrimony and dissatisfaction. Though, the song sounds very submissive and does not contain any sceptical word or phrase or has any hidden transcripts within it, the pathetic position of a forced labourer and shoddier condition of Sikkimese peasantry perceptible in it cannot be ignored.

Another significant and a popular folklore of East Sikkim was:

"रिटिङ रिटिङ नबजाउ बिनायो
काजी ठिकादारको मर्ने दिन लौ आयो
घरमा चै बाल बच्चा भोकाए
आफुलाई चै झार्लङी बोकाए
साइला दाइ...
आइया या ... आत्था ता"

English Translation (Theme)

Do not play *Binayo*
The time of *Kazi* and *Thikadars* is now over
Children back home are striving
And we are asked to carry *Jharlangi*
Oh! Brother
It hurts…it burns

This song composed in *Chudkey* or *Chutkey taal* or beat had huge popularity among the peasants of East Sikkim. It is to be noted that the song was a ditto burlesque of a Nepali song popular in the neighbouring Kingdom of Nepal. The popular song in her western border, with a few alteration, got a broader sphere to grow in Sikkim as the Nepali speaking Sikkimese share a common culture and tradition and are very close to Nepal due to their matrimonial and family relationship. Thus, it appears that, a few alterations were made in the verses pertinently and were widely sung in Sikkim during Second World War. Akin to others, this song was also sung while working as *Jharlangi* labours, or working as *Kuruwa* and carrying *Kalo Bhari*. According to some former *Kalo Bhari* porters, this was the song that had given them relief while carrying loads in the fully snow clad terrains of Tibet.[11] The song resembles long hoarded hidden transcripts of the peasants against the unjust *Kazis* and *Thikadars* of Sikkim in which they are threatening their masters for death. Apart from animosity, the song also carries pains and pricks of the forced labourers along with the love, concern, and worry of a father to his starving children. The song also portrays a clear sketch of the level of hidden transcripts of the peasants against the false feudal foundation. It is worth mentioning that browbeaten peasants of Sikkim continued to sing this song even after the withdrawal of forced labour.

Another interesting verse composed in *Sawai* rhythm of East Sikkim attacks the monopoly of the *Kazi/Thikadars* and held them responsible for the rural distress. Popular in the Aho and its peripheral villages the song manifests monopolistic and authoritarian activities of elites who also had judicial rights in administration[12] as well as on the lands.

"सुन सुन पन्च हो
म केहि भन्छु
भोटे देश सिक्किमको
सवाइ कहन्छु
अन्न बाली पोको पारि
काजिले नै लान्छन्
बोली देउन हे इशोर
प्रजा के खानछन?"

English Translation (Theme)

I am telling *Sawai* of Bhutia Kingdom of Sikkim
All the crops are amassed by the Kazis
Tell me God
What the peasants shall eat?

West Sikkim appears to be the champion in composing satirical and sarcastic songs during feudal years of Sikkim due to its remoteness from the State's capital. Their songs were mostly focused on general condition of the peasants. Peasants of Soreng, Malbassey, Suntaley used to sing such folksongs during *Bethi Khetala* on the fields of their landlords or other village level officials.

"धाराको पानी ध-र-र गर्छ,
कुवा को कुइ रहन्छु,
बाहिरी मन मेरो हासखेल गर्छ
भित्री मन रोइ रहन्छ।
तिम्रो छ संसार साह्रै नै ज्यालो
हाम्रो छ पनेलो
माफी है देउ हे काजी राजा
रोप्नेछु जुनिलों।"

English Translation (Theme)

Stream has a sound
Water in the pond is sullied
I carry smile on my face,
But my heart cries always.
We have a murky world and
You have a bright
Please forgive me my lord
I will cultivate *Junilo*.[13]

This song arranged in *Selo* beat has emphasised on the deteriorating condition of Sikkimese peasantry in which the *Kathakey* had taken up the internal pains of the people. The song pleas probably for the exemption of taxes and also assures his master for the cultivation of maize. The deplorable plight, the perplex situation, and scary and submissive nature of a peasant is well reflected in this composition. Though, the song does not carry any spark of resistance, it highlights the general condition of peasantry crippled under the feudal yoke. Inadvertently, the song has made an evaluation of the two unparalleled worlds, i.e. the *Kazis* and the peasants, which had played a major role in deepening the feudal roots in the Sikkimese soil. Likewise, another significant song of West Sikkim includes:

"बत्ती है बल्यो धिपी मा धिपी राजाको संसारमा
फुल है फुल्यो बुकी फुल जस्तो सुखी कोइ छैन या संसारमा
तिम्रो त संसार हर र बर हाम्रो छ बेकार
जती नै मरे जती नै रोए हाम्रो सुन्छ कसले पुकार?"

English Translation (Theme)

Lightened palace of the King
Beautiful flowers are bloomed

But, no one is affluent in this world.
Your world is happy ours is worse
Even if we die or cry nobody listens to us.

The song composed in *Jhyaurey* prosody attacks the royal lifestyles and it seems that the *Kathakey* had heaved his antipathy against the ruling clique. Cynical in nature the song had resembled daily affairs of poor and hungry peasants who could do nothing to herald a change in their way of life. Similarly, the last sentence indicates a comprehensive hidden transcript of peasants against feudalism which was not in a mood to bend itself even faintly.

Peasants of periphery of Tashiding had composed a folksong which was more rationale and logical than the songs of Suntaley, Soreng, Malbassey and other surveyed villages of West Sikkim. These peasants openly sang songs asking for a natural disaster in the Bhutia Kingdom of Sikkim.

"अरूको भागमा दही र केरा
मेरा भागमा कमिलाका घेरा।
फुटेका हाडिमा खट्टेको ओहिरो
भोटेका देशमा कहिले जान्छ पहिरो?"

English Translation (Theme)

Wealthy have a delicious food
Mine is so unsavoury
In a broken urn the grinded maize is poured
When there shall be a landslide in the Bhutia Kingdom?

The hidden transcripts of the village populace of remote Tashiding are evident from this folksong. Written and composed in *Sawai* rhythm, the song allows us to read the minds of villagers to whom feudalism was not less than a curse. Among all other folksongs, this song had an immense hatred and odium against the unjust feudal system in general and the Namgyal House in particular. Though, the Namgyal House was not actively involved in the distress of these peasants; in ignorance, the *Kathakey* alleged Namgyal dynasty to be responsible for their deplorable condition and was asking for a landslide in the Kingdom ruled by the Bhutias.

Another important *Sawai* composed by the Khas- Brahmin peasants (Chettri-Bahun as they are known in Sikkim) of Sakyong and Gyalshing reflects a sophisticated lifestyle of the aristocrats. The *Kathakey* has highlighted not only the deplorable condition of the peasants but has also got critical in his composition regarding the distribution of lands that, according to the composer, all belonged to the aristocrats.

"पटुकीले पेट बाधि, ठिकादारको सेवा
खेत बारी सबै उसको, हैन हाम्रो पेवा
घोड़ा सवार भइ आउछ, हामीलाई तर्साउन
गिद्धे आखले हेर्छ, सखी नजर झुकाउन।"

English Translation (Theme)

Waists are tightened to serve the *Thikadars*
Lands belong to him, nothing is ours
He rides on a horseback to threaten us
Beware friend; he turns his vulture eyes on us.

It appears that, the composer of this song happened to be a woman as the sentence indicates towards physical exploitation of the rural women by the aristocrats. Similarly, the word *Sakhi* is used to address a friend or mate by a Nepali woman. Therefore, in all probabilities, the composer is warning her friend not to have an eye contact with her master to protect her chastity. Apart from these compositions, the Limboos of Uttarey, Suntaley, Soreng and other villages of West Sikkim composed such songs in their own language known as *Yakthungpan*. The Limboo folksongs appear to be more effective as they were not understood by the authorities.

Likewise, the process of exhibiting peasants' frustration through folksongs was also common among the peasants of South Sikkim. The respondents have informed about their affiliation in singing the sarcastic and scornful songs in their languages against their authorities. The peasants of Temi Tarku were the champions in composing such songs to manifest their hidden transcripts.

"खर्याङ खुरुङ मकै बारी,
बिहा गरौ घर बाकि,
गैरी बारी ढाड बारी,
बोलाउछन हामीलाई कारबारी।"

(English Translation)

The zigzag maize fields,
House would be mortgaged if I marry,
Lower and sterile lands,
The *Karbaris* call us.

This song composed in *Sangini* rhythm had its popularity among the Khas-Brahmin community of Timi Tarku area. This song was usually performed along with a dance by women during religious congregation in the village. It highlights a perplex situation of the young folks who were usually called by the *Karbaris* to carry loads. Further, the song also emphasises on the bewildering circumstances a young peasant had to come across as he had to take care of large fields he ploughs that seemed to be very tough for him. To get a helper in his daily affairs if he wants to get married he had to mortgage his house to his master. The song points towards enormous power of a petty village official like *Karbari* who enjoyed the bottom most position in the feudal hierarchy of Sikkim.

These songs discussed above, were sung in the absence of the feudal officials or on their way as a *Jharlangi* labour. The womenfolk were also very active in singing such songs while collecting fodder for the cattle, collecting firewood, carrying water and so on. The important aspect of such songs was that they differed from one district to the other. These songs manifested the general problems faced by the villagers which were again different from village to village. Whatever the rationale for the divergence in the songs may be, it is important to understand that whenever such rational, reasoned, and radical ideas of the peasantry get suffocated, these begin to precipitate in the forms of hidden transcripts and these hidden transcripts later get impulsive into cohesive resistance.

Hidden Transcript in Spirit Possession

The cult of spirit possession is a universal phenomenon and is widely popular among the shamanists throughout the globe. Though, it is not properly connected to any World Religion, the concept of spirit possession is deeply rooted in all the peasant societies and is widely admired by the peasantry. While studying peasant resistance, we may consider this cult as a mode of social protest by the powerless against the powerful. To quote L.M. Lewis,

> ...persuasively that spirit possession in many societies represents a quasi-covert form of social protests for women and for marginal, oppressed groups of men for whom any open protest would be exceptionally dangerous.[14]

Akin to all other peasant societies, the Sikkimese peasants too were superstitious that gives ample testimonials about the prevalence of this cult among the Sikkimese peasants. If we have to believe Lewis, pretention of being a spirit possessor was the long unexpressed rancour these exploited lot wanted to show in excuse of spirit. However, apart from such bogus possessors there were many others who were devoted in the healing process on which the villagers had their extreme faith. The Lepcha spirit possessors of North district, known as the *Boongthings*, were mostly involved in traditional healing practices. They used to practise traditional methods of healing through their chants conventional medication. Similarly, in the other districts of the Kingdom the *Dhami*, *Jhankri*, *Yeba*, *Bijuwa,* and *Mata* were the Nepali spirit possessors who too practiced the traditional shamanist mode of healing with the sense of utmost dedication. However, apart from such healers, there were others who not only performed the acts of healing, but also made predictions about the coming disaster. Sometimes as coincidence, such predictions would give expected results that would naturally escalate the position of the forecaster. Even if the prediction did not work, the villagers would consider it as wish of god to spare them from a catastrophe. Such predictions can be considered as a form of hidden transcript of the concerned metaphysician that comes out during *Chinta* at the village.[15] Few *Jhankris* performed some mysterious acts on the occasion of *Sansari Puja* and warned the villagers for devastation.[16] Distant from these, there were few others who pretended of having some bizarre power and acted as spirit worshippers and future tellers.

> "Whenever we had to send our people to collect the tax, or for the *Kalo Bhari* we often found them practising some frightening acts and we had to come back as we were scared of their action. The time was like that, we could not prove them wrong".[17]

Most of practitioners in East Sikkim were either tax defaulters or the people who could not serve as a forced labourer. Further, the peasants had an extreme faith on what they called as metaphysical truths; therefore, even the landlords and feudal officials could not take any action against such peasants. Though, less in number, the peasants of East Sikkim had adopted spirit possession as their means to manifest their antipathy against the system. It should be noted that the Sikkimese rural life still has a huge faith on these traditional healers; and in this kind of juxtaposition, it is very hard to figure out the truth or the reality.

Similarly, the peasants of West Sikkim too have narrated about the prevalence of the cult of Shamanism in their district. The Shamanists, too, have an extreme faith on the spirit possessors which according to them is the manifestation of cosmic powers through a human being. They believe that the people having such extraordinary powers are chosen by God and whatever they mutter shivering are the voices of God which could not be ignored. Taking advantage of such beliefs, few peasants evaded their taxes along with *Jharlangi*. It is to be noted that, the peasants of Tashiding and its periphery did not have to carry *Kalo Bhari*.[18] However, they had to serve the State as *Jharlangi* labourers. Hence, while being asked to work as a *Jharlangi* labour, a Rai *Bijuwa* had once beaten one tenant of the local *Kazi* and was left untraced due to the fear of magical power he possessed. It appears that, both the Mongolian and Caucasian stocks of the Nepali community had an extreme faith upon such supernaturalism. Being a social belief, even the feudal officials and the *Kazis* too would believe on the metaphysical issues that naturally provided a little space for the growth of hidden transcripts. The healers were in an advantageous position as even if they uttered something wrong out of their frustration others would take them seriously. Exploiting the common logic of the time, few such peasant healers had escaped working as forced labourers at least once in their lifetime. An 85 years old respondent of Lasso Tashiding says:

> "If they predicted about devastation or a calamity, the peasants along with their feudal officials used to believe in it. But we never witnessed any such devastation in our lives".[19]

The South Sikkim also had a nominal participation in evading taxation and escaping forced labours by adopting Shamanist mode of technique. However, no direct cases of tax evasion by the respondents' forefathers had been recorded from the Southern peasants. Yet, according to their postulations the practice was adopted by the peasants of other villages.

Anonymous Threats as Hidden Transcript

Anonymous in a popular phraseology means nameless or unacknowledged thing or a matter. It can be regarded as the best tool of threatening their masters or to the higher authorities by the peasants throughout the world. The sole intention of the practitioner here seems not to hurt the authority physically. They send letters or messages to the privileged men with whom they had their grudge or in some cases, to avenge them against their misdeeds towards their family. In other cases, peasants do this in order to threaten their superiors so that the tax on them might be subdued in case of agricultural failure. According to James C Scott,

> Anonymous threats are not merely heartfelt expression of anger. They are above all, threats whether they take the form of a letter or an understood sign (the unlit torch stuck in the thatch, the bullet on the doorstep, the miniature cross, and grave near the house) and are intended to modify the adversaries conduct.[20]

The anonymous threats may be an individual or collective act and the peasants who adopt this generally hide their identity to escape from the legal prosecution. The hidden transcripts of the village populace at this stage are not as ripe as to convert it into a full throated movement. Thus, to create a sense of horror among the elites they adopt such anonymous ways. The important aspect of this form of transcript is its leaderless nature and unorganised ways. It was in fact, the independent ways chosen by the peasants or subordinates to avenge their superiors who were responsible for their weathering days.

As far as the case of North Sikkim is concerned, only two cases have been found from the surveyed villages. However, these cases were not related with the sense of resentment against the existing norms of their society. As it was informed, such threats were made by the villagers due to their personal grudge against the concerned, who according to them was not an official. Therefore, such cases do not highlight the existence of hidden transcript against the vices of feudalism.

However, in East Sikkim, a considerable number of the respondents have referred about the anonymous threats made by their co-villagers. Among them 18 people admitted their forefathers' affiliation in expanding such threats against their landlords or other officials. Those threats were basically related to a grave consequence, possibly death, or severe whipping of their landlords or their officials. Further, the villagers often make rumours about the metaphysical power of an individual and make anecdotes and spread among the co-villagers. Such anecdotes would easily get momentum among the superstitious peasants and reached to the ears of their officials with added spices. It is not known if such stories had any impact among the landlords or their officials but it seemed peasants get enormous happiness out of these tomfooleries. The hidden transcripts of peasants were thus coming out showing their strong resentment against the landlordism in the form of anonymous threats. According to Mr T R Upreti of Assam Lingzey village, his father, who was once fined by his landlord for wearing a pair of shoes, was greatly involved in the acts of creating threats against his landlord.[21] He would talk about something frightful against his *Kazi* among his fellow peasants. These listeners would later discuss the same with few of the trusted *Kazi* men and these trusted men would further transfer such threats to their master. However, even after his active involvement the said person was never prosecuted due to the lack of evidence. Such threats were actively made in the far flung villages of Linkey, Bering, and Dongrong of East Sikkim where there was a less surveillance. The Bhutia peasants of Dongrong were significantly implicated in creating anonymous threats against their *Thikadars*. The important feature of anonymous threat was the confinement of such acts within the person or a group of a few who adopted it. In this regard, the person was merely exhibiting his antagonism against the manipulative mechanism as per the level of his analysis. It is not logical to argue that, the individual or a group of a few had ever professed a dream of colossal change by adopting this means of expression. However, such acts can simply be taken as the exposition of long-standing unspoken and muted feelings of peasants against the feudal structure. Moreover, such petty acts of the peasants were literally insufficient to dream about a massive social change that had always accepted domination and suppression since time immemorial.

West district of the Kingdom of Sikkim, too, exhibited its hidden transcripts in the form of anonymous threats as a best tool to harass the feudal authorities. Most of the peasants of the surveyed areas of West Sikkim have confirmed their forefathers' affiliation in creating anonymous threats. It is to be noted that, in almost all the places of the surveyed areas of Sikkim the source of spreading threat was talks or gossip. It comes into light that, the Sikkimese peasants unlike the others, as stated by Scott, did not engage themselves with the understood signs. Rather, they had shown their antipathy through their talks and gossips and they were unknown about the original inventor of such scary issues that could, as they believed, would frighten their landlords or his officials. The remote villages of Uttarey, Suntaley, Tashiding, Sakyong, Nesha were some of the central points where peasants were engaged in anonymous threats. A peasant named Pancha Bir Subba of Suntaley along with few other people made such threat in his village. Later, his identity was revealed and he was physically tortured along with his companions and was also forced to pay a huge fine for his activities.[22] Other peasants of the same village like Kalu Man Tamang, Bir Man Tamang and Athang Limboo were the most influential peasants in creating threats anonymously.[23] Similarly, the peasants of Kabirthang village seemed mild active in this front. There were several people who talked openly against the *Kazis* and about their misconducts. Few of them abused the *Kazis* openly and threatened to beat them.[24] It is thus evident that the villagers in West Sikkim had considerably adopted this mode to expose their long standing hidden transcripts against the asymmetrical set up.

The peasants of South Sikkim also had their affiliation in threatening the *Kazi Thikadars* anonymously. A good number of the total respondents have validated their relations in creating threats against the *Kazi-Thikadars*. Peasants of Temi, Tarku, Nandugaon and Sumbuk had a greater involvement in this activity. None of such anonymous peasants were convicted as they did not leave any traces behind their acts. The peasants of the surveyed villages of Denchung, Nandugaon, Samsebung, Salghari, and Samatar also had a major participation in creating anonymous threats against the Landlords. Peasants like Ratna Bahadur Rai and Dhanapati Sharma of Samsebung, Bal Bahadur Rai of Nandugaon, Santaman Sanyasi of Samatar and Master *Kancha* of South Sikkim were among those creating threats among the landlords. Similarly, peasants of surveyed village of Dambudara in Namchi were not at all indulged in the acts of threats due to a strict surveillance of the *Kazi* and *Thikadars*.

Hidden Transcript of the Peasants in Channel Breaking Activities

Breaking of the irrigational channels was another admired mode of resistance by the Sikkimese peasantry. Amidst greater surveillance, the peasants of East district were greatly involved in the channel breaking activities. The people of Namli village destroyed a channel of Senga *Kazi*, Landlord of their village in the 40's. The peasants of Samlik Marchak village were also active in adopting this mode of resistance. According to an erstwhile *Mandal* of Namin village, such acts were practised by the villagers during the peak hour of cultivation.[25] The peasants of Aho village were also acquainted with this mode of resistance. Being the peasants of a hilly Kingdom they had to put a larger effort to construct a channel for their landlords as *Jharlangi* labourers. Hence, they were well aware about the loopholes of the channel and they would destroy them during nights with a motive of drying the fields of their lords. Apart from the abovementioned villages of East Sikkim, others like Assam Lingzey, Aho, Linkey, and Bering and Manpur villages seemed vulnerable.

Similarly, the peasants of West Sikkim also adopted mischievous technique of breaking channel as a better choice to show their resentment against the prevailing feudal set up. Peasants of Tashiding, who had a great umbrage against their landlord Lasso *Kazi,* had a nominal participation in this form of resistance. However, peasant like Birbal Chettri in the late 80s openly confesses that he destroyed several channels belonged to his landlord. Likewise, the peasants of Uttarey, Soreng and other villages were mostly active in these sorts of activities. They would carry *Ranko* (A lamp made from dried bamboo sticks) to reach the source to destroy the channel of the landlords. People had a fear of *Ranke Bhoot* (a ghost that carries bamboo stick's lamp) and even if officials like *Mandals* and *Karbaris* saw them travelling in nights, they, too, believed that the flames were being carried out by the ghosts. Hence, the fear of ghosts among the ignorant peasantry was a better tool for the resisters to provide a good resistance against the authorities.[26]

The peasants of South Sikkim had also involved themselves in providing a resistance against the unjust feudal system by adopting this mode of resistance. The peasants of surveyed villages of Temi and Tarku were much active in this regard. There were several cases of anonymous channel breaking activities in the village. These villages still have good lands for paddy cultivation that produce a good quality of rice in the State. Mr Kharga Bahadur Chauhan, the erstwhile *Mandal* of Tarku village believes that the activities were mostly carried out by the harassed peasants of his village. They were often tortured without proper evidence and the victims always were in search of an opportunity to harass their Master. Peasants like Devilal of Temi and Janak Sharma of Nandugaon destroyed many channels during nights to show their frustration against the *Kazis* and *Thikadars*. The most active villagers for the execution of these acts were from Temi, Tarku, Nandugaon, and Denchung. However, due to a vigilant authority of a Newar *Thikadar* in the village of Sumbuk, peasants were unknown about this mode of resistance.

Hidden Transcript in Crop Destruction

Apart from the channel breaking activities, Sikkimese peasantry had greatly been involved ın destroying fully grown crops in the farms of their landlords. A considerable number of the respondents from East Sikkim admits their forefathers' affiliation in the acts of destroying ripen crops. Due to a strict surveillance they executed such acts during nights of *Chauthi*.[27] The peasants during their acts got into the orchards and farms of their village officials like the *Mandals* and *Karbaris* and destroyed the available stuffs.

Likewise, the peasants of West Sikkim also engaged themselves in resenting against the corrupt system by destroying the crops of the *Kazis*, *Thikadars*, *Mandals,* and *Karbaris*. Most of such cases were found in the Limboo dominated areas like Uttarey, Suntaley and Soreng. Here, the Limboo peasants after fully getting intoxicated practised the acts of crop destruction. It is to be mentioned here that, the Limboos belong to the Mongolian stock: friendly, sincere, honest, and are a warrior clan who are fond of alcohol. By virtue of their nature, they are fun loving and good peasants. However, the feudal pressure even did not let their fun loving and sincere nature to follow the lawless feudal laws. Most of such destructive acts were executed during marriage of a fellow villager, or during the occasion of *Dasain* and *Tihar*. In other cases, the resisters would wait for an occasion in which the entire villagers were concentrated for a single cause in the village along with their officials.

The peasants of South Sikkim were also greatly engaged in harassing their feudal lords and officials by destroying the ripen crops. The centre of such activities was Namthang which was then a fief of a Newar *Thikadar* Baburam Kasaju. The youths of this area organised a united resistance under the banner of an association founded in 1940 known as Member Party. The members of this organisation were determined to unleash Sikkim from the notorious feudal yoke and they were mostly engaged in destruction of the paddy and other crops of their *Zamindar*. The youths looted the paddy and other crops of the *Zamindar* and distributed the same to the poor farmers.[28] Apart from such united resistance, peasants from Temi Tarku, Denchung, Nandugaon, Assangthang, and Dambudara had also practised individual resistance in the form of crop destruction. The peasants of the surveyed areas of Assangthang village were actively involved in destroying the crops of their landlords. Such tasks were mostly implemented during nights. Unlike the peasants of East Sikkim, the Southern peasants did not wait for *Chauthi* or other occasion for the destruction.

Hidden Transcripts in Other Forms

The dominant class sometime adopts certain measures in order to stop the breeding of hidden transcripts among the subordinates. The measure could be anything as the feudalistic world had no limits of introducing unethical and biased decrees. However, amidst various measures, the east district had a considerable number of people who had different thoughts about the feudal system and were in a mood to deracinate it if they would be supported by a good opportunity. To get a safer way to talk against the officials, peasants used to speak in a *Palsi Kura*.[29] While working in the field of the *Kazis*, *Thikadars*, *Mandals,* and *Karbaris*, the peasants used to talk openly by using this language against their feudal lords. However, it appears that, adoption of the code language was simply meant to pass their time as they were never been able to get unite and combat the set up. Similarly, *Palsi Kura* had its popularity among the peasants of West and South districts as well and they would communicate in this language while working hours in the fields of their lords as *Bethi Khetala*. The process of making violent strategies against the feudal set up were made during *Maghey Sankranti*[30] in January, during *Dhaan Naach*[31] in December and in other festivals like *Dasain* and *Tihar*. However, it seems that, such strategies were never executed by the peasants due to the fear of losing what they had. Conversely, the peasants of the neighbouring villages of the capital did not involve them in intriguing against the system in a greater manner.

Balan appears to be another important platform for making strategies against the feudal set up. It is a religious act mostly performed by the *Chettris* and *Bahuns* of the Nepali community. It was an expensive act in which the whole story of Ramayana had to be featured in three to four hour play. Usually, a peasant who was seeking a birth of a male child would conduct *Balan* at his home. During such acts, the characters always performed from their hearts as the story of Ramayana reflects the victory of truth over injustice. This was indeed the best moment for the peasants to show their anger and antagonism against the feudal officials. Consequently, the artists of such acts projected themselves as the liberators of the meagre. Emboldened with the acts, the hungry and poor peasants began to dream of a better world created by the Hindu God Rama based on the principles of liberty and equality.[32] Encouraged with the victory as reflected in the drama, few peasants had attempted to make violent strategies which were, as it appears, never been executed by the peasants. However, such attempts were playing a vital part in the lives of the peasants in inspiring them to live a respectable life and in aspiring them to dream for a better world to live in.

Thus, it is evident that, hidden transcript is a social product that occurs due to unnecessary encroachment by the state or by its authorities in the daily lives of the people. Like any other social fact, hidden transcript too is a fact which an upshot of social inequity. When the level of suppression reaches its pinnacle, the subordinates began to act offstage giving a shape to their hidden transcripts. The composition and singing of the satirical or cynical songs, spirit possession, anonymous threat, channel breaking acts, crop destruction, adoption of *Palsi Kura*, making strategies to avenge their officials in social gatherings etc. were also the by-product of unfairness and chauvinism and were the hidden transcripts of Sikkimese peasantry. When their feelings got converted into whispers' and those whispers took the shape of voices they began to compose such songs and involved themselves in harassing their officials by adopting disobedience. Further, due to the anonymity of the composers, folksongs and other acts discussed above got impetus among the rural populace of Sikkim with no goal to change the feudal structure. Neither the songs had ever been able to arouse a sense of self respect or astuteness among the Sikkimese peasants to fight against injustice nor did the other mischief have any goals for securing a better government or a system. Therefore, the folksongs and other rural actions during feudal Sikkim were merely an attempt of the poor and meagre peasants to express their unspoken and muted feelings against the system.

Notes

1. Scott, James C (1990), Domination and Arts of Resistance Hidden Transcripts, Yale University Press, p.118.
2. *Ibid.,* p. 7.
3. Central Department, 17th of May 1917, p. 1. According to this Order no Bhutia-Lepcha would be allowed to sell, mortgage or sublet any of their land to any person other than Bhutia and Lepcha without the express sanction of the Durbar, or Officers empowered by the Durbar on its behalf.
4. Administration Report 1914-15, II, 3
5. The language of the Lepchas is known as Rong.

6. *Jhyaurey* is a Nepali folk rhythm used both in poetic writings and folksongs.
7. *Sawai* is a rhythmic poem but in the case of Sikkim the peasants would collectively sing in the original rhythm while working in their farms.
8. *Chutkey* or *Chudkey* is a folk rhythm mostly sung with a musical instrumental *Maadal*.
9. *Sangini*- A dance perform by the Khas-Brahmin (Chettri-Bahun) women during occasions like feast and other social gatherings.
10. *Selo*- a fast beat rhythm widely popular among the Tamangs of the Nepali community of Sikkim is usually sung in the beat of *Damphu*, a musical instrument of the Tamangs.
11. Field Report: 2011-2012.
12. The Kazis and Thikadars had judicial rights and they would dispense justice from the *Adda* Courts stationed at their respective estates.
13. *Junilo* is a variety of maize grown in Sikkim.
14. Scott, (1990), p. 141.
15. Field Report: 2011-2012.
16. Field Report: 2011-2012.
17. Field Report: 2011-2012.
18. Owing to its secluded position, peasants of Tashiding and its periphery were not ask to carry the popular load known as Kalo Bhari.
19. Field Report: 2011-2012: Lasso Tashiding, West Sikkim.
20. Scott, (1990) op cit, p. 149.
21. Field Report: 2011-2012: Assam Lingzey, East Sikkim.
22. Field Report: 2011-2012: Suntaley Village, West Sikkim.
23. Field Report: 2011-2012: Suntaley Village, West Sikkim.
24. Field Report: 2011-2012: Kabirthang Village, West Sikkim.
25. Field Report: 2011-2012: Marchak Busty, East Sikkim. This respondent is an erstwhile Mandal of Marchak Busty.
26. Field Report: 2011-2012: Dara Gaon, West Sikkim.
27. The tradition of practicing *Chauthi* is prevalent among the Nepalese of Sikkim. During *Chauthi* nights the peasants make bands to destroy a little crop of their fellow villagers for fun.
28. Dahal, Dharanidhar (1998), *Sikkim ko Rajnaitik Itihas* part II (Political History of Sikkim) Nirman publication, Namchi, p. 11.
29. *Palsi* language is spoken in the remote villages of Sikkim that can be understood only by the villagers of a particular village. Such languages are different from one village to the other. The language is a corrupt form of Nepali language which is not even understood by a Nepali speaker. In short it was a kind of a code language devised by the villagers to talk freely against the corrupt feudal officials.

30. *Maghey Sankranti* is a Nepali synonym to Sanskrit *Makar Sankranti.*
31. *Dhaan Naach* was common among the Limboo community of Sikkim where people used to gather for the harvest of paddy during November-December.
32. Field Report: 2011-2012: Namin Busty, East Sikkim. This respondent is one of the founding members of Sikkim State Congress.

Chapter 7

Everyday Forms of Peasant Resistance in Sikkim-Assorted Modes

It is evident from the earlier chapter that the Sikkimese peasants had varied forms of hidden transcripts against the manipulative mechanism and they exhibited it time and again by adopting several techniques. This chapter will focus on the resistance they made against the prevailing norms carrying their hidden transcripts in their everyday affairs. It is to be noted that, during the practice of everyday forms of resistance, the subordinates or particularly the peasants, do not have any goal for securing a better government or an arrangement. Therefore, during the entire course of everyday resistance, the peasants seem busy merely in securing their interests devoid of major political ideas and objectives. Importantly, few acts of poaching, stealing, trespassing, migration and tax evasion are not adequate enough to change a cavernous and capricious set up. Therefore, at this juncture, they are not prepared to confront against the State as that may lead to a devastating consequence. Hence, in the case of Sikkim, their tomfooleries, that too, at secluded and inaccessible villages, could not influence the set up. To quote Scott:

> "Most of the everyday resisters are rather like opponents of a law who estimate that it is more convenient to evade it or bribe their way around it rather than to change it. In the case of peasantry, of course, the state and its laws are typically inaccessible, arbitrary, and alien".[1]

As discussed, in everyday resistance, the main motif of the peasants or the powerless is to search out diverse ways and means so that they could escape State's litigation as well as they can safeguard their interests. Such aims are neither formally organised nor do they seek, "self consciously", broad policy goals.[2] Thus, their acts in everyday resistance are less political and more individual and such acts of the peasants are self-guided and personally motivated.

In a popular parlance the term 'Resistance' generally deals with the bearing capacity of an object or an individual or a society. Several scholars have tried to interpret the terminology of 'Resistance' in their own sense of understandings and analysis. Like any other subjects, resistance also has its own sphere, speciality, and history. Every human society, since evolutionary period to present day, has to some extent resisted the existing norms to protect itself from the elite's domination. These elites, since Cognitive revolutions, as it seem, are active in the social theatre, and are always privileged of being a super class in the society. They have framed the social norms, values, and ethics for their own expediency so that their dominance in the society would always remain unchallenged. Such 'asymmetrical equation' of the society has been challenged by the intellectuals from time to time. The father of American Constitution James Madison, even before the birth of Karl Marx has spoken about the existence of class struggle in human society. He argues that there was inevitable conflict in society between those who had property and those who did not.[3] Similarly, Karl Marx points out domination and exploitation of the insufficient by the sufficient as the major cause for class struggle. The privilege class here wants to suppress the unprivileged and the latter being unable to put up with repression began to resist. The resistance of the unprivileged on the one hand and repression of the privilege class on the other leads to a struggle, which is generally, defined as 'Theory of Class and Class Struggle" in the Marxist beliefs.

It is a natural fact that in a power relationship, the subordinate often has to tender somewhat and sometimes has to make a huge deal endangering his whole needs. While discussing about dominance versus resistance in the past, Sherry B Ortner has rightly remarked domination was relatively fixed and institutionalised form of power; resistance was essentially organised opposition to power institutionalised in this way.[4] It is a well observed fact that, status in any society is ascribed by birth; therefore, the minors always have to struggle for their survival against the adversaries posed before them by the elites. While struggling for its survival in an unbalanced world created by them, the subordinates sometimes adopt some techniques to shield it. Therefore, the acts of self-protection like poaching, squatting, deserting, evasion, foot dragging etc. can be regarded as the acts of everyday resistance by an individual.

As discussed in the earlier chapters, the peasants have always played an imperative part for the development of human society by producing agricultural items. Further, by paying tax and rent of the land and agricultural products they make a greater contribution for the economic prosperity of a country. Being the nucleus of human development, the peasants who are always in a larger number have never been treated at par. It is not only a case of a particular province or a state or a country, injustice against the peasant is a phenomenon which is rampant in every nook and corner of the world. The pricks, pains and the wounds the peasants have been subjected to in the past and present are simply irreparable which are very much similar throughout the globe. Their service to mankind in general and their landlords or the governments in particular, the burden of taxation upon them, the yoke of forced labour on their shoulders share a similar nature and feature throughout the earth. In spite of their large contribution, they have been frequently ignored not only by the authorities in the past but by history as well.[5] Further, history of ordinary people which also covers resistance made by the peasants is always regarded as a sundry event by the contemporary historians. This is the major reason why hardships of the peasants in the past have not got their mention in the pages of history. To quote Howard Zinn:

> Not only to the orthodox history of those years, but to the very idea of history told from the point of view of the authorities- a history confined to the "important" people that ignores the struggle of ordinary people.[6]

Major Causes of Peasant Disappointment in Feudal Sikkim

Akin to all other states, in Sikkim too, the major cause of disappointment seems to be unnecessary encroachment of the elites into the spheres of the peasants. Through the study, this is conceived that, most of the descendants of the victims of feudal hegemony believe that their forefathers were severely harassed by the existing social set up of the Kingdom. More than a half of the total respondents believe that the major cause of peasant disappointment was the forced labour like *Kalo Bhari*, *Jharlangi*, *Theki Bethi*, and *Kuruwa*. Likewise, others believe, heavy taxation imposed upon them by the lessee holders as the major factor of the disappointment among the peasants. Finally, a small section of the targets consider unnecessary harassment as the major cause of discontentment among the peasantry. The respondents who held *Kalo Bhari, Jharlangi, Theki Bethi* and *Kuruwa* responsible for the major cause of dissatisfaction further believe that they were severely harassed by their feudal lords without any reason. They were sometimes called by their lords to feed their cattle and for their homely activities like chopping of fire wood, construction of cow shed, pig shed and the like. The mayhem created by the authoritarian government among the minds of the poor peasants is manifested from a Government Notification issued by the General Department bearing No. 8146-08/G dated 19th June 1926 that states:

> "On and from the 1st January in each year, landlords and managers of estates may attach the movable properties of defaulting *Raiyats*, after

serving the usual notice upon them....if the taxes and rents are not paid in within two months after the notice has been served, the landlord or manager concerned should report the defaulting *Raiyats* to the Durbar with a view to obtaining the sanction of the Durbar to sale the attached property."[7]

In their view, the greedy and gluttonous nature of the lessee holders had a major role to play to spark the idea of resistance among the illiterate Sikkimese peasants.

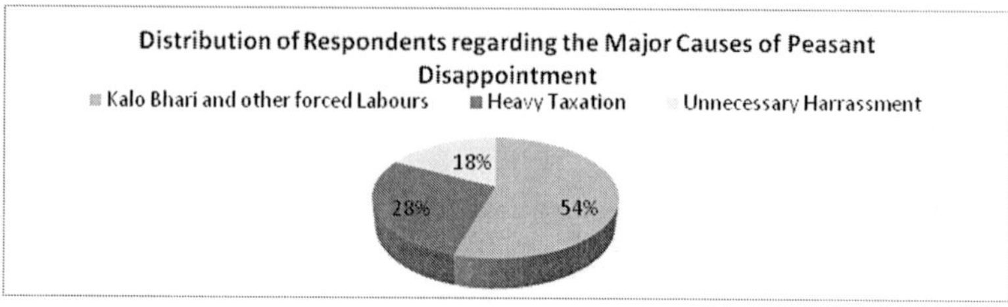

Source: Field Report 2011-12.

Apart from these, the unnecessary toil which the peasants were subjected to confront at the hands of the feudal bureaucracy also added much vigour to the peasant dissatisfaction. The monopolistic policies adopted by the feudal mechanism like the *Mandals*, *Mukhtiyars,* and *Karbaris* were the major factors responsible for the rise of peasant resistance in the former Kingdom of Sikkim. The most important feature of the collected responses is that North District of Sikkim is silent regarding the nature of such severe exploitation of peasantry. Out of the fifty respondents, no one is much aware about the various tools of feudal exploitation like forced labours, unnecessary harassments and heavy taxation. Hence, from the collected responses from the North District, it becomes evident that, with a few exceptions it did not have a major part in the peasant resistance. Therefore, it comes into surface that the exploitative nature of feudalism with a higher magnitude was prevalent only in the other three districts and they played the most striking part in resisting the state.

Mode of Resistance against the Forced Labours

Reiterating here, the collected data indicates about the silence of North District regarding peasant resistance and a very few of the respondents have heard of it. These responses illustrate about a little impact of feudalism in their daily lives

However, it comes to the surface that peasants of other districts of the Kingdom were not fortunate like their Northern counterparts. The responses of other districts viz., East, West, and South throw a good light on the various modus operandi formulated by the peasants to protect themselves from various forms of forced labour. Out of 300 respondents from these districts, 122 (40.66 per cent) of the respondents have confirmed that their forefathers had completely surrendered themselves before the system. It is a clear point to remark that they did not pay any resistance against the feudal set up; rather, they remained a loyal section which was abided by the lawless law of feudalism.

Likewise, 20 respondents both including the direct resisters and their descendents (6.66 per cent) of the East, West, and South districts had defend against carrying *Kalo Bhari*, *Jharlangi*, and *Kuruwa* by hiding in the forests. Few of such respondents had even fled to their relatives' places to escape forced labours. Peasants like Nandalal Bhattarai of Namin village and Pushpalal Sharma of Ranka village in East Sikkim had chosen the way to hide at their relatives' places in some other villages. Unable to bear the physical tortures at the local *Kutcheri* (Police Station), Pushpalal Sharma later on migrated to Banaras and settled there. Identical to the peasants of East Sikkim, the Westerners also practised a similar method to resist the forced labour of *Kalo Bhari*, *Jharlangi*, and *Kuruwa*. Some of the peasants had hide in the agricultural lands (*Kodo Bari*) during the visit of a *Karbari* to pick them as porters and Jahrlangi labourers. Such incidents were common in the areas of Tashiding, Gerethang, Chongrang, Soreng, Sakyong and Gyalshing in West Sikkim. The peasants of South Sikkim had devised a distinct method to resist the forced labour. Unlike the peasants of East and West Sikkim, these peasants used to cross river Rammam and got into the British territory of Darjeeling. They were well informed by the *Karbari* of their villages about the venue of their gathering to carry loads as a wage less porter.[8] Following the information of Karbari, the southern Peasants would opt for a safer option to get relived from the feudal encroachments. It is interesting to note that such resisters were never brought under punishment possibly because of the fear of a

cohesive resistance in the villages. Scott at this point remarks:

> "Resistance at this level requires a more elaborate riposte, one that goes beyond fragmentary practices of resistance".[9]

Apart from such modes of resistance, the peasants also offered resistance against the forced labours by sending a substitute in their place. Though, they had to pay 8 *Annas* to the substitute porter, they preferred it as the safest way to protect themselves from the clutches of feudal torment. Out of 300 respondents from the three districts of Sikkim, 111 (37 per cent) respondents and their forefathers had preferred to send a substitute to carry loads at least once in their lifetimes. It looks to be very simple and an easiest way of resisting the State. However, if we have to believe on the responses, the technique seemed very risky and in case, if they failed to manage a porter they had to face a perilous situation. The norms of *Ghar-Lauri*[10] seemed to be pathetic as it had crippled the daily lives of peasants in a most exasperating manner. As all the men of a village were engaged in payment of free service it was hard to find a proxy porter. It has been known that in such a situation, the peasants had to ask for the substitutes from the adjacent villages in the form of *Parma*.[11] In order to maintain a good and a cordial relationship with the *Mandals* and *Karbaris* and to keep safe from physical torture on *Thinguro*[12] and fines, peasants of South Sikkim had greatly utilised this mode of resistance. Keeping aside the fact of unavailability of the substitute, it is noteworthy that forty six per cent of the 100 respondents both including the direct resisters and their descendants from South Sikkim had employed the substitute to combat various forced labour.

Similarly, the peasants of West Sikkim also utilised the mode of sending a substitute to resist to work as wageless porters of their feudal lords. Forty per cent of the 100 respondents, both including the direct resisters and their descendants, from West Sikkim had resisted forced labours by sending a substitute porter. Most of such techniques were adopted by the peasants of Soreng and Sakyong villages. Likewise, the peasants of East Sikkim too had adopted this method of resisting the strained situation. However, due to its closeness to the capital, it was not in vogue as compared to South and West Sikkim. Even though, 25 per cent of the total 100 respondents, both including the direct resisters and their descendants, have disclosed their association in adopting this mode of resistance. According to them, owing to a very strict law and order, they did not enjoy the space of sending a proxy carrier. Due to the shortage of the porters in their villages, these attempts appear to be occasional. Mostly, the concerned individual himself had to produce before the *Mandals* or *Karbaris* to carry State loads.

Desertion was another admired mode of resistance adopted by the peasants of East Sikkim. Twenty-three per cent of the total responses indicate desertion while carrying the loads on the snow-clad ways to Tibet. Utterly reluctant in carrying the government loads, one Dalbir Rai of Assam Lingzey, as it is said, had thrown off his stack at Tshangu Lake. Scared of the feudal prosecution, he went to Nepal and lived there for seven years.[13] In the other cases, such deserters would go to Darjeeling to get into the British Gurkha Army. Some of the adults of the surveyed village of Assam Lingzey had joined army to escape *Kalo Bhari*, *Jharlangi*, and *Kuruwa*.

Unlike the Eastern deserters, the Western and Southerners chose to live outside the Sikkimese territories. Few of them joined army and served the Imperial Government in various wars. However, majority of them preferred to go to Nepal and Darjeeling to avoid the forced labours in Sikkim. Apart from the desertion of 'peasant soldiers', the real peasants or in the idiom of Mridula Mukherjee, the *flesh and blood peasants*[14] also had followed the process of desertion from their native places for their own convenience. Though, their acts did not make a much difference in the agricultural production or had lessened the pleasure of their landlords, but, such acts of peasants' manifests their level of antagonism against the unjust feudal system. Among 14 per cent of responses from West Sikkim, six *Kuruwa* peasants had left their loads on their midways to Geil Khola, and others made their way to Ilam *via* Chewabhanjyang pass. These deserters, due to the threat of prosecution, had returned to Sikkim only after the abolition of forced labours in 1949.

Only ten responses in the South district indicate adoption of desertion as a way to protect their interest from the forced labour. Out of the ten respondents, only three peasants went to Nepal and remaining seven preferred to join army to get an exemption from carrying *Kalo Bhari*, *Jharlangi*, and *Kuruwa* for their family members. Recruitment in the army had not only provided them an employment but also had helped their family

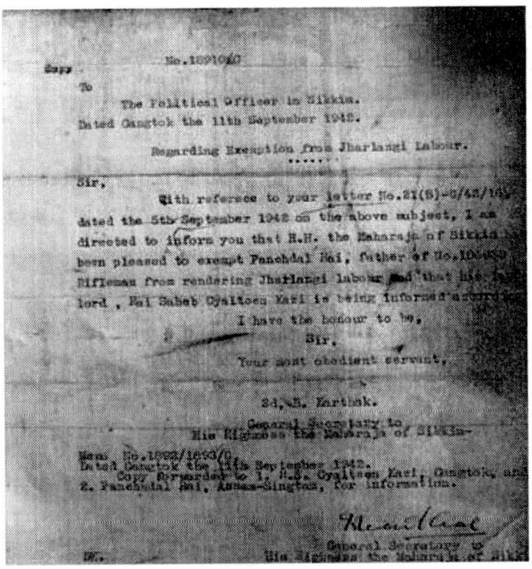

Copy

No. [illegible]

To

The Political Officer in Sikkim.

Dated Gangtok the 11th September 1942.

Regarding Exemption from Jharlangi Labour.

Sir,

With reference to your letter No.[illegible] dated the 5th September 1942 on the above subject, I am directed to inform you that H.H. the Maharaja of Sikkim [illegible] been pleased to exempt Panchdal Rai, father of No.[illegible] Rifleman from rendering Jharlangi labour and that his [illegible] lord, Rai Saheb Gyaltsen Kazi is being informed [illegible]

I have the honour to be,

Sir,

Your most obedient servant,

Sd/-B. Karthak.

General Secretary to

His Highness the Maharaja of Sikkim.

Memo. No.[illegible]

Dated Gangtok the 11th September 1942.

Copy forwarded to 1. R.S. Gyaltsen Kazi, Gangtok, and 2. Panchdal Rai, Assam-Lingtam, for information.

[illegible signature]

General Secretary to

His Highness the Maharaja of Sikkim

Figure 7.1: ***Letter of Late B. Karthak the General Secretary of His Highness the*** **Maharaja** ***of Sikkim to the Political Officer of Sikkim. Dated 11th September 1942, Courtesy: Mr Garjaman Rai Assam Lingzey, East Sikkim.***

to get rid of forced labours. It seems that these children of the peasants had chosen war instead of the feudal clutches. An application of 11th September 1942 bearing number 18910/C forwarded to the Political Officer of Sikkim by the General Secretary of His Highness *Maharaja* Sir Tashi Namgyal provides an authentic testimonial to confirm the abovementioned articulation of exemption from forced labours.[15]

Resistance through Tax Evasion

Tax evasion is regarded as the important implement of the peasant fraternity to show their resentment against the feudal set-up. In every peasant resistance, the peasants have tried to show their dissatisfaction against the unjust and exploitative system by evading their taxes. Even the Holy Bible refers about a charge on Jesus of promoting tax resistance prior to his torture and execution.[16] The reference of Bible makes it clear that the notion of tax resistance among the peasant society is not a new one. Tax evasion, in reality, is a self-protective attempt to overcome or diminish a monopolistic set up by adopting avoidance. Considering this move an appropriate, Karl Marx, in his newspaper, the *Neue Rheinische Zeitung*, published:

> "From today, therefore, taxes are abolished! It is high treason to pay taxes. Refusal to pay taxes is the primary duty of the citizen!" [17]

Ignorant of this Communist decree and Biblical values, the Sikkimese peasantry too evaded their taxes by adopting various means as devised by the whole peasant fraternity worldwide. The easiest and the most admired way for the non-payment of tax were made through migration and the East district had been a leading district in this regard. It is evident from the field study that, the *Mandals* and the *Karbaris* of a village would wait for the tax payment from the defaulters for three years. However, if he fails to pay his dues even during the given time, the officials would confiscate his property.

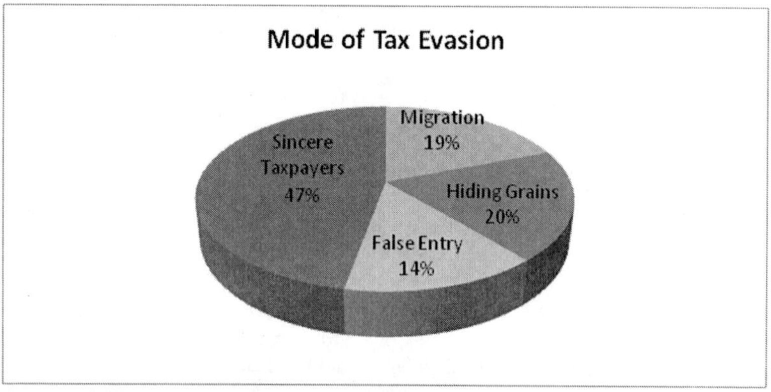

Source: Field Survey 2011-12.

The amount whatever the officials would acquire from the auction of the defaulter's possessions was to be transferred to the lessee holder. Similarly, such lands were to be merged into the Government farms.[18] Frequent delay in the payment of dues was one of the major causes of migration among the Sikkimese peasants.

In all probabilities, owing to their inability for the timely payments, peasants preferred to migrate from their villages to the other. Among Thirty Four such migrated peasants of the East district, Twenty six were the tax defaulters whereas the other eight peasants blamed then set up for anomalies that caused their migration. These eight families migrated because of the unnecessary harassments they met from the authorities. Such families preferred to remain in Kalimpong Sub Division, Darjeeling, and Assam and after the abolition of forced labour and heavy taxation, they came back to Sikkim.

Tax resistance through migration among West Sikkim peasantry was not a popular feature. Only 15 per cent of the respondents have confirmed about their ancestor's migration due to heavy taxation. The migration process in the West district varies from its Eastern counterparts. Out of such migrated peasants, only two families migrated to the plains of Siliguri and other made their inter-district migration. Four of such peasants remained in the villages of South Sikkim like Mangley, Namphing and Salghari and only after the abolition of *Dhurikhajana*, they returned to their native places. Remaining nine families made their way to East Sikkim and stayed as cow tamers in various jungles. They too came back to their native places after the abolition of *Dhurikhajana* and are presently staying in different villages in and around Soreng, Tashiding, Sakyong and Uttarey villages of West Sikkim.

Similarly, 18 per cent of the tax defaulters' migration has been revealed through field survey from the South district. Like in the case of resistance against forced labours, they adopted the technique getting into the British territory by crossing river Rammam. Seven of such cases were found in Timi village which had a cunning *Mandal* called Chulay *Mandal*[19] who never accepted failure of tax payment. Therefore, peasants who could afford to pay the tax would stay in the village and who did not had to make their way towards another village in search of a new land. Likewise, the village of Tarku had also witnessed the migration of the tax evaders. Most of such peasants got their exit from the village during nights.[20] The defaulter peasants also made inter-district migration like in the case of West Sikkim. Most of them went to the villages of East district and settled there as tenants. Two of such cases were also found at Ravi Tar under Namchi sub-division. The family papers of late Nar Dhoj Subba, whose family currently resides at Chota Singtam village in East Sikkim, point out the migration due to their inability to pay tax. From the documents, it is understood that from 1927, his family had stopped paying taxes to the Turuk *Thikadars* which led to their migration to Chota Singtam village. During their move towards East Sikkim, they insisted one Karma Jit Tamang, who was also a defaulter to accompany them.[21] Since then both the Subba and Tamang families are residing in East Sikkim. Correspondingly, three of such cases were also found in the surveyed village of Sumbuk under Namchi Sub-Division.[22] Different from all these migration, few peasants of Samatar, Denchung, Nandugaon of South Sikkim got migrated to the villages beyond river Rammam.[23] There were three such cases, each one in the villages of Samatar, Denchung and Nandugaon. These defaulters, later on, came back to their native places after the abolition of *Dhurikhajana* in 1949. Four other cases were at the surveyed villages of Assangthang and Ghurpisey under Namchi Sub Division. These four peasant family migrated to Nepal and never retreated.[24]

Tax evasion through hiding the grain was also an admired feature of Sikkimese peasant resistance. It was mainly put forward by the *Adhiadars*, *Kutdars* and other varieties of peasants of various villages. It is to be noted here that, peasants who had their lands had to pay their taxes in cash to their local *Mandals*. Likewise, the tenants who were mainly the *Adhiadars* or the *Kutiyars* of the *Kazis* and *Thikadars* had to pay their rents or taxes in the form of grain as per the agreement they made with the former. However, their rents too were assessed by the local officials like *Mandals* and *Karbaris*. The most important contributors of these sorts of resistance were the *Adhiadars* and *Kutiyars* forms of tenancy in Sikkim.

Though, 57 per cent of the total respondents' ancestors did not possess any land in East district; yet, the case of hiding of grain during harvest was very negligible. It comes into surface that, only 13 per cent of the respondents have accepted the adoption of this mode of resistance. They would hide a sack of rice or so before the visit of a *Mandal* or *Karbari* at *Khale Gara*.[25] The *Adhiadar* and *Kutiyars* tenants of the adjacent villages like Assam Lingzey, Aho, Namli, Namin etc. had a very little chance of hiding a huge quantity of the produce. However, people in excuse of keeping seeds for next cultivation used to hide crops in the secret cabin of their houses.[26] Such acts of hiding of the crops are considered as self-interest acts of the peasants and may be regarded as the domination or ascendancy of the peasants over the State. Conversely, for Scott such resistance is not the monopoly of lower classes.[27]

The West District played a vital role in resisting the feudal system by hiding grains. Being situated in remote pockets, such villages were out of surveillance from the higher level authorities. Therefore, as it seems, the Western peasants exploited this advantage to the highest level. 29 of the total 100 respondents admitted about the hiding of crops by their forefathers. The active villages seemed to be the villages of periphery of Soreng. During the absence of the *Mandal* and the *Karbaris*, peasants of these villages never let the opportunity to go futile. During *daai* (day of harvest), all the peasants helped each other to carry the sacks of paddy in the absence of the *Mandal* or *Karbari*.[28] Almost Thirteen of such cases were found in the villages of Suntaley, Pakkigaon and Malbassey villages under Soreng sub-division. Likewise, the peasants of Uttarey, Tashiding, Chongrang, Gerethang, Nesha and other villages had resisted the cruel feudal yoke by adopting this technique. All other remaining Sixteen cases of crop hiding occurred in these villages of West Sikkim. The feudal lords of these villages used to reside in the Capital or in other District Headquarters; therefore, the absence of the landlord from his estate provided a broader opportunity to hide crops during or before the harvest.

The South district of the Kingdom also played a considerable part in resisting feudalism by hiding crops. Among 100 respondents, Fourteen had spoken about their role in hiding the crops before harvest. Here too, these acts mainly took place in the remote parts of the district. Four peasants from the villages of Temi and Tarku had accepted their families' indulgence in hiding crops. The method of hiding was alike to the East and West districts. The peasants of these villages also remained active during nights to hide crops.[29] Similarly, the peasants of Samsebung, Salghari, Samatar, Denchung and Nandugaon had also a bit of their involvement in adopting this mode of resistance. Remaining ten cases were found in these villages of South Sikkim. The village of Assangthang had also shown its resentment against feudalism by hiding crops. The most important factor for such resistance in these villages was lack of surveillance. It is to be noted that, resistance through hiding crops was popular among the tenants of the *Kazis*, *Thikadars*, and among the *Adhiadars* and *Kutdar* tenants. Rest *Chaar Daam* peasants had never made such attempts as they had to pay a fixed tax to the State according to area they possessed.

False entry of the possessed land was another form of resistance technique adopted by the Sikkimese peasantry. As we are aware that the peasants had to pay land taxes in various forms and such attempts of false entry appears to be a measure to lessen the burden of land tax. They had to pay taxes of wet land and dry lands separately and the amount they paid seemed almost similar. So, if they could get exemption from paying either of the two, they could live a hassle free life at least for a year. Keeping this very fact in mind, peasants took this opportunity to exploit in every possible manner. There was only one such case in the North district which too was after the land survey of 1952. Hence, no cases of false entry have been recorded in the surveyed areas of North Sikkim in the feudalistic phase.

The East district of the Kingdom, amid various legal hurdles had Eighteen cases of false entry. Though, the Administrative Reports of Sikkim State makes a clear idea that no lands in Sikkim were scientifically measured during World Wars, yet there were several cases in the villages. As stated earlier, all the measurements of lands were made through *Nazar Jaanch* by a *Mandal* or a *Karbari* in the villages. The villagers who were smart enough could make such false entry in an agreement with the village officials.[30] Many villagers of the surveyed areas of Assam Lingzey, Namli, Namin, Marchak, Linkey, Barapathing, Dongrong, Bering, Tareythang, Manpur, Aho, Kadamtam, Chota Singtam, and Central Pendam have given us information about such acts. In these villages of East Sikkim, at least one case of false entry could be found.

Despite its remoteness, the West district of the Kingdom had a less involvement in making a false entry regarding the area of cultivation. There were only eight per cent of peasants who were involved in resisting the heavy taxation of the State. In the surveyed villages of Suntaley, Pakkigaon, Soreng, Malbassey, Tashiding, Chongrang, Nesha, Gerethang, Sakyong, Uttarey, peasants seemed to have been innocents as compared to other two districts of the Kingdom. Only three cases were found during field work under Soreng subdivision where peasants made false entry to lessen the burden of State taxation. Likewise, the peasants of periphery of Tashiding made such attempts due to the long absence of the *Kazi* from their respective villages. There were five such cases in Tashiding area. The process of making a false entry was similar to the East district. To lessen the burden of taxation, peasants of West district had not only offered a grand treat but, they had also presented their livestock like goat, chicken, and pigs to their concerned officials.

The peasantry of South Sikkim had played a major part in resisting feudal taxation by adopting the mode of false entry of their lands. The district had the largest resisters who paid less tax by showing less area of their possession than the real one. The villages like Denchung, Samsebung, Salghari, Samatar, and Nandugaon had 17 per cent of total respondents who made a false entry to pay less tax to the State. One of such case was noticed at the village of Dambudara under Namchi subdivision. Likewise, other two cases were from the village of Tarku. In South district, all of such acts took place in those villages where there was a least observation. The village of Sumbuk is unknown about this sort of resistance as it was under the direct watch of the feudal official stationed at the village.

Apart from such resisters, there were many other peasants throughout Sikkim who paid their taxes sincerely. These peasants tolerated the feudal pressure without any confrontation. Almost all of the respondents of North district paid their taxes on time. Out of 50 respondents 46 (92 per cent) peasants made timely payment of taxes. Likewise, 35 per cent of the peasants from East district had sincerely paid their taxes due to the threat and intimidation they had witnessed in time and again. Forty-eight per cent of the peasants from West district had honestly paid their taxes to their officials. Similarly, 42 per cent of the Southern peasants paid their taxes to their officials without any resistance. Hence, in totality, the numbers of the resisters and sincere tax payers were almost equal in Sikkim during feudalism.

Peasant Resistance in Sikkim through Poaching

The literary meaning of the term 'poach' is to catch, trespass, and encroach and the act of poaching is generally understood as an act of theft.[31] This mode of peasant resistance was quite popular in the Kingdom of Sikkim. The collected data indicates that almost all the districts of the Kingdom had a good number of poachers. The surveyed areas of North district, though, was not under any feudal exploitation had also shown 90 per cent of its involvement in poaching. The poachers of these areas were mainly involved in hunting and collecting firewood from the reserved lands. It is revealed that the acts of the peasants of the surveyed areas were not due to the feudal pressure. Rather, their motive of encroachment into the reserved land was for hunting that has always been the favourite time pass for the rural Lepchas of Sikkim.

Unlike the Northern peasants, the peasants of East, West and South districts of the Kingdom had resisted the feudal exploitation by adopting various techniques. It was on them the feudal yoke was hooked up in a heavier and a stronger manner. Hence, they reacted in a similar manner to counter the feudal oppression. The peasants of East district had exhibited their bitter antipathy by poaching into the lands of the feudal lords. 15 per cent of the total respondents' ancestors had poached into the landlords' domain to meet their daily needs. Such acts of poaching in East district included hunting, chopping of trees, getting into orchards etc. However, if they were caught by the *Lal Feteys* maintained by the landlords, they had to face a serious consequence. They would be fined or taken to the *Kutcheri* for physical torture or in some cases; the poachers had to bear both. In spite of these obligations, as the exigency of time, the peasants of East district poached into the landlords and government lands. They not only utilised the private lands of their lords for hunting and firewood, but, they also sent their cattle for grazing. The *Adhiadars* and *Kutdars* of the landlords too had poached in both government and their master's land. The most active villages to adopt poaching mode of resistance were Dongrong, Linkey, Bara Pathing, and Parakha which were situated in the remote corners of the district. The villages adjacent to the Capital did not have an active participation in poaching.

According to the field survey, the West district had the largest number of poachers in the private farms of the landlords. Thirty-five per cent of the responses points out towards an active involvement of the peasants in poaching. As stated elsewhere, most of the feudal lords having their estates in West Sikkim had their residence in the District Headquarters or in the State's Capital. Taking full advantage of their absence, the villagers in West Sikkim poached in their private farms for hunting without caring other village officials.

Due to the presence of other subordinates like *Mandal* and *Karbaris*, the villagers got into the private lands during nights for chopping trees. Only three per cent of the cases were related poaching in the Government Land. As in East district, this category of the poachers comprised of the tenants of the *Kazis* and *Thikadars* and the nature of poaching was almost similar with the peasants of East. However, there were a few cases of confrontation between the caretakers of the *Kazis* and the commoners in the periphery of Tashiding estate.[32] The active villages of poaching concerned in West Sikkim were Soreng, Suntaley, Uttarey, Gangyap and Sakyong.

The South district of the Kingdom also had a good number of poachers during feudalistic Sikkim. Twenty per cent of the respondents in the various villages of South Sikkim had confirmed their involvements in poaching. Their activities included hunting, collecting firewood, chopping of trees, grazing their cattle in the government and private lands of the Katis. Few cases were also collected from the closely watched village of Sumbuk where people hunted in a day light in the private lands of their Newar *Thikadars*.

The other villages which were out of the surveillance had repeated the similar features like in West and East districts of the Kingdom. However, they differ in their ways as most of the poachers of South district had made it in the government lands. They seemed more active in collecting honey from the reserved forest lands. In the excuse of honey, they sometimes killed deer, wild pigs, and wild chicken and the like. Adopted by few peasants, the act of poaching appears to have played an important part in the daily lives of Sikkimese peasantry. If we exclude the North district of the Kingdom, peasants of the other three districts played a considerable role for their survival against hegemony as poachers.

Apart from these usual modes of resistance, the peasants of West Sikkim had devised a new mode to safeguard their interests to counter the feudal pressure that includes transformation of caste. This was indeed a new and an unusual form of peasant resistance in Sikkim. It is believed that, the peasants of Sombarey and its periphery had left their original castes and adopted the customs of the Bhutias and the Lepchas. As it was informed, almost all of the Limboo peasants of a village under Sombarey block adopted Lepcha customs and traditions and became the Lepchas.[33] Likewise, few Tamang peasants of the same village and its periphery adopted Bhutia ways of life and became the Bhutias. While doing so, they made their marriage vows with the Lepcha and the Bhutia families and after a lapse of two or three generations they began to call themselves as Bhutias or Lepchas.[34] It is to be noted here that, the Lepchas and the Limboos of Sikkim share similar features and along with their appearance, their clan names also sound same.[35] Likewise, the Tamangs of Sikkim had their religious similarity with the Bhutias. Hence, with their affinities with the Bhutia families, they, too, claimed their Bhutia ancestry and got liable to pay a bit lesser amount of tax. It is interesting to note that, this mode of resistance was popular only in the villages of Sombarey and its periphery. Therefore, this mode of peasant resistance is a unique and a new mode adopted by the peasants of West Sikkim to counter the feudal laws.

Resistance through Bribe and Sexual Temptation

The peasants due to famines, droughts and natural calamities, sometimes, could not pay their due taxes on time. To get rid of the danger of paying double tax or being tortured, they had also employed other forms of resistance. Bribing of an official was the last option left to a peasant to run his livelihood during the sandwiched moments of feudal pressure and natural disaster. The Sikkimese had a little participation in bribing the feudal officials to get exempted from the tax payment and forced labour. The surveyed areas of North Sikkim did not have to bribe the concerned officials as it was away from the feudal yoke. Even East district of the kingdom had a nominal participation in bribing their feudal officials as just seven responses indicate the indulgence in adopting this mode of resistance.

The peasants of West district had a major participation in bribing their feudal officials as ten respondents confirmed their about their families' engagements in bribing the feudal authorities. They had to give *Koseli*[36] to their officials to get exempted from the payment of taxes for once. The *Koseli* comprised of cattle and other valuable edibles like paddy, buckwheat, and millet but were bound to pay their interest during their next tax payment. During the next payment, they again had to visit their officials with other *Koseli* to show their gratitude.

> "We had to offer them curd, chicken, vegetable and country beer locally called as *Jaad*, *Saptu* or *Chhang* to the *Mandals* and the *Karbaris*".[37]

The major reason for the little participation of the peasants in this mode of resistance was due to the provision of gifts and souvenir which had to be presented to the feudal lords. A peasant who was not able to pay his taxes to the government would be never in a position to offer valuable gifts to his officials. Hence, owing to financial constraints, it appears that, the peasants were least interested in bribing their officials.

The South district, too, had a mild affiliation in bribing the feudal officials. Eight cases were found in the surveyed villages of South Sikkim. Similar causes were traced out during field survey about the causes for bribing the feudal officials. The most important of such villages were Temi, Tarku, Samatar and Nandugaon. These peasants were engaged in bribing their officials to get exemption from the taxation and forced labour. For these, they had to work wage less in the farms of their officials or had to send their children to work as slaves in their houses. Nevertheless, the main motif of the peasants was almost similar in all the three districts which were to get relaxation from paying taxes and serving as a forced labourer.

Resistance through sexual temptation was not at all a popular form of peasant resistance in Sikkim. The non-involvement of Sikkimese peasantry in resisting the feudal norms through sexual temptation was mainly because of its social norms where sex is regarded as a taboo in the society. Further, even if the practice was in vogue the respondents were not so open to speak in a large volume as they regarded the matter as filthy and confidential. Therefore, in totality, resistance through sexual temptation was not a popular form of peasant resistance in Sikkim.

The Administrative Reports of the Sikkim State have not made reference of any of the resistance made by the peasants. As the matter got extra complex, it appears that, the peasants made complaints about their unwillingness to comply with the wishes of their *Mandals* and other feudal officials against forceful *Jharlangi* in 1911.[38] Similarly, the administrative reports of the World Wars period have stated about the occasional complaints of over taxation were received from the ryots of Mamring, Amba and Pathing.[39] To short out the problems of the peasants, the palace tried to abolish free labour with a system of compulsory paid labour.[40] However,

Balikci suggests that the landlords did not comply with the royal orders to be implemented.[41] She further informs that owing to the objection of British Political Officer the Durbar could not abolish the entire system of free labours.[42] The silent and a hushed attitude of the Palace and the British Political Officers, the faulty and a confused administration that lacked division of power between the Palace and Political Officers, the repressive and exploitative nature of the *Kazis* and *Thikadars* were some of the major factors responsible for the peasant discontentment in Sikkim. Further, the Administrative Reports have several cases of fraud and cheating made by the *Kazis* and the *Thikadars*. However, amidst such allegations it emerge that the *Kazis* and *Thikadars* were never punished for their gluttonous acts. In the year 1930-31, there was a decline in Land revenue of ₹ 39,800 under household taxes.[43] Though, the Political Officer of the State had asked for an explanation from the concerned *Kazis* and *Thikadars*; yet, the explanations given by the alleged *Kazis* and *Thikadars* has never got its place in the succeeding Administrative Reports. There were several cases of fraud and cheating made by them as the tax of the lands which they were holding was practically fixed at a level. Indisputably, such cases were suppressed by the *Kazis* and *Thikadars* with their power and money.

Further, the peasants could not appeal to the *Adda* Courts and even if they appeal their voices went unheard. According to the Administrative Report of 1931-32, there were 57 *Adda* Courts in Sikkim.[44] The *Adda* Courts were invested with some class of judicial powers both on civil and criminal parts. They were neither honorary nor stipendiary courts as they used to keep to themselves the half of the Court fee released or half of the fines imposed on the peasants.[45] Hence, it seems that when all the doors for justice were closed, with a sense of keeping themselves in a justified position, the Sikkimese peasants devised various modes to resist them from the all-round attack of feudalism.

Owing to the above stated factors, the lower class discontentment gradually changes its mode of resistance and sometimes gets rebellious and that may also bring an open confrontation against the state. In this context, the peasants of Sirwani in East Sikkim had beaten a son of a *Kazi* to death and as it is said, the family members could not even recover his body.[46] Likewise, the peasants of Barapathing had beaten their *Kazi* during his visit to the village.[47] In the same way, a peasant Brihaspati Parsai, who later became an important leader of Sikkim State Congress, had beaten up his *Mandal*. Similarly, Jatan Das Rai of Namin village had thrashed his *Kazi* while he was ploughing, and as it is said, he had even destroyed his crops.[48] A peasant named Dal Dhoj Rai of Assam Lingzey along with his friends made an attack on his *Mandal* Chatursingh. Later, all these accused were made to pay fines.[49]All these methods adopted by the Sikkimese peasants to resist the feudal encroachments in their daily lives, were indeed the '*weapons of the weak*' as illustrated by James C Scott. From these incidents, it is evident that the resentments of the entire Sikkimese peasantry were at its pinnacle. Therefore, when the cohesive movement began in the Kingdom, these depressed and frustrated rural lots made a greater contribution towards the expansion of democratic ideas among other fellow peasants.

The history of peasant struggle against the state reveals the fact that they resisted the State only when their interests were endangered. To safeguard themselves from the unnecessary encroachment of the State they took up a variety of methods for their survival. Adoption of various modes in irregular and individual ways was their attempts to get rid of the unjust and unethical set-up and these modes of resistance do not bear the creed of violence. Hence, with the exception of few cases, the everyday forms of peasant resistance are non-violent which even lacks open demonstration and defiance. Such modes of resistance are considered as the stubborn bedrock upon which other forms of resistance could grow.[50] With the advancement of time and with the breeding of some new and radical ideas among the peasants, these very forms of resistance could even take the shape of a political philosophy. Few educated people among peasantry then begin to dream for a set up where they could enjoy equal power relationships.

With the commencement of Second World War, the nature of peasant resistance in Sikkim also began to take a different curve. The exploitation of the *Kazis* and *Thikadars* reached its highest watermark during this period that consequently resulted in enhancing the pace of struggle against the State. During the turbulent phase of Second World War, Sikkimese peasantry was battling in the two fronts i.e. the native exploitation at the hands of *Kazis* and *Thikadars* and the exploitation by the British *Sahibs*. Consequently, the individual acts of the peasants began to take shape of a united movement and few uncontrolled peasants of Assangthang and Namthang started violent acts against their feudal officials. Their involvement for a unified resistance to unleash the Sikkimese peasantry from the cruel yoke of the *Kazis*, *Thikadars*, *Mukhtiyars*, *Mandals,* and *Karbaris* shall be discussed in the next chapter.

Notes

1. Scott, James C, '*Everyday forms of Resistance*' Copenhagen Papers, p. 57.
2. Scott, James C (July 1987), '*Resistance without Protest and without Organization: Peasant Opposition to the Islamic Zakat and the Christian Tithe*' Comparative Study in Society and History, Vol. 29 Issue 3, p. 421.

3. Zinn, Howard, (2007) A Power Government Cannot Suppress, City Lights Books, Sa Francisco, p. 35.
4. *'Resistance and the problem of ethnographic refusal'* (1995) Comparative study in Society and History, Vol. 37, No.1, p. 174.
5. Guha, Ranajit (ed) (2010), Subaltern Studies Vol. I Arnold David '*Rebellious Hill men: The Gudem-Rampa Risings 1839-1924*', Oxford University Press, pp. 88-89.
6. Zinn (2007) op cit, p. 228.
7. General Department, 8146-08/G, 19th June 1926.
8. Field Report: 2011-2012: Nandu Gaon, South Sikkim.
9. Scott, James C (1990), *Domination and Arts of Resistance Hidden Transcripts*, Yale University Press, p. 118.
10. As per the Ghar Lauri norm every householder had to send a male member to carry government loads.
11. *Parma* is a form of labour among the villagers that was made in exchange. If a peasant was unable to carry loads he would ask for help from his neighbour or from the person of another village and send him instead. For this he would not pay to the substitute but, he would help him carrying loads during the latter's engagement as a porter.
12. The *Thinguros* were made up of wooden planks, the culprit had to put his legs inside the hole made at the middle of the plank, with this the mouth of the *Thinguro* would be tighten by a rod or an iron, thus, leaving the culprit standing in utter pain. *Source:* Field Report 2011-2012.
13. Assam Lingzey, East Sikkim.
14. Mukherjee, Mridula, '*Peasant Resistance and peasant consciousness in Colonial India Subalterns and Beyond*', Economic and Political Weekly, Oct 8, 1988.
15. Documents collected from Mr. Garja Man Rai (91 years) a Second World War Veteran of Assam Lingzey during Field Survey.
16. Holy Bible, Luke 23: 2.
17. Marx, Karl, (November 1848), "*No Tax Payments!*" *Neue Rheinische Zeitung* #145, Www. Marxists.org. date of access 19 September 2011.
18. Field Report 2011-2012: Assam Lingzey Saureni village, East Sikkim.
19. Field Report 2011-2012: Tarku village, South Sikkim.
20. Field Report: 2011-2012: Information collected through personal interview from erstwhile *Mandals* of feudal Sikkim.
21. From the tax receipts preserved by Mr. Harka Bahadur Subba of Chota Singtam Village in East Sikkim.
22. Field Report 2011-2012: Sumbuk village South Sikkim.
23. Field Report 2011-2012: Sumbuk village South Sikkim.
24. Field Report 2011-2012: Assangthang village, South Sikkim.
25. *Khale Gara* is a flat tract of land which has been used by Sikkimese peasantry for keeping un husked rice before the harvest.
26. Field Report 2011-2012: Central Pandam village, East Sikkim.

27. Scott, James C (1985), *Weapons of the Weak everyday forms of peasant resistance*, Yale University Press, p. 295.
28. Field Report 2011-2012: Suntaley village, West Sikkim.
29. Field Report 2011-2012: Tarku village, South Sikkim.
30. Field Report 2011-2012: Assam Lingzey, East Sikkim.
31. Scott, James C, (April 1989), '*Everyday Forms of Resistance*', Copenhagen Papers pp. 37-38.
32. Field Report: 2011-2012: Information collected from the related peasants of Tashiding West Sikkim.
33. Field Report 2011-2012: Munew village, West Sikkim.
34. Field Report 2011-2012: Munew village, West Sikkim.
35. Field Report 2011-2012: Munew village, West Sikkim.
36. *Koseli* is the Nepali synonym to a valuable gift.
37. Field Report 2011-2012: Middle Chongrang, West Sikkim.
38. Land Revenue Department, File No. 37, 21st January 1911, Sikkim State Archives
39. Administrative Report 1917-1918, II, p. 2.
40. General Department, 5814/G, 15th July 1924.
41. Balikci, Anna (2008), *Lamas, Shamans and Ancestors- Village Religion in Sikkim*, Brill, Leiden, The Netherlands, p. 51.
42. *Ibid.*
43. Administrative Reports 1931-32, V, 30.
44. *Ibid*, 23.
45. *Ibid.*
46. Field Report 2011-2012: Tarku village, South Sikkim.
47. Field Report 2011-2012: Linkey village, East Sikkim.
48. Field Report 2011-2012: Namin village, East Sikkim.
49. Field Report 2011-2012: Assam Lingzey, East Sikkim.
50. Scott, (1985) op cit, p. 273.

Chapter 8

The Era of Cohesive Peasant Resistance (1930-1947)

As stated in the earlier chapters, the feudal oppression in Sikkim was at its highest level during Second World War and the resistance made by the peasants were the individual self protective measures to ensure their survival. Basically, the dissatisfaction among the rural folks was, as it appears, due to the failure of the State to redress the minimum grievances of the hungry and the needy. As stated elsewhere, even if the monarch wanted to eliminate the rural injustice the Political Officer would have his objection owing to which a larger section of the society had to live a perilous life. When the common interests of the villagers were frequently disregarded by the State they began to organise and act, resulting into a unified mode of resistance. The earlier, though few, violent and acts of insubordinations proved to be the gateway for a larger political goal to achieve their common interest. The unbending motives of both the ends eventually led to a conflict between the 'affluent' and the 'meagre' heralding a new era in the Kingdom. The earlier individual resisters had now organise themselves under various associations and clamoured for the elimination of all social nuisances. Collectively, the peasants were now determined to achieve the world of their choice, and they seemed ready to attain it even through violence. At this juncture, they had given up their earlier everyday mode of resistance and became vocal in securing their rights through petitions and, if it was needed, through demonstrations. However, in their later course of action they came under the political influence and continued their resistance against the State following the principles of a political party. James Madison, the father of the American Constitution justifies such conflicts as,

"... Conflict between those who had property and those who did not."[1]

The study reveals that, peasant resistance of Sikkim had taken a different curve after 1930's and reached its uppermost echelon during Second World War. When the entire world was busy in winning each other, the rural lots of the erstwhile Himalayan Kingdom seemed busy fighting with their own destiny. As we have seen, apart from the families of few Sikkimese army men, the rest had to follow the orders of their officials to carry the State loads[2] and were also obligated to pay a high rate of taxation. Thus, the majority of the peasants, without much change in their everyday affair, had to live their lives as their forefathers lived, in utter distress and poverty. In contrast to the peasantry, Indian independence brought a new dimension for the ruling cliques as the Kingdom got a special position in the Constituent Assembly of India.[3] With the signing of the Standstill Agreement on 27th February 1948 Sikkim retained her previous status of Protectorate.

Expansion of Individual Resistance into Rural Secret Societies

Entirely, if we have to access, Sikkim, on the eve of Indian independence, was a closed book as far as the social reformations and political mobility were concerned. Few violent acts in distant places of Sikkim did not have much impact on the political expansion of the Kingdom. Such acts may be considered as the acts of noncompliance by the peasants against their feudal lords and were crushed down with iron hands. However, in the midst of this oblivion, the attempts of the few villagers to go against the monopolistic set up deserve appreciation, no matter how their attempts did got foiled. Apart from them, it is thus obvious that, majority of the peasants was living under the feudal yoke and were enduring it due to their illiteracy and poverty. However, from their everyday resistance it can be perceived that, peasants were eager to get rid of the exploitation they had been subjected to in their daily lives.

Many scholars hold the view that the political awakening of Sikkim took place due to the inspirations drawn by the Sikkimese people from Indian independence. Of course, the Indian independence was a major event not only in the Indian sub-continent but, also in the international arena. Nevertheless, to believe that Sikkim got inspired entirely because of the Indian factor is an unjustifiable point. Certainly, the neighbouring Indian activities were playing impacts on the Sikkimese hearts also. Yet, we cannot undermine a variety of native factors in abundance to create a political awakening in Sikkim. Obviously, Sikkim had also an open and independent sky under which stars were calculating their revolving around the orbit.

As we have noticed in the preceding chapters about the native factors responsible for the peasant resistance. We are now also aware of the Sikkimese society before the era of cohesive resistance, with no equal distribution of lands, and the condition of the poor peasants, left entirely at the mercy of their landlords. The indignant attitude of the landlords and their officials had wounded the sentiments of thousands of rural souls.

However, no authority was there to listen to their problems and to heal their emotional sores. Apart from those of elites, as it appears, economic condition of the people in Sikkim was not better than the poorest peasant society of the world. Squeezed in between feudal pressures and daily needs the peasants had hardly ever thought of a world of freedom and independence. It emerges that; entire countryside psyche was limited in between their relations with their masters and other officials. Therefore, there was no issue of going beyond the whimsical landlords who seemed to be the fate writers of these paupers.

With the introduction of modern schools, people of the capital and its periphery got its benefits. The rest and the majority of the marginalised were standing far away from advantage of education. The available documents indicate adoption of repressive measures by feudal officials against the opening of schools in far distant places.[4] Moreover, education is a compulsion to those who are aware of it. For the marginalised lot of rural Sikkim, it may be assumed that, it was not the part of their flavours. Besides, they were struggling for their survival against domination where one fistful grain was much more soothing than the philosophies of Marx, Engel, Gandhi, and Socrates. However, in spite of such a miserable circumstance, it comes to light that a few peasants had sent their children to the schools run by a village committee. Likewise, in all probabilities, imitating their landlords, as education consciousness among them seems very little; few affluent peasants had even sent their children to the neighbouring state of West Bengal for their study.[5]

Birth of Rural Secret Societies

As an exigency of time, the calm and quite rural masses began to flow against the current ignoring every threats and intimidation. Moreover, the lower class antagonism and their participation have always played a crucial role in determining the destiny of a State. The hidden transcripts of the Sikkimese peasants were on their way of transformation when the level of suppression reaches its apex and something like a confrontation was utterly inevitable. Their sense of repulsion and revulsion were getting actualised when they started to oppose feudal norms collectively. To secure their interest, they began to struggle together with a prime motive to uproot feudalism along with its vices. The torments they received in their lives, the humiliation at the hands of their masters and other officials, their pathetic and shoddier conditions, their sense of freedom and their radicalism, their needs and necessities were some of the igniting causes to go against the system. Thus, with a motive, to secure their little interests, the masses rose against suppression of the *Kazi-Thikadars* without caring about their lives and property.[6] Their escalated enthusiasm paved way for the birth of rural secret societies, determined to unleash their fellow brethren from the clutches of the *Kazi-Thikadars*. Howard Zinn observes:

> "The uneasiness grows and grows and the citizenry gathers in resistance in larger and larger numbers, which becomes too many to control; one day the top-heavy empire collapses."[7]

The *Danthey* Party

The first of unwritten and unmentioned cohesive resistance in the form of a secret society was posed upon by the peasants of Assangthang in South Sikkim. Field study drops a light on the harassments and sufferings met by them at the hands of feudal officials especially during payment of their *Dhurikhajana*. Apart from these browbeaten lots, the *Kazis* and *Thikadars* had even cheated a gentle Lepcha *Mandal* who was in charge of the collection of revenues at Assangthang. It is said that, the Lepcha *Mandal* had regularly deposited the collected revenues to his *Kazi* however; owing to a personal difference, he was accused for the non-payment of taxes. Subsequently, the *Kazi* made a petition to the palace stating about the *Mandal's* unfaithfulness and got the arrest warrant and was prosecuted. After a prolonged trail under the lawless laws, the Lepcha *Mandal* got acquitted and in annoyance, he left his village and migrated to Kalimpong in the British territory.[8] If the vindication is true, one can imagine the actual condition of peasantry that belonged to the lowest strata of Sikkimese feudal society.

Therefore, to get rid of such nuisances' at least from their village, peasants of Assangthang village joined their hands in wiping out the manipulative forms of feudalism. It was during pre-Second World War period, a person named Bhadru Magar of the village, formed a secret society known as *Danthey* Party, with a motive to go against the tide viciously. We are not much aware about other agendas of this society however; from the information it is so far known that its primary goal was to dismantle the feudal edifice. It is also said that, Bhadru Magar was very critical in evaluating existing equation and encouraged his fellowmen to stand and to speak up and also insisted them to get violent if it comes as necessity. It is believed that, the members of *Danthey* Party would carry sticks or *Dantha* to fight against asymmetrical feudal decrees and therefore, this society got its name as *Danthey* Party. They organised few groups to attack feudal lords during their visits to the village.[9] The members of this society seemed eager to petrify system and to get themselves in the lightened positions. Few such efforts were made by them to whisk away the officials during the assessment of taxes. Owing to his violent design to dismantle feudal structure, that appeared not less than the rock of Gibraltar, Bhadru Magar became a popular name in the peripheries of Assangthang and Namchi. Through his radical talks and zeal he had induced among his fellow brethren, a sense of self-respect and courage to go adverse to the forged foundation of feudalism. At Assangthang, Bhadru seemed to be no more a name, as he was now regarded as a *synonym* of hope of many paupers. It may be assessed that, when the level of suppression reached its pinnacle, sufferers like Bhadru began to retaliate in a violent manner paving a way to their hidden transcripts for a full throated expression. It is worth to mention that *Danthey* Party of Assangthang village in South Sikkim was a first society of the Kingdom of its kind to counter feudal yoke. Though, Bhadru and his society could not eradicate feudalism from the village; but, the endeavour of ignorant peasants to eliminate such evils is a matter of endorsement. Regarding such collective acts of the peasants Scott observes:

> "... a particular peasant may be a tenant of a landlord whom he regards as particularly oppressive. He may grumble; he may even have fantasies about telling the landlord what he thinks of him or even darker thoughts of arson or homicide. If this is an isolated, personal grievance, the affair is likely to stop there at fantasy. If, however, many tenants find themselves in the same boat, either because they share the same landlord or because their landlords treat them in comparable ways, there arises the basis for a collective grievance, collective fantasy, and even collective acts".[10]

The Members' Party

The disobedience of Bhadru Magar and his associates had inaugurated a new sphere in the rural lives of South Sikkim. Their rebellious ideas of insubordination had a deep impact among the people of Assangthang and Namchi and the course of defiance continued. It is believed that, they were never arrested and prosecuted for their opposition probably due to fear of rural uprising. In all probabilities, such cases of rebellions were fixed up by the concerned *Kazis* as they have not got their mention in available administrative reports. Conversely, such rebellious acts had far reaching consequences among the other villagers to adopt a similar way to get rid of system. It is uncertain to determine if the pioneers of other societies of South Sikkim were strictly driven by the ideas of Bhadru. However, it can be articulated that the phase of insubordination and noncompliance inaugurated by *Danthey* Party gained momentum in other parts of the district as well. The youths of Namthang, organised another secret society against the exploitative set up. They founded a secret village group known as Members' Party in 1940, under Dahal brothers, Khadananda Dahal and

Dharnidhar Dahal.[11] According to Dharnidhar Dahal, other remarkable members of the secret society were Maha Singh Limbu, the Sapkota brothers namely, Jai Narayan Sapkota and Trilochan Sapkota, and Jerman Lepcha.[12] Analogous to *Danthey* Party, main objective of the 'Members Party' was also to unleash Sikkim from the evil socio-economic practices of feudal Order.[13] Dahal, further informs that, they held a meeting at Namthang Bazar in April 1945 (date unknown) and delivered their speeches before the villagers.[14] This was arguably first political speech given by any rationalist Sikkimese. The summary of the speech is as under:-

> "Now the time has been changed. We are no more tolerating atrocities and discrepancies of *Kazi-Zamindars*. We all must arise, awake, and should join our hands to uproot *Kazis*. Henceforth, without wage, none of the *ryot* will carry paddy sacks of Baburam Kasaju (the *Zamindar*). This is a warning to all the peasants of Namthang, if anyone dares to do; their home will be turn into ashes. Apart from this, we are not going to carry *Kalo Bhari, Jharlangi*...We are ready to give our lives for us, but, we will never obey their orders... Down with *Kazi Zamindars*, Long Live People's Power!!"[15]

Alarmed with such radical speech, repressive measures were taken up by the concerned *Thikadar* Baburam Kasaju to extinguish sparks of rebellion. It is stated that, a police force was sent to arrest the youths with charges of sedition as they had projected themselves as the liberators and urging insubordination against their master. Somehow, the judicious youths managed to escape and got underground and became more active in their designs. It is also known that, prowling of paddy fields of *Zamindar* by the youths of Members' party became a common feature at Namthang and its periphery. Moving a step further, they distributed robbed paddy sacks among the poor farmers, who according to them were the real masters of lands.[16] The course of speeches at Namthang Bazaar continued and gained impetus among the peripheral peasants. However, in the course of time, one of its active members, Maha Singh Limbu, was arrested and tortured in a most inhuman manner and was banished from Sikkim.[17] Conversely, even after such stiff action from the part of State, course of speech continued and the earlier scared lots began to attend such speeches fearlessly.[18] To elucidate such acts of subordinates, Howard Zinn comments:

> "Public consciousness starts with low level discontent, at first vague, with no connection being made between the discontent and the policies of the government. And then the dots begin to connect, indignation increases, and people began to speak out, organise, and act".[19]

Thus, the idea of cohesive resistance in the form of secret societies got ignited in remote pockets of the Kingdom mostly focusing on the removal of unjust, noxious, and inequitable policies of the State. Night meetings were held to find out ways and means to do away with the suppression and injustice for a new horizon in the history of the Kingdom. Proving itself as an apt 'anti thesis' of the hegemonic foundation, the Members' Party clamoured against inequalities rampant in the Kingdom and ignited a spark of rebellion. With the foundation of such defiant societies, we may now assess that in spite of theocratic and feudal political structure, certain aspects of rebellious acts were in the mounting stage in the rural ways of life.

Tendong Secret Meet

Arguably, secret societies of Assangthang and Namthang initiated by a few, had a deep impact among the peasants who began to feel the currents of change from their nearby areas. It seems, peasants of other parts of the Kingdom, began to feel that they too were staking on the same horse that was heading towards their ultimate devastation. Owing to their intuitions, they also, began to appear in bands and groups with a fierce cry to knell down feudalism along with its vices of torment. Consequently, a secret meeting under Dhan Bahadur Tiwari and Goverdhan Pradhan was held at Tendong Hill, Damthang in South Sikkim. It is believed that, the secret meeting had a huge support from the peasants of nearby villages. Available sources inform that, famed Bhadru Magar of Assangthang village was also among the participants of this secret meeting.[20] Though, we are unknown about its resolutions and decisions taken up by the meeting, as almost all of the participants do not exist, but, it is now evident that, peasants were in no mood to carry on with biased state policies. Similarly, it seems, being a meeting of the mistreated and marginalised lots no body felt importance of keeping records in writing. Accordingly, in the absence of the sources it is not possible to get into the matter in a reliable manner.

However, even if that meeting was a gathering of the most secluded, neglected, segregated, and politically isolated section of Sikkimese society; desperate attitude of the State in redressing their grievances seems the most common factor to wind them up. Similarly, the lawless laws that were dispensed through several *Adda* Courts in the villages or in the estates along with exorbitant taxation and feudal exploitations were some other factors that guided them to stand up together. In precise, this morsel of consciousness among these rural dwellers was not because of education rather it was the consequence of experience they achieved through their State since long. Therefore, to come out of the boiling frog situation they started to resist the State in a cohesive manner. In all probabilities, to keep themselves away from State's surveillance they selected an isolated Tendong hilltop which is surrounded by thick forest.

Growth of descent societies- Pre-Sikkim State Congress Associations

Subsequent to the Tendong meeting, peasants of Timi Tarku village in South Sikkim initiated to form *Rajya Praja Sammelan* under the leadership of Dhan Bahadur Tewari and Goverdhan Pradhan in 1946.[21] Certain resolutions, seeking new avenues for the entire peasantry to prosper, were passed by the meeting and were forwarded to the palace with a request to bring an end to all the rural woes.[22] However, it comes into light that authorities had a silent and numb attitude towards the resolutions of *Rajya Praja Sammelan*. Such approach from the State had naturally escalated the level of united resistance in a highest manner. Ignorant from the general will of rural populace, the State kept on discounting their wishes that proved to be a vital cause for a cohesive resistance. The initiatives of *Rajya Praja Sammelan* soon gained impetus among the villagers of other districts and they too were on their ways for the formation of an association that could speak for a common purpose.

Thus, following the steps of the peasants of South Sikkim, western tract of the Kingdom too plunged itself against autocratic policies of *Kazi – Thikadars*. Peasants in the peripheries of Chakhung in West Sikkim had manifested gusto to establish a forum that could listen to their grievances and would even forward the same to the authorities concerned. The common zest of peasantry got its shape as a village level meeting that ultimately paved its way for the formation of a new peasants' body popularly known as *Rajya Praja Mandal*.[23] It is worth to mention that the leader of *Rajya Praja Mandal* was *Kazi* Lhendup Khangsarpa, who happened to be an aristocrat and had a historic antagonism with Sikkim's ruling *Chogyals*. Sceptical may argue that the sole motive of *Kazi* Lhendup to join hands with the peasants was to avenge ruling house for his personal gains. Whatever his intentions might be, but, it appears that few insightful aristocrats had begun to feel the perforated and pitiable proviso of rural Sikkim. Keeping cynical assumptions apart, it may be assumed that, *Kazi* Lhendup was genuinely concerned about the socio-economic and political miseries of rural populace and he was determined to bestow justice to the peasantry. Some of the important objectives of *Rajya Praja Mandal* were to sabotage feudal system and to unleash peasantry from the clutches of *Kazis* and *Thikadars*.[24] In spite of these activities, Sikkim witnessed the opening of another peasants' association named *Praja Sudhar Samaj* at Gangtok under Tashi Tshering.[25] Basnett illustrates:

"The *Praja Sudhar Samaj* had the benefit of the reasoned counsels of Tashi Tshering, who alone of the all champions of change had good education, understood politics, and administration and had the gifts of being able to articulate views".[26]

To reiterate, the formation of various peasant organisations in the latter half of 1946 in different parts of the Himalayan Kingdom appears due to the 'least bothered' attitude of the palace and its aristocrats towards the grivances of their subjects. As these organisations or in a truer sense, peasants clubs started to come up, the frustrated peasants rendered their unconditional support to them changing the very face of rural life. The vast affiliation of the rural folks also shows their infinite level of hidden transcripts against the administrative system. However, in their earlier days, due to the lack of such bodies, their hidden transcripts were merely confined within their tomfooleries they made in their villages against their lords or other officials.

As stated, the major objectives of these organisations were to eliminate the monopoly of *Kazi Thikadars* and to uproot several forced labours that made their lives crippled. Immediately after their foundation, at their neighbourhood, people of Darjeeling experienced democracy under independent India and this development had naturally inspired thousands of freedom loving souls in Sikkim as well. Politically speaking, these associations did not have much policies, agendas, programmes, or ideologies which are the basic elements for a strong political party. Consequently, in the absence of some concrete agendas, they may be regarded more or less as welfare bodies or the descent societies with a common ideology. Nevertheless, we can assume that formation of these associations was enough to disturb the monopolistic attitude of the State. From the activities of these societies, as it appears, the State had a fear of a cohesive tax resistance in the rural areas. To avoid any adversities, the government issued a Notification stating non-payment of *Khazana* (tax) would be treated as disobedience and would be dealt in a severe manner. According to it, a defaulter was liable for persecution and was also liable for expulsion from the Kingdom, or imprisonment up to two years or he might have to face the both.[27] However, from the activities of the associations, it emerges that they were not in the process of compromising further. Despite of such tough laws, few peasants had openly defied the notification and evade their taxes in those areas where the associations had their existence.[28] Such attempts of the peasants provide testimonials to know the wholeheartedness of rural souls to dump away the oppressive mechanism into the pages of history. Ram Rahul access:

> "The socio-political set-up of the country was such that, despite the majority position of the Nepalese in total population of the country, the Bhutias controlled the government and owned large land holdings."[29]

Thus, being in majority, the Nepali population had a larger amount of grievances and keeping that fact in mind, they were guided by the leaders who also belonged to Lepcha-Bhutia stock. It appears that, in the initial phase, apart from personal gains and attainment, these leaders were truly concerned for the improvement of rural plights. Therefore, they made several petitions to *Durbar*, appraising condition of the peasantry and urged the State to show a sense of obligation to resolve rural distress. On the contrary, despite several petitions, palace seemed inactive to introduce benevolent measures to do away with the rural sufferings. The firm and a passive attitude of the State indicate an augmentation in the authoritarian set up, that had done nothing to solve the problems of the peasants. The muted role of the State had naturally mounted level of bitterness among the subordinates and served in a better way to get determined in their motives.

However, a little later, probably with a motive to solace rural aspirations, Sikkim *Durbar* made some changes in the State Council. The State Council was expanded to include each representative from three different communities of Sikkim, the Lepchas, the Bhutias, and the Nepalese.[30] Conversely, the council failed to include rural representatives to formulate a policy for a solution of the countryside issues. Moreover, demands of the peasantry were simply related to their distress and were eager to wipe them out from their lives and consequently, expansion of the State Council had no impact in their daily affairs. Therefore, this political reformation had a very little role to play in the spheres of peasantry. However, this reformation may be accessed as a sign for a political process that would incorporate unuttered voices of the masses in the later days.

Determined in their motives, the peasants as it appears were in a full mood to deracinate the feudal structure that had thoroughly paralysed their lives. Probably, considering political resistance as the need of the hour, the earlier torchbearers had strongly felt the need of a political party. With a motive to represent the common interest they engaged themselves for the formation of a broader political gathering that could open a gate to attain their long awaited goals.

It is thus obvious that, before the formation of a strong political party, the associations discussed above were the secluded entities and the only common factor in between them was their anti-feudal approach. Amidst hefty zeal to uproot feudal forces, as it is revealed that, the peasants of surveyed villages of East Sikkim did not have an active participation for the establishment of *Praja Sudhar Samaj*. Though, being in proximity to the Capital, they were real scapegoats of the hegemony, yet, they kept themselves away from the association probably due to the fear of feudal laws. Hence, perhaps, to avoid any form of adversaries in their daily affairs, it is conspicuous that peasants in the east district preferred to remain silent. Field study makes us to understand that, peasants of West and South districts were more open and active owing to their secluded positions. Further, they had the advantage of their isolation to provide a stiffer cohesive resistance against the State. As they could hide themselves in the thick forests or could even get into Darjeeling even if they made some offences against the authorities. Owing to these advantages, ideologies of such associations got their chance to prosper in West and South district in an inclusive manner.

During the course of field study, ten respondents of the surveyed villages ascertained about their affiliation to the association *Rajya Praja Sammelan* founded by their co-villagers Dhan Bahadur Tiwari and Goverdhan Pradhan. According to their opinions:

> "We had an extreme faith on them for the eradication of forced labour of *Kalo Bhari, Jharlangi, Tekhi Bethi* and *Kuruwa*".[31]

It is assumed during the study that, almost all the peasants hailing from Temi and Tarku villages were ardent supporters of *Rajya Praja Sammelan* and were determined to throw feudalism into nothingness.[32] The peasant leaders of the village appear to have been very much concerned about the exploitation they met in their daily lives. Attempts were also made by them to appraise the State through petition regarding the pathetic condition of the villagers. However, such attempts were nullified by the feudal officials and it is said that, such petitions never reached to the office of His Highness *Maharaja* Sir Tashi Namgyal.[33] An old associate of *Rajya Praja Sammelan*, Mr Bishnu Dhungel states:

> "Peasants were now fearless; they began to talk in a voluminous manner against the system as they were now aware about their importance to the State. Without them the state could have been paralysed".[34]

It is worth to discuss that, few unsuccessful attempts were made by the feudal officials to threaten the peasants in order to suppress their ideas of united resistance.[35] They were even threatened and harassed by their officials for conducting meetings at their village and made report against them to the higher authorities. Due to fear of prosecution, the peasants began to hold secret meetings during nights.[36] However, this attempt of the peasants was also not an easy idea as the officials would keep a strict watch on their movements through their espionage. Ignoring, all such obstacles, the peasants of Timi and Tarku villages had come forward to get their demands secure through their affiliations with *Rajya Praja Sammelan*.

Apart from the villages of Timi Tarku, the *Rajya Praja Sammelan* had attracted a lot many peasants of its periphery. The peasants of other surveyed areas like Namchi, Dambu Dara, Denchung, Samatar, Assangthang, and Nandugaon had also a bit of influence of the association. Though, these villages did not have any leader to lead them; however, few of such peasants from these villages had also taken part in the meetings at Timi Tarku. Peasants like Jiba Nath Sharma of Samatar, Thar Man Jogi, Ravi Chandra Pradhan and Karna Bahadur Bishwakarma of Nandugaon village had attended such gatherings on the call of *Rajya Praja Sammelan*.[37] They too revealed fear from the part of their village officials to attend such gatherings.

> "We went there on foot; our main motive was to listen to the enlightened talks of peasant sympathisers who were determined to uproot the very base of feudalism. However, we never revealed before other villagers due to fear and fright of the local village officials".[38]

Though, the participation of these peasants was not recurrent as their villages were situated at a far off place, yet, their eagerness to get rid of feudal mistreatment is praiseworthy. The relevant data indicates that, foundation of *Rajya Praja Sammelan* not only marked the beginning of a peasant politics in Sikkim, but, it also contributed in arousing a sense of self respect among the neglected lots.

The *Rajya Praja Mandal* of Chakhung had also a larger participation of peasants of West District. Even being an association formed by a *Kazi*, *Rajya Praja Mandal* dragged the attention of socially secluded section with a determination of dumping 'privileged few'. Peasants of Chakhung and Soreng would admiringly call Lhendup Dorjee as *Kancha* (youngest) *Kazi*. The epithet of *Kancha* itself makes us to understand about the villagers' admiration and love for him. Seventeen respondents from the surveyed areas had their affiliation with the association founded by *Kancha Kazi*. It is said that, the peasants in the periphery of Chakhung were greatly engaged in propagating message of this association meant for the elimination of feudalism along with its fraudulent practices. With a motive to arouse sense of self respect many young peasants took membership and propagated principles of the party to others. It is also said that, a person named Purna Singh Limboo, a son of a village *Mandal*, also had joined the league of *Praja Mandal* to unleash other villagers from the prevalent forced labours. Overwhelmed with the ideas of *Praja Mandal*, he protested against the misdeeds of his father against his fellow villagers and supported the cause of majority. Later, as it is believed, he got his father convinced to deal the villagers in a lenient manner.[39] The other young peasants of Suntaley village like Pancha Bir Limboo, Nar Bahadur Limboo, Birbal Rai, and others were actively engaged with secret meetings and strategies to fight back the lop-sided State. After the formation of Sikkim State Congress in 1947, peasants like Pancha Bahadur Limboo and Chandra Bahadur Limboo became village level leaders.[40]

The anti-feudal ideas of the peasants of Chakhung and Soreng had a huge popularity among other peasants of West District. Field study reveals that, there were lot many who were stirred by the ideas of *Rajya Praja Mandal* and were eager for a change. Peasants of Burikhop village of Soreng sub-division, like Dhan Prasad Gurung, made their active participation in convincing the illiterate peasants about the torments of feudalism. He urged these uncared lots to join their hands for the common cause initiated by *Rajya Praja Mandal.* Due to his time pertinent, though extreme ideas, Gurung was imprisoned for 27 days at Kalimpong by the *Kazis*.[41] Gurung's only crime appears to have been his radical ideas against the monopolistic set up. Similarly, a peasant of such gusto named Athang Khewa of Tharpu village was murdered by the agents of the *Kazis* at Gangtok.[42] Thus, it appears that, when the activities of *Rajya Praja Mandal* became vibrant in terms of feudalism, *Kazis* and *Thikadars* began to suppress in a cold-blooded way. Adoption of every possible way to suppress the rising tide of antagonism by the State indicates its perplexing position to save itself from rural fury.

The peasants of Tashiding and other villages in its periphery, too, had a little participation in supporting the ideas of the *Rajya Praja Mandal.* As this village was located far away from Chakhung, it did not have a major participation in adopting the principles of *Rajya Praja Mandal.* Only a few peasants were in touch with the activities of the *Rajya Praja Mandal.* According to the participants, one of such meetings was held at Chakhung *Kothi*.[43] It is worth to mention that, even before the birth of the *Praja Mandal*, the area of Tashiding and its surroundings had manifested utter abhorrence against the 'domination of a few'. It comes into view that, peasants of Sakyong village had taken the lead to let their authorities to feel rural psyche. In 1934, a peasant named Kharga Bahadur Khatiwara of Sakyong village had deracinated a *Thinguro* from the *Kothi* of his *Kazi* and carried it before the *Maharaja* in Gangtok. With the help of three fellow villagers namely, Badaley Sanyasi, Laxman Kharel and Ghyampey Sanyasi he attempted to apprise the King about the domination of feudal lords in far distant villages.[44] It was indeed a great attempt made by a common peasant to expose the faulty administration before the King about rural realities. Gauley illustrates:

> "In 1934, they burgled the building of Sakyong Kazi, and with unimaginable courage they carried away the "Thinguro" to Gangtok undercover. They spent their first night at Damthang forest. After spending the second night at Sirwani, they reached Gangtok. They went straight to the *Maharaja's* palace to leave the Thinguro..."[45]

The efforts of Kharga Bahadur Khatiwara did not go futile as the King assured him to abolish all such means of torture from every estates hold by the *Kazis* and the *Thikadars*.[46] Accordingly, as per assurance of the *Maharaja*, all such *Thinguro* possessed by the *Kazi Thikadars* were confiscated and they were surrendered to the palace. For this bravery the palace awarded them with ₹ 5 each as a reward.[47] The boldness of Kharga Bahadur Khatiwara on the one hand and the assurance of the King on the other had naturally encouraged other peasants to swim against the tide. Unfortunately, assurance of the King to Kharga Bahadur Khatiwara about the abolition of forced labours never achieved practicality until the Sikkim State Congress took a lead to abolish feudalism from the Kingdom. Likewise, the surveyed village of Uttarey in West Sikkim did not have much experience with anti feudal approach of *Rajya Praja Mandal*. None of the respondents have discussed about their involvement in *Rajya Praja Mandal* of Chakhung. Owing to secluded location of the village, the villagers were not much aware about the objectives and goals of the *Rajya Praja Mandal*.

As stated, peasants of East district were not so open to be a part of *Praja Sudhar Samaj* under Tashi Tshering. A very less number of people had revealed their dealings with the principles of the *Samaj*. Akin to Kazi Lhendup Dorjee, Tashi Tshering was also admiringly called as Tashi *Babu* by his followers. Few peasants of surveyed villages of Assam Lingzey, Namli, Namin and Marchak would go to attend the meetings called by the association.[48] The influenced peasants believe that Tashi Tshering was genuinely concerned with the deplorable plight of the rural folks.[49] It is also interesting to note that, most of the peasants who joined *Praja Sudhar Samaj* were the erstwhile poachers, channel breakers and the tax defaulters. For this section of peasantry, as it seemed, *Praja Sudhar Samaj* had offered an opportunity to illustrate their long nurtured hidden transcripts in a full fledged manner. Hence, it is palpable that, *Praja Sudhar Samaj* was only able to influence peasants of the nearby villages of the Capital. It is noticed during the course of study that, peasants of far off villages like Linkey, Manpur, Bering, Angkuchen, Tareythang and Bara Pathing were not much familiar with the principles of the *Praja Sudhar Samaj*. Few peasants of Tareythang and Bering villages were aware about its existence but, that too, in a not clear approach. This is not a surprising issue as these villages were existed in the remotest part of the Kingdom with no roads and means of communication. Further, apart from political agenda, for them, as it seemed, other survival issues were relatively important. Therefore, they found it appropriate to be loyal than to be branded as dissenters. However, it is evident that, with the foundation of Sikkim State Congress, peasants of East district began to join the union in more open manner. The district had been able to produce many peasant leaders who were committed to uproot feudalism from the Sikkimese soil.

Owing to the frequent petitions and appeals of the associations, the State made some decisions in resolving the rural woes. According to the notification dated 31st December, 1946 the State had completely abolished *Jharlangi* labour. The notification read thus:

> "It has come to the notice of the Sikkim *Durbar* that there is some confusion regarding requisition of Jharlangi labour resulting in public agitation. It is therefore notified for the information of the public that whosoever unlawfully compels any person to labour against the will of that person shall be punished with imprisonment of either description for a term which may extend to one year, or with fine, or with both (Sec 374 I.P.G)."[50]

The same notification also stressed over the immediate implementation of the Royal Order.

> "It is again notified that no Landlord, Manager, or their *Kamdaris* shall employ labour otherwise than by his consent, but for any administrative purpose and ceremonial occasions *Jharlangi* labour which also includes transport may be requisitioned on payment of wages at standardised fixed rates fixed by the Durbar from time to time. Fuel and fodder shall also be supplied to persons travelling on State duty on payment at rates fixed by the Durbar. Any person travelling on duty is entitled to those privileges".[51]

It may be assumed that, the State had eventually shown a bit of sympathy to the people who were the backbone of its economy. Consequently, extractions of various forced labours were done away with in the Kingdom. Even if the implementation of the new orders had to travel a long route yet, some signs of contentment could be felt in the rural horizons. Indeed, a new epoch was on its way to come to the lives of Sikkimese peasantry. An indescribable reality was in the process to knock the doors of the browbeaten, a day approaching to them without *Kalo Bhari*, a morning coming nearer devoid of *Jharlangi* and an evening with the meaning of togetherness.

After the implementation of the notification, it emerges that, there was a shortage of the state porters as the peasants denied to cooperate with the State. Following to this, the government issued another strict notification to secure uninterrupted supply of labours from among the rural populace.[52] However, according to the new order, the word *Jharlangi* was substituted by 'State Labour' and a porter would receive 14 *Annas* as his wage.[53] Similarly, forceful engagement was avoided and all the concerned were to get approval of the porter before his engagement as a State Labour. Hence, it is known that the forced labour of *Jharlangi* was simply altered in the way it sounded, whereas, the reality was far away from idealism. Similarly, the Government of Sikkim again issued another notification for the abolition of the *Kuruwa* labour. The Notification of Sikkim State General Department (Misc. Branch) had abolished the awful *Kuruwa* practice with effect from the 31st of January 1947.[54] The new notification states:

> "It is hereby notified for the information of the public that His Highness the Maharaja has been pleased to order the system of "*Kuruwas*" in the whole of Sikkim to be abolished with effect from the date of Notification".[55]

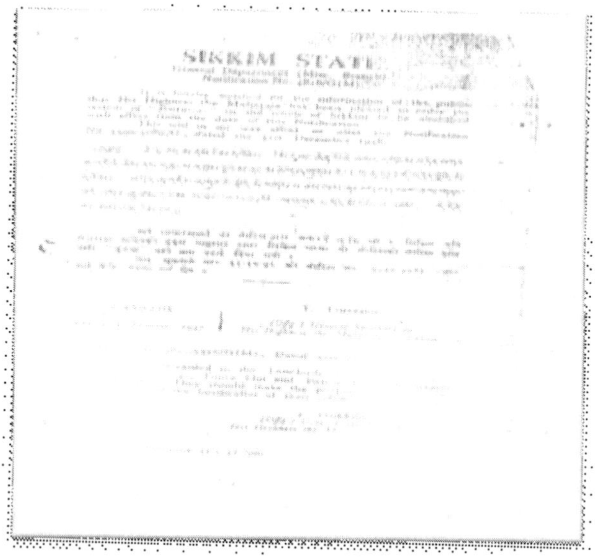
SIKKIM STATE

Figure 8.1: Notice for the abolition of Kuruwa Date of publication 31 January 1947. Ram Gauri Sangrahalaya Rhenock East Sikkim.

The Notification issued on a single page in three different languages i.e. English, Nepali, and Tibetan was forwarded to every lessee holders and to the police and patrol outposts. However, the erratic *Kazis* and the *Zamindars* had never let such Notifications to be implemented accordingly.

The field study indicates that, none of such notifications were properly put into practice as it had to go a long and descending way via *Kazis*, *Thikadars*, *Mandals,* and *Karbaris* to reach to the doorsteps of the peasants. The peasants of the surveyed villages believe that forced labour was practically abolished only after the political resistance made by Sikkim State Congress. Thus, efforts of the *Maharaja* were never taken seriously by the feudal officials leading to an all round rural dissatisfaction. Further, the ignorance poised by them for the execution of the Royal Orders provided a larger avenue for the petty peasant associations to expand further. The vacuum created by those landlords later on swelled in a gigantic way paving its way for the formation of Sikkim State Congress.

It is thus obvious that, the associations discussed above came into exist due to the one sided policy of the State machineries. The marginalised lots in order to ensure their survival began to seek their alliance with such associations. Undoubtedly, such bodies were petty objects to the age old feudal edifice yet, from the points of the subordinates, they were the steps to reach to the world of freedom, equality, and respect, which were till now appears to be confined just in the words. Consequently, with a hope of justice the ignorant peasants began to associate themselves to those associations founded by their sympathisers. The course of peasants' affiliation kept on increasing securing new heights to form a larger and a descent society known as Sikkim State Congress.

Notes

1. Zinn, Howard, (2007), *A Power Government Cannot Suppress*, City Lights Books, San Francisco, p. 35.
2. Letter of General Secretary to His Highness *Maharaja* of Sikkim to the Political Officer for the exemption of *Jharlangi* to Panchdal Rai of Assam Lingzey Dated 11th September 1942, Memo No 1892/1893 G.
3. Constituent Assembly of India DEBATES (Proceedings) Vol. II Wednesday 22nd January, 1947, p. 11.
4. Draft Letter of Tashi Wangyal Lassepa, Namchi Kazi, to the Judicial Secretary to the HH Maharaja of Sikkim in Reference to Memo No. 5058/J, 2nd February 1937.
5. Field Report 2011-2012: Assangthang village, South Sikkim.
6. Gauley Gopal (et'al) (First published 2002), *History of Democratic Movement*, Department of Information and public relations, Govt. of Sikkim, p. 20.
7. Zinn Howard (2007) op cit, p. 39.
8. Field Report 2011-2012: Assangthang Village, South Sikkim.
9. Field Report 2011-2012: Assangthang Village, South Sikkim.
10. Scott, James C. (1985), *Weapons of the Weak, Everyday Forms of Peasant Resistance*, Yale University Press, London, p. 44.
11. Gaunley (2002) op cit, p. 20.

12. Dahal, Dharnidhar, (1998), *Sikkim ko Rajnaitik Itihas Part II* (Political History of Sikkim) Nirman Publication Namchi, p. 16.
13. *Ibid.*
14. *Ibid.*
15. *Ibid.,* p. 11.
16. *Ibid.*
17. *Ibid.*
18. *Ibid.*
19. Zinn, (2007) op cit, p. 15.
20. The secret meet of Tendong hill was attended by Dhan Bahadur Tiwari, Goverdhan Pradhan, Jus Lal Rajalim, Bishnu Bhakta Dhungel, Kharga Bahadur Basnet, Chuk Tshering Bhutia of Yangyang, Bala Das Sinha, Bhadru Magar, Chatraman Rai of Wok, Bagbir Rai, Nar Bahadur Karki and Tenu Das Rajalim. Gauley, (2002) op cit, p. 20.
21. *Ibid.*
22. *Ibid.*
23. *Ibid.*
24. *Ibid.*
25. Basnett, Lal Bahadur, (1974), *Sikkim- A short Political History,* S. Chand & Co. (Pvt.) Ltd. New Delhi, p. 76.
26. *Ibid.*
27. Land Revenue and Forest Department,. 3254-753/G, 20th September 1947.
28. Field Report 2011-2012: Tarku Village South Sikkim.
29. Rahul, Ram (1978), *The Himalaya as a Frontier*, Vikash Publishing House, New Delhi, p. 50.
30. Basnett, (1974) op cit, pp. 75-76.
31. Field Report 2011-2012: Tarku Village, South Sikkim. This respondent was one of the founder members of Rajya Praja Sammelan.
32. Field Report 2011-2012: Tarku Village, South Sikkim.
33. Field Report 2011-2012: Tarku Village, South Sikkim.
34. Field Report 2011-2012: Tarku Village, South Sikkim.
35. Field Report 2011-2012: Tarku Village, South Sikkim.
36. Field Report 2011-2012: Tarku Village, South Sikkim.
37. Field Report 2011-2012: Nandugaon, South Sikkim.
38. Field Report 2011-2012: Nandugaon, South Sikkim.
39. Field Report 2011-2012: Suntaley village, West Sikkim. This respondent was a founding member of Rajya Praja Sammelan.
40. Field Report 2011-2012: Suntaley village, West Sikkim. This respondent was one of the founding members of Rajya Praja Mandal.
41. Field Report 2011-2012: Suntaley village, West Sikkim.
42. Field Report 2011-2012: Pakkigaon Village, West Sikkim. This respondent was a founding member of Rajya Praja Mandal.

43. Field Report: 2011-2012: Information collected through personal interview from the respondents of Tashiding West Sikkim.
44. Field Report 2011-2012: Gerethang Village, West Sikkim.
45. Gauley, (2002) op cit, p. 180.
46. Field Report 2011-2012: Lower Chongrang, West Sikkim.
47. Gauley, (2002) op cit, p. 180.
48. Field Report 2011-2012: Aho Village, East Sikkim.
49. Field Report 2011-2012: Ranipool Bazaar, East Sikkim.
50. General Department 3590-4089/G, dated 31st December 1946:Ramgauri Sangrahalaya Rhenock.
51. *Ibid.*
52. Education and Transport Department 600-780/E.T, 23rd June 1948 circulated in English, Tibetan and Nepali languages.
53. Education and Transport Department, 2035-780/E.T, 15th February 1949, circulated in English, Tibetan and Nepali languages.
54. General Department (Misc. Branch) 4816/G(M), 31st January 1947, circulated in English, Tibetan and Nepali languages.
55. General Department 4816/G(M), 31st January 1947, Ramgauri Sangrahalaya Rhenock East Sikkim.

Chapter 9

The Era of Political Resistance-Peasants' under Political Patronage

The scattered or in a truer sense individual rural activities had crossed many milestones till history of Sikkim reaches into the phase of political resistance. The smaller and dotted secret societies, without proper guidance and specific objectives were nothing but the first instinct of political consciousness in politically barren minds of the Sikkimese. Politically speaking, ideas of liberty, equality, justice, and overall development of the State were yet to conceive in the minds of State bearers. However, it appears that, temper of far off villages were not in a position to bargain with the State to get their natural rights. Consequently, rural activities gained air and began to swell in a much broader manner. The peasants who were simply considered as compelled lots, as now it seemed, had realised their role and importance to the State. To reach Sikkimese history to this juncture, this stratum of the society had tolerated many extraneous forms of agonies and miseries. The monopolistic taxation, hunger, mortgage, confiscation of properties, injustice, abuses, physical torture at *Thinguro*, humiliation, slaps, cheating, and many other unimagined sketches coloured with fluid of feudalism, were a few to name them. It emerges that, the smell of their warm sweat, their cut marks on their hands and bodies, tattered piece of cloth, and cracks on their heels had never been captivating factors to draw attention of the State. Therefore, to make authorities to acknowledge their contributions for the development of State, this half stomached lots began to organise themselves in a broader manner. All the petty associations, confined within remote villages, had now felt to join their hands with each other for a larger interest. Consequently, with the consent of other two associations, *Praja Sudhar Samaj* of Gangtok decided to hold a public meeting at the Capital. Scott observes:

"First, people experience deprivation and oppression within a concrete setting, not as the end product of large and abstract processes, and it is the concrete experience that moulds their discontent into specific grievances against specific targets".[1]

Foundation of Sikkim State Congress

With a motive to incorporate all the marginalised interests, the three important associations decided to meet at Polo Ground (now Palzor Stadium) on 7th of December 1947. The historic day of this congregation is also known as 'Red Letter Day'.[2] It seems that, the leaders had a frame of mind to bitterly criticise the loop sided State and were also eager to speak wholeheartedly against the prolonged suppression and exploitation in a capacious manner before the gathering. This is evident from a pamphlet circulated among the people on this pioneering day.[3] The radical approach of the leaders to get into real issues and their appeal to get united against State machinery were some of the major issues included in the pamphlet. We are not sure about the consequence of the notes among illiterates; however, to get such a sharp criticism from commoners justifies a serious governmental malfunction.

Figure 9.1: Peasants attending Foundation Day of Sikkim State Congress at Polo Ground, Gangtok on 7th December 1947, Courtsy Mr N.B. Parsai, Namin.

On 7th December 1947, leaving all their everyday affairs, peasants of Sikkim began to gather at Gangtok with enthusiasm and nervousness. They were excited, as for the first time they were listening to liberal talks and were nervous due to the fear of repression that might come from the part of State.[4] The small town of Gangtok, considered to be the powerhouse of feudal force, was thus filled up with the most neglected and ignored section of society. It comes into view that, the Sikkimese peasantry, unknown of its strength totally remained stunned with the huge crowd meant for a common purpose. Dugo Bhutia, an immature member of the meeting reminiscent the event in the following words:

> "That was our first experience and we realised that if we got united we could not only throw out feudalism but, we could even think of changing the entire set up."[5]

It is believed that, this momentous day of the political history of Sikkim, was attended by nearly five thousand peasants with a common agenda to stand against feudal machineries.[6] In vociferous voices, the speakers criticised past sufferings of the peasants, inequalities heaped on them by the administration, and the growing transgressions of the landlords.[7] The important speakers of the meeting were Tashi Tshering, Sonam Tshering, Kazi Lhendup Dorjee, K.D. Roy Chaudhari,[8] and Mrs. Helen Lepcha[9] *aka* Savitri Devi.[10] However, centre of attraction among the speakers was a 24 years old Chandra Das Rai, a son of a peasant from Namchi who highlighted about most relevant and radical topics rampant in the society like *Kalo Bhari*, *Jharlangi Theki-Bethi* and *Kuruwa* and demanded the immediate removal of such evils.[11] Regarding the flamboyant speech of Chandra Das Rai A.C. Sinha writes:

> "His eloquent Nepali speech was a novel experience for politically indolent Sikkim".[12]

To reiterate, the State had abolished aforesaid rural evils through notifications published on 31st December, 1946 and 31st of January 1947 for abolition of *Jharlangi* labour and *Kuruwa* respectively. However, such notices did not reach the villages as it appears that, they missed their ways and became the virtual prisoners of the *Kazis* and *Thikadars*. The disregarding attitude of the *Kazi-Thikadars* to the royal orders had naturally multiplied peasants' grievances to many folds making them furious. Similarly, the monopolistic policies of *Kazis* and *Thikadars* show the level of their influence in the administration of the State. It emerges that, *Maharaja* Sir Tashi Namgyal was undoubtedly a benevolent and a generous King however; his aristocrats were not complying with his orders and working at their whims. It signifies a compelled and constrained position of the King who was merely considered as a figurehead with absolute powers at the hands of his nobles.

All the speeches in the meeting were made in Nepali language, the language of the majority of Sikkimese population and the unofficial *lingua-franca* of the Kingdom.[13] The people of West district had a major involvement in the meeting. Almost all the peasants associated with the earlier *Rajya Praja Mandal* had made their ways to Gangtok with a motive to sabotage feudal practices.

> "We had to travel for more than three days to reach Gangtok. In the midst of troubles, we went there to see our *Kancha Kazi* addressing the masses".[14]

This statement of the respondent manifests his immense faith on his leader who always had encouraged them to flow against the tide keeping their sense of pride alive.[15] Similarly, peasants from far off village of Kabirthang in the periphery of Gyalshing had also made their participation in the huge gathering of 7th December 1947. In Gyalshing, the task of gathering peasants was taken up by peasants like Bhim Bahadur Subedi and Kharga Bahadur Khatiwara *aka Bhalukey Buda*, the same man who deracinated the *Thinguro* back in 1934. They motivated their fellow villagers to go to Gangtok and to attend the meeting.[16] Correspondingly, peasants of Tashiding and its adjoining areas too seemed eager to reach Polo Ground. It is noteworthy that, the peasants were so keen to stand against the State that they made all their arrangements at their own and proceeded to Gangtok.[17] It is also said that, on their ways they encouraged others to accompany them and with a huge crowd moved towards the capital. Their spirit to oppose the monopolistic attitude of the State in a united manner was exemplary.

The silent and the hushed activities of peasants of East Sikkim during pre-Congress era had an overnight change leading to their mass support for Polo Ground Meeting. It is said that, at least one from each household from almost all the villages of East Sikkim had participated the meeting.[18] It appears that, the *modus operandi* of collecting the peasants was made in an organised manner by their leaders. By now, every villages of East District had at least one influential that could explain and convince the villagers about the prevailing situation. Similarly, such influential could also induce them the spirit of unity and could urge them to strike back the State, which led to a mass participation from the district. The task of gathering peasants from the villages was taken up by the influential like Brihaspati Parsai of Namli village, Nandalal Bhattarai of Namin, Man Prasad Upreti of Assam Lingzey village and the like. Most of the peasants of Aho, Assam Lingzey, Kadamtam, Marchak, Rumtek and Namli of East Sikkim appears to be the supporters of Late Brihaspati Parsai. His well-expressed and unblemished speech dragged peasants to the meeting who, according to the villagers, was a great orator and a polished statesman. With an urge of self realisation he could inculcate sense of revulsion against the State among the suppressed lots.[19] Late Parsai was later appointed as the publicity Secretary of the Sikkim State Congress. Similarly, apart from the physical support, Man Prasad Upreti of Assam Lingzey village had even extended financial support for the formation of Sikkim State Congress.[20] It emerges that, late Upreti was using this chance of a united resistance against the State wholeheartedly. It is said that, once he was severely humiliated and was asked to pay ₹ 5 as fine to Gyaltsen Kazi, the landlord of his area, for wearing a pair of leather shoe.[21] Thus, at this juncture, he seemed committed to demolish the false notion of superiority to the ground. He was later made the President of Assam Lingzey and Aho villages of the Sikkim State Congress. Likewise, a peasant Sher Bahadur Subba from the village of Saureni collected the peasants of his and surrounding villages.[22] He was a retired British army man and had witnessed both extreme and moderate movements in India. However, he wanted to follow Gandhi in gaining the support of the peasants and working class to eliminate monopoly of the State.[23] As per the information, peasants of Saureni, Tamla, and Chota Singtam villages followed Sher Bahadur Subba to Polo Ground for the grand and the historic meeting. Similarly, Sangay Tshering Bhutia of Dalapchand took a lead to bring the peasants from Rhenock to Gangtok. He played a crucial role during the foundation of Sikkim State Congress.[24] Others like Keher Singh Karki of Ranipool area collected the peasants of his village including Setipool, Jalipool, Chinzey and Samdur villages to drop the powers enjoyed by the *Kazis* and *Thikadars* by making the peasants to join the mainstream.[25] Many peasants from other villages of East Sikkim also came forward as curtain raisers of the revolution against the corrupt State. Tikalal Nirola of Central Pendam village took the lead of gathering peasants of his village for the meet that could play a vital role for the eradication of forced labour, feudalism and *Dhurikhajana* from the Kingdom. After the formation of Sikkim State Congress, he too was given the charge of Publicity Secretary of the Party along with Brihaspati Parsai of Namli.[26] Owing to its larger participation, the contributions of peasants of east district for the political transformation cannot be taken on a miniature scale.

The peasants of South Sikkim who were earlier associated with *Rajya Praja Sammelan* and Member Party threw their allegiance to the meeting organised by *Praja Sudhar Samaj*. Peasants like Krishna Bhakta Dhungel of Tarku village along with few other peasants collected the villagers and inspired them to attend the meeting.[27] However, even with a major grudge, it appears that, the district was unable to manifest it's detest on the day of foundation of Sikkim State Congress. Very few peasants, who had their association with the earlier *Rajya Praja Sammelan,* had only made their participation. The involvement of the other peasants in the 7th December meet seems ostensible. Almost all the respondents who had witnessed the foundation day of the Sikkim State Congress were from the villages of Temi Tarku and Namchi. A peasant named Bishnu Bhakta Dhungel of Tarku village took the lead in guiding other fellow villagers to go to Gangtok for the meeting. He informs

> "I was one of the office bearers of the *Rajya Praja Sammelan* and hence many villagers were there in my circle to accompany me to attend the meeting".[28]

Apart from the surveyed villages, there were many other peasants from other villages who had their active involvement for the common cause. Gyampo Bhutia, a peasant of Ben village in South Sikkim became a frontline leader after the foundation of Sikkim State Congress. It is said that, he stood always against the injustice and suppression of *Kazi Thikadars*, yet, he entered into active politics only after 1947.[29] Similarly, peasants like Bhagiman Rai of Mickhola village in the fringe of Namchi insisted people to attend the meeting at Gangtok. Amidst low participation, the South district had been able to create some of the good leaders like C.D. Rai, Chuk Chuk Sangdarpa, Adhar Singh Lepcha, Durga Prasad Rajalim and the like.[30] Considering the huge public response, the three different societies namely *Rajya Praja Sammelen*, *Rajya Praja Mandal*, and *Praja Sudhar Samaj*, decided jointly to form Sikkim State Congress on the very day of 7th December, 1947.[31] Tashi Tshering, the founder of *Praja Sudhar Samaj*, got elected as the President of the new Party.[32]

It is worth to mention that, modes of everyday forms of peasant resistance in Sikkim were, in fact, the nucleus of the political ideas which were later on transformed into political ideologies. The remarks made by Karl Marx about the peasants 'they cannot represent themselves; they must be represented'[33] is thus corroborated by the formation of Sikkim State Congress. The formation of the Sikkim State Congress was a landmark in the political history of Sikkim in general and peasants in particular. The smaller peasants' societies, both secret and descent, were merged into a broader union with the name of Sikkim State Congress. The initial attempts of peasants throughout Sikkim to give an appropriate retort to feudal oppression were now taking a figure of exposition.

With the inauguration of a party, resolutions were also adopted at the same meeting for political and economic reforms. A five member delegation called on the *Maharaja*, Sir Tashi Namgyal, and presented a memorandum incorporating the three demands formulated at the meeting.[34] The three fold demands of the State Congress were as under:

(a) Popular or responsible Government should replace the present non-descript oligarchy with the abolition of Landlordism as sine qua non and that no time should be lost in bringing this about;

(b) An interim government should be formed and installed as early as possible as a necessary precursor of the democratic form of government to come;

(c) And that, immediate steps may be taken to accede to the Government of the Dominion of India, if this has not been done already. The reasons for this are obvious and we need not expatiate on the many advantages accruing from it.[35]

The delegation met the *Maharaja* on 9th December 1947, and presented the three fold demand formulated on the meeting. The *Maharaja*, probably to avert confrontation, promised for an immediate reformation, for the abolition of landlordism.[36] Similarly, to pacify the rising tempo of political activity the State agreed to appoint 'Three Secretaries to the *Maharaja*', belonging to three major communities- the Lepchas, the Bhutias, and the Nepalese.[37] On the issue of 'accession of Sikkim to India', his stand was a clear 'NO'.[38]

In contrast, within one month of the foundation of Sikkim State Congress, probably bearing in mind the wobbly gesticulate of the peasants, the State had curtailed some of the privileges of landlords that include right of registering documents and the privilege of being a sub-register.[39] The State, at this point, as it seems, was trying to invalidate the cause taken up by the Sikkim State Congress. The demand of Sikkim State Congress was a complete elimination of feudalism along with all privileges enjoyed by the landlords. Abolition of this little power of landlords would not have a broader impact on the daily affairs of common people. They were fighting for the corrupt practices, malfunctions, and against the highhandedness of landlords. These very issues related to the rural populace had not got their mention in the said notification. Therefore, the hasty decision taken up by the State emerges merely as a measure to solace rural lots and to slower the pace of resistance.

As regard to the political expansion, Sikkim State Congress nominated three members namely, Sonam Tshering, Capt. Dimik Singh Lepcha, and Raghubir Singh Basnet one each from the three communities, to function as Secretaries to the *Maharaja*.[40] It is said that, the three Secretaries soon completely identified themselves with the administrative machinery; and had forgotten the charges that were directed on them by their party.[41] However, realising to have been boarded on a wrong train, the Nepali nominee resigned from the government in obedience to the Party's call.[42]

The activities of State Congress, directed along peaceful and legitimate lines, exercised a considerable influence throughout Sikkim. It sought changes in the social and political structure of the Kingdom. A series of deputations were sent to the authorities for abolition of slavery, protection against forced labour and demanded that people should be allowed to pay their taxes direct to the state instead of landlords who had often cheated them in recording the payments.[43] However, with unrelated alteration in the powers of landlords, the State seemed too content in a way as if it had eliminated a century old nuisance in a single stroke. The State at this juncture had failed to realise the popularity of Sikkim State Congress among the downtrodden and, as it appears, had miscalculated its huge popularity among the subjects. It also emerges that, the State had utterly failed to sense the forceful wind of frustration blowing from far distant villages with a fury to brush off the entire set up. Therefore, considering the rural grievances as sundry events, the State continued a neglecting glance on the rural issues. Sceptical may argue that, the State was then busy in securing a separate identity from falling into Indian hands[44] and it got diverted from redressing the rural grievances. Contradictorily, according to the demands of Sikkim State Congress, a few politically aware Sikkimese had even sighted warmth and kindliness on the Indian lap. Prevalence of such elements in the State indeed would prove adverse and the State would have taken some swift measures to gratify them. However, it did not happen when the State continued to pursue its authoritarian policies enhancing disarray among its subjects. Therefore, the sceptical assumption at this point gets invalid and measures taken up by the State seemed worthless which were simply meant, as it appears, to ensure the protection of its shaky throne. The current psyche of the signatories of the 7th December resolution indicates that they could go to any extent if their demands were not seriously considered. The serious miscalculation to the endeavours of the peasants by the State with a content, calm, and quiet attitude was in fact playing a key role to enhance the mounting level of bitterness in the villages. The absolute failure of the State to feel the gravity and vastness of the people's aspiration ultimately led to a serious conflict between them.

On the other hand, the Sikkim State Congress embarked on its move of the administrative and policy reforms. From its constitution, it appears that the Congress was determined to abolish feudalism from every corner of the Sikkimese society and was also determined in achieving what the majority of the State had dreamt for since long. As a full fledged political party, the Congress began to work in a meticulous manner with an intention to bring all the scattered peasantry under its banner. With the framing of a constitution, it urged the villagers to get abided with the guidelines

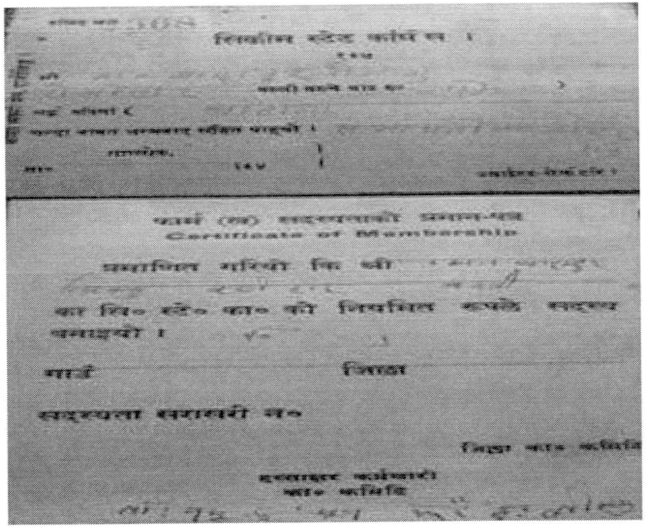

Figure 9.3: *Membership card and certificate of membership of the Sikkim State Congress of Late Man Bahadur Limboo of Rabitar Namchi South Sikkim.*

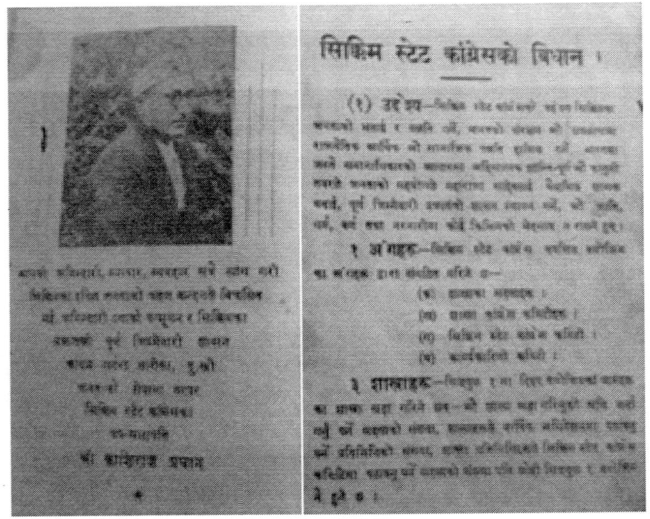

Figure 9.2: *The Constitution of Sikkim State Congress. Courtesy Mr B.B. Lohrung Rai, Kazitar, Namchi, South Sikkim.*

enunciated by the party. The lone motive of the party seems here was to get a larger participation of rural folks in the decision-making process of the State. With zeal to reach to the doorsteps of peasants, the party had strictly directed its members to set up a block level committee in every block.[45] Such blocks were further divided into several villages to ensure a maximum affiliation of the peasantry. Funds were raised from the villagers and other subordinates ensuring their membership to the party. It is known from the available documents that, a peasant had to pay ₹ 1 in securing a general membership. Similarly, few peasants like Man Bahadur Limbu of Rabitar in South Sikkim were made permanent members by acknowledging them with a certificate. However, the process of securing a permanent membership in the Sikkim State Congress is not known.

All together, there are 12 Articles with many other clauses which were basically meant for maintaining discipline among the cadres and holding of Annual Meetings of the Party.[46] Few peasants still possess their membership card that ensures their payment of ₹ 1 as a membership fee to the Sikkim State Congress.[47]

Intended with a full throated political conflict against the adverse set up, movement under State Congress went ahead gaining momentum. It seems that the wide popularity of the party had literally put the State into a complete confusion and to make its position secure made some important decisions. Among such decisions the liquidation of landlordism along with its vices occupies prominence. The cruel feudal faces like *Jharlangi*, *Kalo Bhari*, *Kuruwa*, *Theki Bethi* and other forms of sufferings were eliminated. The litigation rights of the landlords and other influential were done away with without much haggling and their courts popularly known as *Adda Courts* were abolished.[48] In lieu of the *Adda* Courts, Panchayat tribunals were established throughout the Kingdom that consisted of four nominated representatives of the peasants and one the landlord of the area as the representative of government.[49] The Lessee system was dropped and the people were given right to pay tax directly to the state.[50] On the contrary, the government had also put a ban on further clearing of forests lands for cultivation purpose.[51] Similarly, in all probabilities, sniffing a threat from the newly founded Sikkim State Congress, government issued notification prohibiting agitation to stop payment of *Khazana* by the peasants.[52] Likewise, terrace cultivation was made compulsory by the Terracing Ordinance of 1949 and if a peasant cultivates in contravention of this Ordinance had to pay fine of ₹ 1000 or imprisonment for the period of six months or had to face the both.[53] However, as stated, these reforms simply got their spaces in the papers of notification and were far away from actuality and therefore, the State was regularly criticised by State Congress in vociferous manner.

Apart from these, other philanthropic moves were also taken up by the State to regain its lost faith among the peasants. Ration Cards commonly known as *Luga Pauney* Card, were provided by the State with a motive to provide cheaper clothing to the rural folks. To avail subsidy, a peasant had to pay 25 paisa or *Chaar Anna* in securing a card from the Textile Commissioner. In one disburse the card holder was allowed to obtain six meters of subsidised cloth for an adult and three meters for a child.[54]

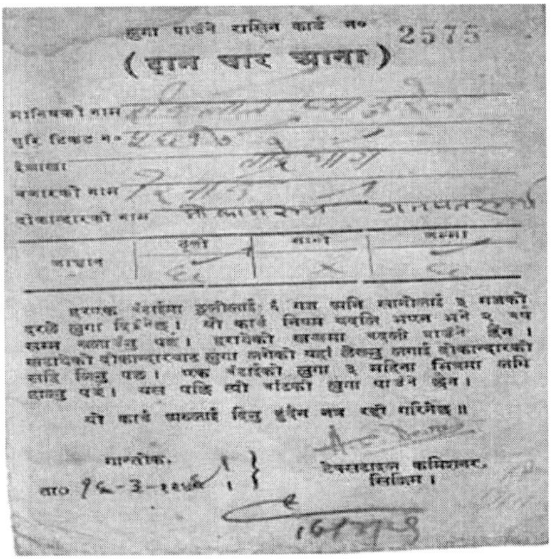
2575

Figure 9.4: **Luga Paune** ***Ration Card issued to Late Ravilal Pyakurel of Tareythang Busty East Sikkim on 16th March 1949 by the Textile Commissioner, Government of Sikkim.***

From the study of few such Ration Cards it becomes evident that it was strictly issued to the person who paid *Dhurikhajana*. Though, most of the *Dhurikhajana* payers had secured their *Luga Pauney* Ration Cards but had hardly availed the cheaper clothe.[55] Thus, it emerges that, the ambitious aim in winning the hearts of rural Sikkim had a very mild popularity among the peasants. Consequently, the Ration Card Mission adopted by the State simply appears to have been a small pouch of ointment for an utterly burnt body.

The State Congress on the other hand took ultimate advantage of the situation and kept itself engaged in gaining the faith of the peasants. From the available documents, it is palpable that the party was committed to provide a better and a threat free life to the commoners. Pertaining to the sentiments and issues of the peasants, the State Congress plunged itself in securing the basic rights through many agendas, concrete goals, tangible objectives, and solid and firm resolutions. Politically speaking, the Sikkim State Congress had by now grown up as a fully matured political party endorsed with political agendas. In all probabilities, being associated to the lowest stratum of the society, the State, on the other hand seemed still unbending in resolving the pending matters associated with feudalism in a practical manner. It is to be noted that, even with a full political objectives, the State Congress had been so far engaged in the Sikkimese political sphere as a welfare body. The resolutions passed by the Congress on 7th Day of December 1947 were basically meant for the liquidation of feudal elements. Similarly, resolution related to the formation of an interim government with the representation of people was based on the principle of equality and liberty. The only political demand made by the Congress was accession of Sikkim to India. Therefore, keeping these facts in mind, we may access that, till the foundation of Sikkim National Party, the State Congress had a *modus operandi* of a welfare body that later got transformed into a political ideology.

The Sikkim State Congress began to act as a political party of the peasants only after the foundation of pro-feudal party known as the Sikkim National Party in April 1948. With the establishment of Sikkim National Party, the State Congress became more vocal for the elevation of peasantry in the Kingdom. Along with the earlier peasant centric demands, State Congress began to demand for larger participation of the peasants in the state affairs. This led to the conversion of a peasant union into a political party with the cardinal principles of liberty, equality, justice, and fraternity. On the other hand, the Sikkim National Party began to act as the bulwark of age old feudalism that forced Sikkim State Congress to become more determined to dismantle the authoritarian order. The face-to-face quarrel between the pro- and anti-peasant parties commenced a new epoch in the history of Sikkim which was now more open and united confrontation between the pro- and anti-feudal elements.

Establishment of Sikkim National Party

After getting the 'Secretaries to the Maharaja of Sikkim' into its court, the State made further efforts to sabotage the idea of resistance at its shoot. Being aware of the fact that, to secure favour of the Secretaries was insufficient to crush the rising tempo of opposition, State played a vital role for the establishment of a Party. It is said that, the *Maharajkumar* and a group of landlords gathered a number of Bhutias, Lepchas, and the Nepalese, with a view of forming a new 'Sikkim National Party' to oppose the Sikkim State Congress.[56]

In the meeting held on 30th April 1948, the party adopted the following resolutions:-

1. "Resolved that, with regard to the question of abolition of landlordism in Sikkim, the Party should approach His Highness the *Maharaja* in writing, praying for an early consideration. It has been unanimously agreed that a time honoured institution, like the one in question, cannot be suddenly wiped out of existence, root, and branch, without giving rise to grave consequences such as administrative difficulties and disruption. The House has, therefore, been to the opinion that any development with respect to the question of abolition should progress by gradual process and not by a sudden stroke of policy."
2. "Resolved that the proposal of introducing responsible Government in Sikkim, at the present juncture, is not administratively possible. For under the existing state of circumstances, a responsible government would be quite impracticable. Universal political consciousness with all round development in general standard of education must precede enfranchisement or responsible government. In the absence of this essential and unavoidable condition, a popular government, if ever attempted to build up, will presumably raise an undesirably poor and inefficient government run by ignorant and illiterate classes. The ultimate result would be that the people themselves suffer the most and in time, anarchy and confusion might almost certainly crop up. Democracy cannot come into being unless the people are fitted for it and the many essential requisites are present to ensure a success. In this connection the House quoted the very works that were uttered in no uncertain terms by the Honourable Minister, States Department of the Government of India which runs "Democratic Government in a small state is a farce."
3. Resolved that Sikkim shall not under any circumstances, accede to the dominion of India. The arguments levelled against the question of accession have been found numerous, of which the weighty ones are:-
   (a) Historically, socially, culturally, and linguistically, Sikkim has closer affinities with Bhutan and Tibet.
   (b) From the geographical ethnic points of view Sikkim is not a part of India. She has only political relations with the latter, which were imposed on her.

(c) From the religious point of view, being Lamaist, she is quite distinct from India.

(d) The policy of the party is to maintain intact be all means the indigenous character of Sikkim and to preserve its integrity.[57]

The resolution further declared that the party would make all out efforts to keep a separate identity of Sikkim. It states:-

> "From India's point of view, a happy Sikkim as a buffer State would be great advantage than an unhappy Sikkim in India on one of her future international boundaries of great importance, which would be disadvantage, indeed a danger to India".[58]

The first resolution of Sikkim National Party regarding feudalism was a severe blow on the demand voiced by Sikkim State Congress. The State Congress opposed to the preservation of any form of feudalism and was determined to liquidate the same from Sikkim without any compromise. On the other hand, the Sikkim National Party was eager to protect this bulwark of exploitation, against the wishes of the common people. From the resolution adopted by the party, it appears that, the leaders had labelled them as the 'truer nationalists', even if not, the 'Nationalists' of Sikkim. Further, Sikkim National Party was totally opposed to the formation of a popular and responsible government which was the final goal of State Congress. The party raised a counter-Slogan demanding the retention of effective powers in the hands of *Chogyal*. The Sikkim National Party, by its very nature established to be an anti-thesis of the Sikkim State Congress. Thus, with the birth of Sikkim National Party, an 'ideological tug of war' between the 'accepted force' backed by the Sikkim State Congress and the 'ostracized force' of the State commenced. Owing to its proclivity towards the State, the leaders of the State Congress had dubbed the Sikkim National Party as a 'Party of the Palace'.[59]

On 22nd October 1948, the Sikkim State Congress with a firm motive to dismantle the remnants of feudalism, held a huge meeting at Namchi.[60] Following the resolution of the meeting, Tashi Tshering and C.D. Rai, the President and General Secretary of the party went to Delhi to meet the Indian Prime Minister. While discussing on their list of demands, the Prime Minister Nehru said to have stated:

> "...Do not worry the insignificant *Zamindari* System prevalent in your Kingdom will easily vanish, our government will give full support to the democratic government of your State.[61]

With its little pro-peasant programmes, on the other hand, the National Party too had begun to counter the State Congress in winning the hearts of the masses. Probably, with a view to spread repugnance, the leaders of

State Congress were denigrated as the Indian agents who were intent on selling Sikkim.[62] Despite of several attempts, it comes into surface that, almost all the peasants had sealed themselves inside the sanctuary of Sikkim State Congress to get their rights secured.[63] Within one year of its formation, the party had successfully reached to the courtyards of the poor with its gospel of salvation from *Kazi/Thikadars*. Several petitions and representation were made by the party with a plea for the adoption of reformation. As usual, the State was too numbed to go ahead with the demands of the State Congress. Probably, the State was in a notion that it could counter any issues of State Congress seeking help from the National Party. Finding the State insensate towards their demands the party decided to hold its first Annual Conference.

The First Annual Conference of Sikkim State Congress (February 1949)

With a view to chalk out plans to counter the cold attitude of the State, the Sikkim State Congress decided to hold an Annual Conference at Rangpo on 1st February 1949.[64] All the party cadres were intimated through notices sent to the block level committees. A considerable crowd was gathered at the bordering town of Rangpo with zeal to find out ways and means to cripple feudal arrangement and to secure their position in the administration. The demand of the State Congress for the establishment of an interim popular government had gradually gathered momentum. Therefore, to ensure their participation in the government through their party, peasants reached the venue of the session barefoot. It has already been stated that, the government had put a ban on staging any form of agitation by peasants for non-payment of their *Khazana*.[65] In spite of prohibition, the party in its first Annual Conference proposed a 'no rent' and 'no tax' campaign as a part of its programme of agitation.[66] Stepping ahead from the rural core issues, the Conference took momentous decisions to intensify steps for achieving popular ministry.[67] With far reaching decisions, the annual conference was concluded on 6th Feb 1949.[68]

Apart from an overwhelming response from the people some unhappy moments were waiting for the leaders at Gangtok. It is said that, when the party members reached the capital, six important leaders were arrested and jailed[69] for having defied the government notification, while the warrant against Tashi Tshering was not executed.[70] However, from the record of a firebrand orator, Brihaspati Parsai, it is revealed that he was arrested by the police immediately after his deliberations at Rangpo. His narration reveals the harsh dealings by the State against the leaders of the State Congress.

Figure 9.5: An unknown Sikkim State Congress Leader addressing the gathering at Rangpo. Pic Credit, Mr N.B. Parsai, Namin Busty, East Sikkim.

"I was taken into custody immediately after finishing my deliberation to the gathering. It was not known to me where they were taking us. With handcuffs, I was told to board on a Jeep standing at Rangpo Bazaar. We were charged for creating nuisance among the peasants and put behind the bars. We were ruthlessly tortured and continuously threatened with our lives and properties".[71]

Figure 9.6: Late Brihaspati Parsai addressing the gathering at Rangpo, Pic. Credit Mr N.B. Parsai, Namin Busty.

The arrests of the Sikkim State Congress leaders were followed by the protests following the government to issue curfew (144 Section) at Gangtok town however, the protestors did not care of such obligations.[72] Basnett illustrates, on 9th February 1949 a 5,000 strong procession defied the curfew and there was a continuous flow of people from all over the Kingdom at the Capital.

Nandalal Bhattarai, a participant of the agitation of 9th February 1949 interprets:

> "We made Duki Paan Dokan located near the palace as our base camp; later, many others from different villages joined us to show our anguish against the State".[73]

On 11th February 1949, the number of demonstrators had swelled to 7,000. In sympathy with the arrested leaders of State Congress, the business community went on an indefinite strike. On 12th February, the arrested leaders were released unconditionally.[74] Thus, in the first round of open confrontation between the peasants and the State, the former come out as victorious. After the protests were over, prolonged negotiations took place between the State Congress leaders and the Sikkim *Durbar*. The talks failed to arrive at a mutually acceptable solution to the political problems clouded in the Kingdom.[75]

Peasant Demonstration at Gangtok on 1st May 1949

As the dialogues failed, the State Congress decided to resume its agitation, which was impeded on the advice of Hareshwar Dayal, the Indian Political Officer in February.[76] The most frustrating issue for the party seemed to be the muted approach of the State to their demands. The initial demonstration was called off with an assurance from the State to resolve all the rural distress. However, once everything got normal, the State adopted the same policy to overlook the issues of the villagers. Much determined in their motives, rural folks under the guidance of Sikkim State Congress began to reach the Capital. On May 1st, 1949, more than 10,000, followers of the Congress gheraoed the palace with a slogan of "*Bari Kasko jotneko.... Ghar Kasko potneko*"[77] meaning land belong to those who plough and house belong to them who take care of it. It appears from the slogan that, the peasants were not in a compromising disposition to maintain any authoritarian ascendancy. Early in the morning, a 3,000 strong procession went up to the palace, shouting- "*Down with the landlords,*" "*Long live Democracy,*" "*We want rule of people*" etc.[78]As the number of protestors engorged, the *Maharaja* had taken Shelter in the Indian Residency and the administration had stopped functioning.[79] For an amicable agreement with the agitators, the *Maharajkumar* P.T. Namgyal made his way towards the protestors in a jeep. The participants of the demonstration observe:

> "We were deputed by our party to protest at the palace gate. The *Maharajkumar* had come to know the prevailing situation in front of the palace. He was trying to cross the human barricade on his jeep. Our leader Chandra Das Rai put the tri-coloured flag of Sikkim State Congress and forbade him from crossing the human blockade".[80]

It is said that, the agitating crowd forced him to get down and to make his way on foot.[81] It is important to remember that the Indian army rescued the ruler to its protection in the Indian Residency and an ugly situation was averted.[82] On the same day, the State came forward for a negotiation with an assurance for the establishment of a responsible government at the earliest and to do away with the vestiges of feudal machinery. The agitating peasants, confident of the promise of His Highness, retreated shouting *Shree Panch Maharaja Dhiraj ko Jai hos, Maharaja Tashi Namgyal ko Jai* (Hail to the *Maharaja*!! Long live *Maharaja* Tashi Namgyal).[83]

The agitation was the first instance of the peasant movement in the State that had raised a current on the calm surface of life in the mountain ringed Kingdom. It is evident thus, that the fear and suppression of state machinery was omitted from the minds of Sikkimese people. The very same poor people, who were once neglected by the state and its authority, had united themselves in a gigantic way against the unnecessary encroachments of the State in their daily lives. With their support to the Sikkim State Congress, they made the State to come forward for a settlement that would be acceptable to the both. With a positive assurance from the State, the State Congress now became more anxious for the formation of a popular government.

Redress of demands by the State through Sikkim State Congress

When the rural whispers became voices and those voices turned into slogans and started reverberating in Gangtok, His Highness the *Maharaja* of Sikkim, on the advice of the Indian Political Officer Hareshwar Dayal, agreed to set up a council known as 'Popular Ministry'. This ministry was formed on 9th May 1949 and was headed by Tashi Tshering as Prime Minister.[84] The State Congress members in the Council of Minister recommended the palace to reduce the house tax from ₹ 6 but, the State rejected their recommendations.[85] Deeply hurt by the rejection, the Congress nominees find it very hard to go parallel with the State. Several loopholes had their place in the said popular ministry. Firstly, there were no clear defined powers at the hands of the members of the Council. Similarly, in every sphere of their dealings, they had to seek the agreement of the State. Inspired from the liberal ideas, the State Congress nominees soon found the Ministry too constraint and started to oppose its functioning. On the other hand, they might have felt that, they had a clear mandate to go ahead with the issue of abolition of landlordism, forced labour, and house tax. However, under these adverse circumstances, it was not possible to secure their demands being in the Council as the State seemed committed to continue the rural evils.[86] The difference of opinion in terms of rural issues and division of power resulted in chaos and the whole administration seemed to be heading towards a downfall. Thus, on 6th of June 1949, the Political Officer Hareshwar Dayal summoned the Sikkim cabinet to inform its members about their dismissals and taking of the administrative charges by him.[87] In this context, it appears that, Government of India was simply imitating the colonial approach of the British in dealing with the matters of a 'protectorate'. Moderately speaking, instead of dissolving the ministry established on the advice of the Political Officer, India was supposed to assist the *Durbar* to settle the matter amicably. The sudden installation and dismissal of the Popular Ministry, at the fancy of the Political Officer indicates the hegemonic and majestic attitude of independent India.

It is to be noted that, the dismissal of the popularly ministry by Government of India inaugurates a new epoch of interference of a sovereign State by its protecting power. The move of Government of India was for no doubt, a precautionary measure to prevent Sikkim from getting into disorder. However, such sudden move of the Political Officer had not only dismissed the infant 'Popular Ministry', but also had shattered the long awaited aspirations of democratic and popular government of the subjects. The public was demoralised and it is believed that, the palace heaved a sigh of relief.[88] It comes into luminosity that no protest, no agitations were seen in any parts of the Kingdom regarding the untimed demise of the Popular Ministry. Owing to their extreme faith on Government of India and its leaders, State Congress leaders too had remained as passive spectators. Unquestionably, they too were stunned from the sudden decision of the Political Officer but, their sense of loyalty to the Indian Government and its leaders had probably stopped them from criticising interference in a voluminous manner. Incontrovertibly, most of the leaders of State Congress belonged to the neglected section and were not aware of the conspiracy hived against them. However, keeping these ignorant lots aside, the party was also guided by the people like Tashi Tshering, L.D. Kazi, C.D. Rai, and others who were the selected faces among the subordinates. Conversely, no voice of opposition was heard from the Sikkim State Congress that eventually opened the gates of Indian interference in the administration of Sikkim. At least, these leaders could have apprised Government of India that, they were the subjects of the *Maharaja* of Sikkim and their major objective includes liquidation of feudalism and to establish a democratic government. No such attempts were made either by the State or by the State Congress against such interference rather they stood happily anaesthetized.

After the dismissal of short lived popular ministry, a new mode of administration was institutionalised with the appointment of *Dewan*. The Government of India, appointed a *Dewan* John S. Lall on 11th of August 1949, with imaginative powers that could even exceed the enormous powers of the first British Political Officer.[89] Lall, on taking his charge as *Dewan* found everything rampant in the Kingdom. It has to be stated further that, the State Congress had not called off 'No Rent' Campaign as decided by the First Annual Conference in February 1949. Owing to the decision of the Congress, the Lessees had not collected revenue since last two years due to chaos.[90] With a view to streamline the rampant situation he made his visit to Namchi where he was greeted by a huge demonstration.[91]

Many peasants from the villages of Namchi were gathered at Alley Tar, at the call of Chandra Das Rai to oppose the notorious forced labour and other feudal evils that still had its existence in the villages.[92] He took the opportunity to discuss with the State Congress leaders for their co-operation with the administration.[93] Surprisingly, immediately after the meeting, at a single stroke of the *Dewan*, the House Tax of ₹ 6 was deducted to ₹ 1.[94] Thus, after the appointment of the *Dewan*, prolonged struggle of *Dhurikhajana* instantly got eliminated and the age old feudal edifices got dismantle within a second by the sharp and the pointed nib of an Indian pen. This indicates the level of trust and dependence the Kingdom of Sikkim had with India. The State, in consent with the British Political Officer, could have made it possible even before the Indian independence. However, considering the rural dissatisfaction as an inconsequential issue, the State continued to ignore, that provided a space for the growth of political resistance. Such mistakes from the part of the State and the political parties' later on provided a larger avenue for the Indians to have their control in the Sikkimese administration. Assisting Sikkim for the elimination of feudalism seemed to be an Indian scheme to get the Sikkimese peasantry into its confidence and to separate the State from its subjects. However, at this juncture, the State seriously lacked intuition of disastrous consequences in the future and continued itself in pleasing the protecting power. Likewise, *Tehsils* were established for East and West Sikkim and a new officer known as *Tehsildar* was appointed with magisterial and executive purpose and was also entrusted with the charge of the collection of revenue.[95]

Apart from these developments, Sikkim witnessed a sluggish progress even in politics after the Indo-Sikkim treaty of 1950.[96] After the Treaty, a delegation of Sikkim State Congress went to Delhi for further discussions with Government of India. However, it seemed, at least for this time, Delhi was unenthusiastic to support Sikkim State Congress for a democratic and responsible government in Sikkim.[97] Amid reluctance, owing to the recurrent pressure and resentments of Sikkim State Congress, Indian Government asked the *Dewan* to clear up the way for the people's participation in the Government. Consequently, in May 1951, the matter of Communal representation was discussed and eventually adopted, that ultimately led to the birth of communalism in the Kingdom. In the discussion, it was decided to adopt a 'parity formula' for a proportion between the Lepcha-Bhutia and the Nepali subjects. The Sikkim State Congress was represented by Capt. Dimik Singh Lepcha and Kashi Raj Pradhan, a Lepcha and a Nepali respectively.[98]

It is interesting to note that, formerly Sikkim had two conflicting interests, the State with its feudal train and the Sikkimese peasants; now, since the peasants had apparently been divided into two communal groups, Sikkim had three different interests- the *Maharaja*, the Lepcha-Bhutia group, and the Nepalese. Through a proclamation dated 23rd March 1953 'parity formula' was adopted as a basis of the succeeding elections in the Kingdom. Accordingly, it was also decided to hold elections for a State Council consisted of twelve elected members six of them would represent Sikkimese Bhutias or Lepchas and the other six would represent the Nepalese. In addition to this, as it was decided, five members were to be nominated by His Highness the *Maharaja* at his discretion.[99]

The National Party won all six Lepcha-Bhutia seats and was thus confirmed by the electorate as a sentinel of the Lepcha-Bhutia interests. Similarly, the winning of all six Nepali seats by Sikkim State Congress had reflected the Party as a protector of the Nepali interests.[100] It may be accessed that, from the beginning of the political process, the three ethnic groups of Sikkim adopted a narrow approach based on communal issues. Instead of voting to a candidate who belonged to their community, the voters were supposed to choose the party that was committed for the progress and development of the Kingdom. However, possibly due to the growing mindset of pro-community approach of their leaders they got seriously misguided and voted the candidates belonging to their communities. The leaders on the other hand, were too, some way or the other, influenced by the parity formula of ethnic balance. Therefore, without caring much about the grave consequences they put every effort to win the election. Their neglecting views in this regard, had planted the embryos of communalism in the political farm of Sikkim in a wider scale leading to a breach between the three communities. Thus, apart from all other outcomes, Sikkim was gifted with the souvenir of communalism in the form of parity formula designed and indented by Government of India. The parity formula seems to be an altered version of the 'divide and rule' policy of British. This imperial policy had divided the Indians between the Muslims and the Hindus to secure effective rule over the subcontinent. Proving as an apt child of the British mechanism, Government of India too, had adopted the same blueprint with an altered version of 'parity' to divide the three ethnic communities. The complicated voting procedures and elections result has thus confirmed that Sikkim still had a long way to walk to attain a popular and responsible government as dreamt by the political pioneers.

Thus, the earlier symphony of Sikkimese peasantry that consisted of Lepcha, Bhutia, and Nepali peasants, during the period of everyday resistance, was seriously disturbed with the politicisation of peasants' issues by the State. Now, after the reformation in administration they had a different importance to the State as well as to the political parties they were affiliated to. During everyday resistance, they were considered as porters, a peasant, a subordinate, and an inferior, and most importantly, a lucrative being to spin money for the landlords. Similarly, they had to spend all their lives in pleasing their Masters sometimes as *Jharlangi* labourers and often as subordinates. Though, they had been able to achieve unimaginable after they came under the influence of State Congress. However, they were now in the process of losing their identity as peasant folks. For a political gain and as an 'ethnic balance' measure they had been divided according to their communities and were now merely being treated as a voter by their respective parties and a subject by the State. Although, their journey from porter to voter, and from subordinate to subject, had many turns and twirls, whereupon they were guided by their leaders who were eager to uplift their plights. However, situation began to take unpleasant turns and dwindled from bad to worse when the State adopted an unbalanced parity formula.

During their course of everyday resistance, the very same peasants who were then leaderless were free to live and to resist the State by adopting several techniques discussed in the preceding chapters. Undoubtedly, that was an individual effort to resist the State and they themselves were responsible for the disturbances they created or achievement they could attain. Being leaderless they were their own guides and philosophers and worked according to their consciences in a time apposite manner. However, circumstances were totally different after history reaches at this juncture, and now it is evident that, the State was very much eager to set an ethnic balance by adopting parity formula. Therefore, on the advice of the

Political Officer, the State adopted it without keeping a second thought in its mind. The State at this point, had even forgotten the attachment and intimacy these elements shared in establishing harmony in rural Sikkim. To reiterate, all these elements had resisted feudalism and its evils at the best ways they could devised. Conversely, immediately after achieving a very little from their prolonged resistance they got bifurcated into two halves just because they belonged to varied communities. Incorporating a very little interest of the peasantry by the State, they were made the victim of a political conspiracy hacked by its protecting power. The very parity formula had become a core issue in the succeeding elections and when it was still undone, the peasants rose in a revolt that had not only eliminated the remnants of feudal structure but had also swept away their sovereignty.

Notes

1. Scott, James C. (1985), *Weapons of the Weak, Every day Forms of Peasant Resistance*, Yale University Press, London, p. 43.
2. Grover, B.S.K, (1974), *Sikkim and India-Storm and Consolidation*, Jain Brothers, New Delhi, p. 34.
3. Tshering, Tashi, "A few facts about Sikkim" a pamphlet issued by the Sikkim State Congress on 7th December 1947.
4. Field Report: 2011-2012: Information collected through personal interview from the participants of the Meeting.
5. Late Dugo Bhutia, had served as an MLA of the first Sikkim Legislative Assembly (1974-1979).
6. Field Report: 2011-2012: Information collected through personal interview from the participants of the meeting of 7th December 1947.
7. Basnett, Lal Bahadur, (1974), *Sikkim- A short Political History,* S. Chand & Co. (Pvt.) Ltd. New Delhi, p. 76.
8. K.D. Roy Chaudhari was a Bengali from Kolkata (then Calcutta) who met a friend Bishnu Bhakta Dhungel of Temi Tarku while he was studying in Benaras. It was Bishnu Bhakta, who called Roy Chaudhari from Calcutta to come to Sikkim. After Roy Chaudhari reached Temi Tarku, he remained at a temple as a Sadhu. It was Roy Chaudhari who played a vital role for the foundation of *Rajya Praja Sammelan* of Temi Tarku and *Praja Mandal* of Chakhung. (Gauley 2002, pp. 67-69).
9. Helen Lepcha hailed from Kurseong; Gandhiji renamed her Sabitri Devi when she went to Sabarmati Ashram on Bapu's invitation. She was the first Lepcha women freedom fighter and was put behind the bars at Darjeeling jail for three months. Sinha, Dr. Gokul, (2006), *Role of Gorkhas in making modern India,* Mark printers New Delhi, Published by Bharatiya Gorkha Parisangh, p. 32.
10. Bhattarai Nandalal, unpublished diary, late Bhattarai was a founding member of Sikkim State Congress.
11. Field Report: 2011-2012.

12. Sinha, A.C., "*Sikkim of Yesterday*", The Sikkim Times, Gangtok, Saturday June 9th 2007.
13. Field Report 2011-2012.
14. Field Report 2011-2012: Suntaley village West Sikkim. This respondent was among the participants of the Meeting of 7th December 1947 from West Sikkim.
15. Field Report 2011-2012: Suntaley village West Sikkim. This respondent was one of the founding members of Sikkim State Congress.
16. Field Report 2011-2012: Kabirthang Village, West Sikkim. He was among the participant of 7th December Meeting.
17. Field Report 2011-2012: Tashiding, Arithang Chongrang, West Sikkim.
18. Field Report 2011-2012: Namin village East Sikkim. This respondent was one of the founding members of Sikkim State Congress.
19. Field Report 2011-2012: Aho Village, East Sikkim. Personal interview from a participant of the meeting of 7th December 1947.
20. Field Report 2011-2012: Assam Lingzey, East Sikkim. He is among the participants of the meeting of 7th December 1947.
21. Field Report 2011-2012: Assam Lingzey, East Sikkim.
22. Field Report 2011-2012: Assam Lingzey Saureni village, East Sikkim. This respondent was one of the attendee of the meeting of 7th December 1947 at Polo Ground.
23. Field Report 2011-2012: Assam Lingzey Saureni village, East Sikkim. This respondent had attended the meeting of 7th December 1947 at Polo Ground.
24. Gauley Gopal (et al) (First published 2002), *History of Democratic Movement*, Department of Information and public relations, Govt. of Sikkim, p. 22.
25. Field Report 2011-2012: Assam Lingzey, East Sikkim. After his retirement late Garjaman Rai from Imperial service joined as the first teacher of newly opened school nowadays known as Assam Lingzey Sr. Sec School.
26. Field Report 2011-2012: Namli Village, East Sikkim. He is the son of late Brihaspati Parsai, Publicity Secretary of Sikkim State Congress.
27. Field Report 2011-2012: Tarku Village, South Sikkim, a participant of the meeting of 7th December 1947.
28. Field Report 2011-2012: Tarku village, South Sikkim. This respondent was among the founders of Rajya Praja Sammelan of Temi Tarku and was also a key participant of the meeting of Sikkim State Congress on 7th December 1947.
29. Gaunley (2002) op cit, p. 125.
30. Field Report 2011-2012: Ranipool Bazaar, East Sikkim.
31. Sinha, A.C., "*Sikkim of Yesterday*", The Sikkim Times, Gangtok, Saturday June 9th 2007.
32. Dhamala, Jay (1983), *Sikkim ko Itihas* (History of Sikkim) Shyam Prakashan Darjeeling, p. 72.
33. Mridula Mukherjee, (Oct 8 1988) '*Peasant Resistance and peasant consciousness in Colonial India Subalterns and Beyond*', Economic and Political Weekly, p. 2119.

34. Kotturan, George, (1983), *The Himalayan Gateway- History and Culture of Sikkim*, Sterling Publishers Pvt. Ltd. New Delhi, p. 95.
35. Bhattarai, Nandalal, (Unpublished Dairy), Namin village, East Sikkim.
36. Basnett, (1974) op cit, p. 78.
37. Kotturan, (1983) op cit, p. 95.
38. Gaunley (2002) op cit, p. 22.
39. Notification, Sikkim State General Department, 5186-085/G, Gangtok 3rd January 1948. This Notification forbade the landlords from registering documents along with their rights to act as sub Registers.
40. Parsai, Brihaspati (Unpublished Notes) He was the first Publicity Secretary of the Sikkim State Congress.
41. Basnett, (1974) op cit p. 78.
42. Grover, (1974) op cit, p. 36.
43. Goyal, Narendra (Second Edition 1966), *Political History of Himalayan States-Tibet, Nepal, Bhutan, Sikkim and Nagaland since 1947*, Cambridge Book and Stationary Store, New Delhi, p. 141.
44. The Indian authorities had first submitted the "Instrument of Accession" form which was used for signing by the rulers of Indian princely states on their merger with Indian Union. But, when Sikkim objected to this format, India agreed to use the terminology of "Standstill Agreement", which had been suggested by the Sikkimese representatives. This rendered an implicit recognition to Sikkim's special status by the Indian Union as well as providing an early but clear indication of India that would not insist upon Sikkim's complete merger with the Union unlike other states. The Standstill Agreement was signed on 27th February 1948. Grover, B.S.K, (1974), *Sikkim and India- Storm and Consolidation*, Jain Brothers, New Delhi, pp. 87-88.
45. *Sikkim State Congress ko Vidhan* (Constitution of Sikkim State Congress).
46. *Ibid.*
47. Membership Card of Sikkim State Congress, 1948 to Harka Bahadur Subba *aka* Khukuri Bajey.
48. Notification, Judicial Branch, 3054-254/PS, Dated 24th January 1948 Gangtok.
49. Notification, Judicial Branch, 3054-254/PS, Dated 24th January 1948 Gangtok.
50. General Department, 5186-085/G, Dated 3rd January 1948.
51. Forest Department, 5093/F, Gangtok, Dated 13th September 1948.
52. Land Revenue and Forest Department, 433-633/L&F, Dated 8th April 1948.
53. The Terracing Ordinance 1949, Gangtok Dated 23rd November 1949 p. 1.
54. *Luga Paune* Ration Card, 16th March 1948, Ravilal Pyakurel of Tareythang Busty East Sikkim.
55. *Ibid.*
56. Grover (1974) op cit, p. 35.
57. Moktan, R.(2004), '*Sikkim: Darjeeling Compendium of Documents*,' Resolution passed by the Sikkim National Party on 30th April 1948, Himadri Printers Gangtok.
58. *Ibid.*

59. Grover (1974) op cit, p. 36.
60. Gaunley (2002) op cit, p. 22.
61. *Ibid*, p. 32.
62. Basnett, (1974) op cit, p. 85.
63. Field Report 2011-2012: Assam Lingzey, East Sikkim.
64. Parsai, Brihaspati (Unpublished Notes), Publicity Secretary, Sikkim State Congress.
65. Land Revenue and Forest Department, 433-633/L&F, Dated 8th April 1948.
66. Basnett, (1974) op cit, p. 86.
67. Grover (1974) op cit, p. 37.
68. Parsai, Brihaspati (Unpublished Notes), Publicity Secretary, Sikkim State Congress.
69. Grover (1974) op cit, p. 37.
70. Basnett, (1974) op cit, p. 87.
71. Parsai, Brihaspati (Unpublished Notes), Publicity Secretary, Sikkim State Congress.
72. Dhamala, (1983) op cit, pp. 74-75.
73. Field Report 2011-2012: Namin village, East Sikkim.
74. Basnett, (1974) op cit, p. 87.
75. *Ibid.*
76. *Ibid.*
77. Field Report 2011-2012: Pakki Gaon, West Sikkim.
78. Dhamala, (1983) op cit, p. 75.
79. Sinha, A.C. "*Sikkim of Yesterday*", The Sikkim Times, Gangtok, Saturday June 9th 2007.
80. Field Report 2011-2012: Namin village, East Sikkim. This respondent had been a leading member of the agitation of 1 May 1949.
81. Field Report: 2011-2012, Namin Busty East Sikkim.
82. Grover (1974) op cit, p. 38.
83. Field Report 2011-2012: Namin village, East Sikkim.
84. Gaunley, (2002) op cit, p. 32.
85. *Ibid.*
86. Basnett, (1974) op cit, p. 89.
87. Bhattarai, Nandalal, (Unpublished Dairy), Namin Busty, East Sikkim.
88. Bhattarai, Nandalal, (Unpublished Dairy), Namin Busty, East Sikkim.
89. Basnett, (1974) op cit, p. 91.
90. Order No.11, Collection of Khazana from the Lessees, August 30th 1949.
91. Dhamala, (1983) op cit, p. 76.
92. Field Report 2011-2012: Tarku village, South Sikkim. This respondent had participated in the demonstration of Sikkim State Congress at Namchi supporting "No Rent" Campaign.

93. Basnett, (1974) op cit, p. 92.
94. His Highness *Maharaja* of Sikkim, Notification No. 318, dated 17th October 1950.
95. Order No.4, Revenue Administration, Dated 19th August 1949.
96. Indo-Sikkim Treaty of 3-12-1950 Article I-XIII, the treaty was signed between Hariswar Dayal Political Officer in Sikkim and Sir Tashi Namgyal, His Highness, the *Maharaja* of Sikkim and was certified by Palden Thondup Namgyal, the Maharajkumar of Sikkim at Tshuklakhang royal chapel, Gangtok. The treaty of 1950 had cancelled all the earlier treaties signed between Sikkim Government and British Government.
97. Cohelo, V.H, (1970), *Sikkim and Bhutan,* Indian Council for Cultural Relations, Vikash Publications, New Delhi, p. 29.
98. Basnett, (1974) op cit, p. 95.
99. Sikkim *Durbar* Gazette (Extraordinary) Proclamation of His Highness *Maharaja* Tashi Namgyal, *Maharaja* of Sikkim, Dated 23rd March 1953, Composition of Council, Clause 3, p. 1.
100. Basnett, (1974) op cit, p. 102.

Chapter 10

Political Eclipse on the Peasants' Issues

In the lapse of nine years (1940-1949), the peasantry of Sikkim had come across a several phases in terms of their relations with the State. Their sense of antagonism, resentments, hidden transcripts during the period of their everyday resistance, had taken several curves according to the need of the hour. The outbursts of their hidden transcripts in the forms of speeches, and the repressive policies adopted by the State to eliminate the rebels, the underground meetings, and its resolutions had eventually made their ways to establish an association for a common cause. The same everyday resisters had taken their seats as the member and the leaders of the association owing to their eagerness to live a hassle free life. Their individual efforts to fight back the State, and the assistance they received from few of the influential had thoroughly changed the rural mind set. Now, they seemed very determined to achieve what they had dreamt throughout their lives. Indeed, the patronage they received from Sikkim State Congress had further elaborated their dreams to achieve a world of their choices. The issues of bread and butter that had paralysed the entire peasantry after the British were not yet over. However, along with their primary issues, they began to work for the emancipation of the entire fraternity. The self-centred acts they practiced during everyday resistance were thus transforming. It appears that, at this phase of events, the conventional notion of being the subordinates was replaced by an undeclared awareness of being the contributors to the State.

The marginalised lots who had recently thrown off the thick blanket of feudalism seemed more committed and vibrant to get their position secure in the State. After a prolonged resistance the Sikkimese peasantry had achieved a new milestone subsequent to the May agitation of 1949. Undoubtedly, the credit for the massive agitation clamouring for its rights and justice goes to Sikkim State Congress. Consequently, for the first time in the history of Sikkim, the submissive and subservient subjects had made the State to bow and to come forward for a compromise. After the agitation, the unbending and obdurate State too had changed its dealings and guaranteed the elimination of every nuisance from the rural Sikkim. Following the negotiation, on the advice of the Indian Political Officer, a short lived Ministry was installed but lack of defined powers led to its dismissal within 29 days of its formation. After to the dismissal, a strange and unusual formula known as parity with a motive for ethnic balance was devised in May 1951. Accordingly, the first general elections to the Sikkim Council were held in 1953.

Casualness of the State Congress towards the Rural Issues

As either parties failed to secure majority in the Council, a 17-member State Council was constituted on 7th August 1953 with the *Dewan* as its President.[1]

Figure 10.1: Members of the First State Council 1953. Pic. Credit Mr Shital Pradhan, Singtam, East Sikkim.

An Executive Council of three members that included the *Dewan* and the Elected Councillors of both the political parties namely Kashi Raj Pradhan, Sikkim State Congress, and Sonam Tshering, Sikkim National Party was created. However, the first elected councillors failed to act as the representatives of Sikkimese people as a whole. They simply got stuck in the narrow notion of their respective communities and functioned within the outline. The administration of Education, Public Health, Excise, Press and Publicity, Transports, Bazaar, Forest and Public Works were transferred to the Executive Councillors under 'Transferred Subjects' as stated in the clause 21 of the Royal Proclamation.[2] Similarly, the State preserved the administration of Ecclesiastical Affairs, External Affairs, State Enterprises, Home and Police, Finance, Land Revenue, Rationing, Establishment. The Departments under the State were categorised as 'Reserved Subjects' following the Royal Proclamation.[3] The Executive Councillors were made responsible to *Durbar* for the executive and the administrative functions of the government.[4] Similarly, Proclamation had also overpowered the *Maharaja* with a veto and he could forfeit the decision of the Executive Council and substitute his own decision instead.[5] Therefore, it is evident that, the significant departments were all kept by the State leaving a few at the hands of the people's representatives. Similarly, it comes into light that, the Proclamation was designed with a motive to keep the public representatives in a lesser position. Another important noticeable aspect of the Proclamation is that, it seriously differed in aphorism and action that had later on virtually paralysed the entire set up.

On the other hand, the appointment of Kashi Raj Pradhan of Sikkim State Congress as a member of Executive Council left the State Council with no opposition. The party that had a battle cry of elimination of rural injustice had thus assimilated itself with the force that was responsible for the peasant resentments. We are not aware about the compulsion of Sikkim State Congress in joining the Council yet, the action of the Party indicates a plot by the State to purge rural aspirations. The voters got convinced from the rural oriented programmes of the party and had voted for its victory. However, deceiving thousands of souls, the Party had reconciled itself to the 'Constitutional Proclamation' entirely forgetting the pre-election promises. At the same time, Tashi Babu was expelled as the President of the Sikkim State Congress.[6] The expulsion of one of the most revered and acclaimed leader by the party justifies with whom the Party was with. It may be accessed that, as the members of State Congress stepped on the clean and bright floor of the State Council, they had totally forgotten the dirt and mud back in their villages. The office of the State Congress was now transferred to *Kazi* Lhendup Dorjee Khangsarpa. Following the removal of Tashi Tshering *aka* Tashi *Babu*, the course of action of the Sikkim State Congress also transformed. The association which was set up to provide justice to the peasants by forming a responsible government was put in a morgue and the former peasant sympathisers, as appears, had now become faithful agents of the *Durbar*. Hence, the plight of the Sikkimese peasantry with a little reformation was still static at the same point from where the journey of cohesive opposition to the feudal forces was started.

The Executive Council of the Sikkim Council lacked a proper power classification between the State and the elected Councillors. The entire process of the Council, from discussion to decision, was supervised by a five pages document framed as 'Constitutional Proclamation'. The Constitutional Proclamation had left a very limited space for the growth of egalitarian ideas among the rural lots. In reality, not a single issue related to the rural distress was mentioned in this proclamation that could help the Councillors to put forward grievances of the peasantry. Thus, by sabotaging the opposition at the Council and keeping all the key departments by the State and leaving a very little space to the elected representatives, the State, as it emerges, was moving towards absolutism. In such a situation John S. Lall was replaced by Nari Kaikusrav Rustumji as the new *Dewan.*[7] This new *Dewan* had been a friend to the *Maharajkumar*, during their training days for Indian Civil Service. Rustumji managed to get sanctioned 4,315 million US $ from Government of India and launched a Seven Year Plan to Sikkim.[8] The whole amount received from the Government of India was subjected towards launching some developmental plans in the entire Kingdom. However, even in the Seven Year plan prepared by the State the village development programme was not included. Allegedly, the money was carelessly utilised by the State ignoring all the plans and proposals they made to get it sanctioned.[9] The Constitutional Proclamation in its Clause 16 had a flexibility of discussing such expenditures made by the State.[10] Conversely, as it seems, the member of the State Council adopted a muted attitude in this regard and kept on misleading the rural distress. In all probabilities, they did not want to get deprived from the royal 'blessings' and remained quite without raising a single voice of opposition for a larger interest. It is also significant to point out that; the State Council as directed by the 'Constitutional Proclamation' had to be elected for the period of three years.[11] The dubious State policy is evident from another Proclamation, which extended the terms of the members of the State Council till December 1957.[12]

Frustrated with the unvoiced actions of his party men against the monopoly of the State, *Kazi* Lhendup Dorjee resigned from the Sikkim State Congress and joined a newly founded organisation, called *Swatantra Dal*, under Namgay Tshering.[13] It is also said that, *Kazi* Lhendup Dorjee had become a helpless spectator of the erosion of powers of the Executive Councillors. Kashi Raj Pradhan, the Leader of Sikkim State Congress in the Council, lacked courage and conviction to oppose the *Dewan's* encroachment in every affair.[14] Similarly, it is also accused that, Kashi Raj had given the highest positions of the party to his kith and kin. Thus, at this juncture, the earlier peasants' demands and their enthusiasm to form Sikkim State Congress seems heading towards vein. The party determined to unleash entire peasantry from all social and economic exploitations was in the process of wringing into a narrow convention. It comes into view that,

State Congress's principles of equality and egalitarianism had remained a miles away from the dusty and grimy villages as it itself fell on the pyre of despotism. With the resignation of *Kazi* Lhendup Dorjee, the vacant post of the president of Sikkim State Congress was filled up with the appointment of Kashi Raj Pradhan.[15]

In between these, Sikkim went for second general elections following the Proclamation of His Highness *Maharaja* Sir Tashi Namgyal dated 16th March 1958.[16] It would not be unfair to ascertain that, the new system of communal voting, as reflected in the Proclamation, was the brain child of *Dewan* Nari Rustumji. However, the highly complicated system of election, which complicated the actual casting of votes and subsequent counting, was very confusing to the simple Sikkimese electorate.[17] There were reports of political leaders asking to vote for them in various meetings and even rumoured of social boycott in case of voting for the candidates of the other communities.[18] The Sikkim State Congress had focused on the establishment of a responsible government and on the other hand, the National Party was still committed to retain the old system of governance.[19]Apparently, the peculiar mode was to keep India away from criticism for introducing communal system of voting in her Protectorate.[20] Though, the seats in the Council were raised from seventeen to twenty yet, the cling of parity system was still maintained by the State.[21] In a layman's understanding, a simple an uncomplicated voting procedure would have served the uneducated electorate in a better way than a communal, and a knotty system. Conversely, none of the political party had raised their voices against the complicated voting procedures and plunged them in the elections in November 1958. Leaving aside one General Seat, the election of the remaining 13 Seats (distributed on other ethnic formula) were declared as follows:-

> "Eight candidates belonged to the Lepcha, Bhutia, and Nepali communities were elected from the State Congress, four candidates belonging to the Lepcha-Bhutia community from the two factions of the Sikkim National Party and one Bhutia candidate from the Lama or Sangha seat were declared elected".[22]

In contrast, after the resignation of *Kazi* Lhendup Dorjee, Kashi Raj Pradhan himself had assumed the post of the President of Sikkim State Congress. With his appointment, the leadership of the State Congress, as it emerges, was transferred from the peasants to the aristocrats. Further, Kashi Raj Pradhan allowed his own men to occupy the executive posts of the party who belonged to the '*Taxari*' family of Sikkim.[23] *Taxari* were the people who minted coins to the *Maharajas* of Sikkim and were excessively well-heeled and affluent. Therefore, they were unacquainted with the problems faced by the rural masses that symbolises the party had completely identified with the interests of the State.[24] However, in theory, the State Congress was reverberating itself as a promoter of democracy and responsible government in the State. The President Kashi Raj Pradhan, who was also the editor of a Nepali magazine *Kanchenjunga*, once wrote:

> "Sikkim State Congress always had believed that after the second election, they would form a responsible ministry. On the contrary, even after the elections, an executive council was formed instead of a ministry. As had been in the past, half of the departments remained reserved and the administration has turned into a diarchy. So is it right to articulate that Sikkim is progressing in the path of democracy?"[25]

From the writings, it emerges that Kashi Raj was a bit concerned for the cause of people and the ultimate goal of State Congress seemed to establish democracy. However, akin to State, he too fluctuated in his aphorism and action at the same time as he joined the State Council. If this aristocrat could have understood democracy from a rural perspective, the history of those subjugated for a responsible government would have definitely taken a speedy course.

Far from this political front, the peasants of Sikkim were still crashing themselves in the tug-of-war of the political parties and the State. Demand of the peasants for a responsible government in the Kingdom was at a vanishing stage. Similarly, the parity formula, the unequal taxation, land reformation were some of the major issues that were yet unsolved. It emerges that, achievements secured through the agitation of 1949 were now almost diminished and the State was marching back towards complete despotism. The people and the palace were still standing on the two opposite poles as the peoples' representatives were busy keeping the palace pleased with their good dealings. Similarly, the Indian diplomats with their high sounding titles of Political Officer, *Dewan*, and Administrative Officers, instead of scurrying the democratisation process were also busy enjoying the royal warmth. Thus, in the triangle of pleasing each other, the plight of meagre was standing tallest among all yet, no one was there for them to get into the bottom of injustice. No differences were occurred even after the little political development in the daily lives of the rural folks. The stagnation seemed basically due to the laxity of their leaders who in all practicalities were not serious to solve the problems of the masses. Though, the *Thikadari* system was abolished in 1949, peasants still had a threat on their minds of their hilarious past. Still large sections of the people were debarred from possessing landed property and equal distribution of lands was merely hearsay. However, over all, to some extent they were now free from feudal exploitation; still they suffered lack of education, social malpractices, discrimination, and poverty. They were compelled to live with their hardships due to the lack of roads, communication, post and telegraph etc. A major alteration on these social issues was the exigency of time and that were to be dealt by their respective representatives. Conversely, accustomed to the royal etiquettes, these representatives kept themselves engaged in pleasing the royal house than resolving the rural despondency. In a truer sense, they were explicating a Nepali proverb *Mero Tumbi Bharija Aru Jogi Marija* i.e. my bucket is full I need not worry about poor.

The concept of 'one man one vote' enunciated by Bentham and James Stuart Mills in nineteenth century was yet alien to the democracy that the masses had known so far. Even in the mid of the twentieth century, Sikkimese leaders were happy and content with the communal voting procedure that got obsolete long back in Imperial India. This outmoded voting procedure in a real sense of interpretation was digging a grave of monarchy which the State had utterly failed to consider.

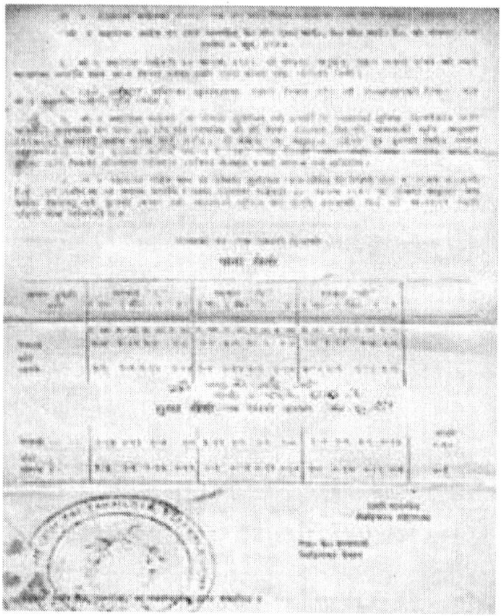

Figure 10.2: Proclamation of His Highness* Maharaja *of Sikkim Sir Tashi Namgyal on 7th June 1957, published by Sikkim* Durbar *Press Gangtok. Courtesy Mr Krishna Prasad Pyakurel of Tareythang Busty East Sikkim.

Apart from this political tug-of-war, the State came up with some rural reformation through a proclamation on 7th June 1957. With a view to lessen the burden of taxation among the subjects a new mode of revenue assessment was adopted through this proclamation. According to it, '50 per cent of the taxation was to be reduced from the peasantry. However, discrepancy was yet established in the amount of taxation to be paid by Lepcha-Bhutia and the Nepali peasants'.[26] The rationale of the diverse rate of taxation among the Sikkimese subjects on the basis of ethnicity is not known. Undoubtedly, lessen of taxation from the shoulders of meagre had provided a new era in the everyday affairs of the villagers. However, the contradiction in the rates made by the State among the three ethnic communities had naturally escalated antagonism among the Nepalese. Such slip-ups from the part of the State were playing vital role among the Nepalese peasants to go against the system in a fierce manner.

Corruption and Neglected Condition of the Peasants

The coronation of *Chogyal* Palden Thondup Namgyal and *Gyalmo* Hope Cooke Namgyal inaugurated a new era in the history of Sikkim. Assured from the territorial integrity by the treaty of 1950,[27] the newly ascended royal couple engaged themselves in maintaining a separate identity of their country. Being born and brought up in a hustle free American society, the new *Gyalmo* found the Indian yoke in Sikkim too strident and outdated in modern perspectives.[28] Encouraged by her liberal, enlightened, and democratic ideas, the *Chogyal,* too, began to work for the economic development which had gathered a good momentum in the Kingdom. As per Cooke, very few unsolved matters were pending in Sikkim before their accession to the throne. She illustrates:

> "...was to work toward ending parity voting, to work for an end of communalism, and to encourage all groups in the country to view themselves as Sikkimese above all, a unity essential for the survival of a small country caught between powerful neighbours".[29]

However, it appears that, the realism was a miles away from its remedy. The political parties and their leaders, with a new hope and aspiration were waiting for a greater participation with the accession of the new King and the Queen. Apart from the two Sikkimese interests involved in maintaining sovereignty and attending supremacy in the Council, another interest that was fighting for its survival was that of the peasantry. Ignored and exploited by both the earlier interests, they were still living a combatant's life. Reforms during the reign of *Maharaja* Tashi Namgyal were the only thing they had been able to achieve so far from the administration. Still a majority of the peasants were share croppers, *Adhiadars*, *Kutdars* and many of them were landless agriculturists. The successor of *Maharaja* Tashi Namgyal remained more active in safeguarding his crown from felling into the Indian hands than to standardise the plight of the peasants. Though, some measures for the elevation of Sikkimese peasantry were initiated by *Chogyal* Palden Thondup Namgyal yet, they seemed to have remained ineffective among the peasantry. Some of the important initiatives were loans for agriculture and animal husbandry development,[30] the Sikkim Panchayat Act,[31] Compensation in advance before acquisition of land of a peasant[32] etc. Apart from these, many such acts and amendments were initiated during the 10 years of rule of *Chogyal* Palden Thondup. However, as they seemed were not having much influence over the peasant related issues. Thus, due to his mild approach towards the betterment of the peasantry their condition began to deteriorate. No doubt, contributions of *Chogyal* Palden Thondup Namgyal for maintaining sovereignty of his Kingdom cannot be overlooked yet; his approach to uplift the plight of is peasants appear to be nominal. It is revealed that, even during the reign of the last monarch, *Chogyal* Palden Thondup, a large number of the peasantry did not possess landed property. It is evident from the tax receipts of Rumtek monastery estate that still revenues of such estates were collecting in a fluctuating manner.[33] It is worth to mention that, the monastery estate too had a large number of tenants and the rate of taxation was similar to the earlier *Chaar Daam* peasants and the former too had to pay their taxes regularly. Conversely, it becomes visible that there is a difference in the amount of taxation paid by the concerned *Kazi* to the government for an unknown reason. According to the receipts, the *Kazi* made a payment of ₹ 135 of Rumtek estate in 1966. However, in 1967 he deposited only ₹ 114 to Jethmull and Bhojraj, the state bankers of Sikkim. [34] Whatever the actuality may be, it is evident that the *Kazis,* who were now powerless, still have their upper hand in Sikkimese administration even though their excessive rights were curtailed in 1949.

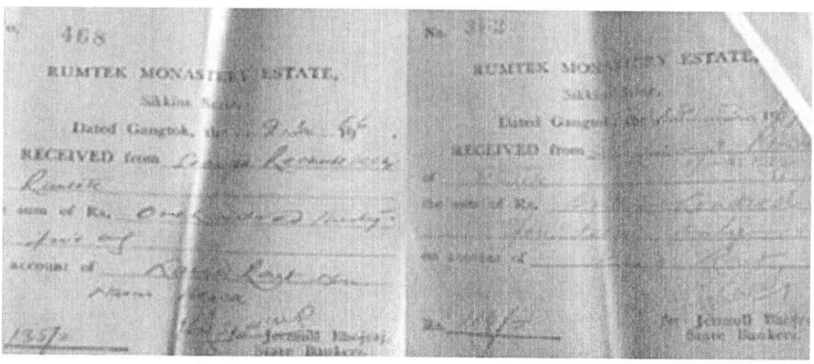

Figure 10.3: Land Rent receipts issued to Senga Rechuck Kazi of Rumtek Monastery Estate in 1966-67 by the State Bankers Jethmull and Bhojraj. Courtesy Mr Passang Tshering Bhutia of Namin Busty.

On the other hand, even if they had a solid reason there was no ebb and flow in the payment of taxes by a common peasant. Ravilal Pyakurel, a peasant of Tareythang Busty East Sikkim had made ₹ 17.45 as his land tax in 1965 and the same amount was paid on his behalf in the consecutive year to his concerned *Mandal*.[35] From an observation of these two documents, belonging to two varied interests, one cannot overrule the prevalence of rampant corruption in the rural areas even after the accession of *Chogyal* Palden Thondup Namgyal.

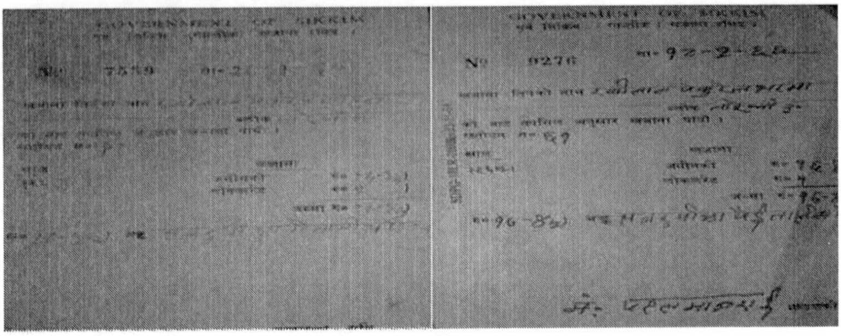

Figure 10.4: Land Tax Receipts of Late Ravilal Pyakurel of Tareythang Busty paid in 1965-66. Courtesy Mr Krishna Prasad Pyakurel Tareythang, East Sikkim.

Conversely, the political parties' vocal with the pro-peasant demands too had a silent approach in the established inconsistency in the part of the government. Many unsolved political problems were far from their solutions. Some of the important issues were divergence in the Sikkim Subject Regulations, abolition of 'Parity System', Land reforms that included confiscation of the *Kazi* lands and its distribution among the peasants, elimination of private estates, eradication of nepotism, and the development of villages.[36] Thus, it is Palpable that, Sikkimese peasantry was still squashed in between the policies of the big giants and assurances of their political leaders. It also becomes discernible that, the peasants were heavily exploited by the political parties to gain their seats in the Assembly than to uplift their condition. During feudalism the same peasants were operated by the Sikkim State Congress to secure popular ministry and election and still they were using them to vote in their favour. The tenure of Third Sikkim Council (1967-1970) had also heavily shattered the interests of peasants as some of its members were engaged in siphoning the allotted budget meant for the development. Bhim Bahadur Gurung, an Executive Councillor, was charged with misappropriation of money from the contractor.[37] He was later forced to resign on 5th September 1969 from his councillorship but was again appointed as an Executive Councillor by the *Chogyal* on 2nd January 1970. Crippled in between such circumstances, it would not be an overstatement to say that, the peasants were in a stagnant position where they were during reign of Tashi Namgyal. In fact, the entire reign of *Chogyal* Palden Thondup Namgyal remained busy in resisting unnecessary Indian encroachment in the administrative affairs of Sikkim. The political parties meant for the betterment of the peasants, too, remained silent, that forced the peasant grievances to remain in a back stage till it culminated into the revolt of 1973.

Notes

1. Goyal, Narendra (Second Edition 1966), *Political History of Himalayan States-Tibet, Nepal, Bhutan, Sikkim and Nagaland since 1947*, Cambridge Book and Stationary Store, New Delhi, p. 143.
2. Proclamation of His Highness *Maharaja* Tashi Namgyal, 23rd March 1953, Clause 21.
3. *Ibid.,* Clause 14, p. 3.
4. *Ibid.,* Clause 20, p. 4.
5. *Ibid.,* Clause 26, p. 5.
6. Basnett, Lal Bahadur, (1974), *Sikkim- A short Political History,* S. Chand and Co. (Pvt.) Ltd. New Delhi, p. 105.
7. Rustumji, Nari K (1971), *Enchanted Frontiers*, Oxford University Press, p. 20.
8. Dhamala, Jay (1983), *Sikkim ko Itihas* (History of Sikkim) Shyam Prakashan Darjeeling, p. 82.
9. Parsai, Brihaspati (Unpublished Notes), Publicity Secretary, Sikkim State Congress.
10. Proclamation of His Highness *Maharaja* Tashi Namgyal, *Maharaja* of Sikkim, 23rd March 1953, Clause 16.
11. *Ibid.,* Clause 20, p. 4.
12. Dhamala, (1983) op cit, p. 82.
13. Cohelo, V.H, (1970), *Sikkim and Bhutan,* Indian Council for Cultural Relations, Vikash Publications, New Delhi, p. 31.
14. Basnett, (1974) op cit, p. 108.
15. Dhamala, (1983) op cit, p. 83.
16. Proclamation of His Highness, Sir Tashi Namgyal, KCSI, KCIE, *Maharaja* of Sikkim, 16th March 1958, Clause 2 (i) (b) p. 1.
17. The candidate securing the highest number of votes of the community which he represents will ordinarily be required to have secured also at least 15 per cent of the total votes of other community for which seats have been reserved to entitle him to return. If however, he fails to secure 15 per cent of the votes of other community, the candidate securing the next highest votes of their own community and who have also succeeded in securing 15 per cent of the votes of the other community will be eligible to be returned, provided the difference between the

number of votes of their own community secured by them and the highest candidate does not exceed 15 per cent of the total votes secured by the latter. If the difference is in excess of 15 per cent the latter will be regarded as returned, notwithstanding that he shall not have secured 15 per cent of the total votes of the other community.

18. *Kanchenjunga*, Gangtok, Vol. II, No.3 15th November 1958, p. 62.
19. *Kanchenjunga*, Gangtok, Vol. II, No.1 15th September 1958, p. 18.
20. Basnett, (1974) op cit, p. 110.
21. *Kanchenjunga*, Gangtok, Vol. II, No. 8, 15th April 1958 p. 125.
22. *Kanchenjunga*, Gangtok, Vol. II, No. 5 15th November 1959, p. 61.
23. Gauley Gopal (et. al.) (2002), *History of Democratic Movement*, Department of Information and public relations, Govt. of Sikkim, p. 33.
24. Basnett, (1974) op cit, p. 111.
25. *Kanchenjunga*, Gangtok, Vol. II, No. 5 15th November 1959, p. 63.
26. Proclamation of 7th June 1957 (Published in Nepali) by His Highness *Maharaja* of Sikkim Sir Tashi Namgyal, published by Sikkim *Durbar* Press Gangtok, Point No. 3.
27. Indo-Sikkim Treaty, 5th December 1950, Tsuklhakhang Royal Chapel, Article I-XIII.
28. Basnett (1974) op cit, p. 124.
29. Cooke Hope, (1980), *Time Change-An Autobiography*, Simon and Schuster, New York, p. 117.
30. Sikkim *Durbar* Gazette, Vol.XIV, No. 2, Date (unavailable)July 1964, Gangtok.
31. The Sikkim Panchayat Act 1965, Sikkim *Durbar* Gazette, Ex. No. 3, Dated 24-12-1965, Gangtok.
32. Circular '*Acquisition of Land-Payment of compensation in advance before occupation*', 1/LR (S) Dated 10-08-1970, Gangtok.
33. Tax Receipt of Rumtek Monastary Estate of year 1958, 1966, and 1967 paid in favour of Bhojraj and Jethmull Bank, Gangtok, collected from Mr. Passang Tshering Bhutia erstwhile *Mandal* of Namin village on 29th of January 2012.
34. Tax Receipt of Rumtek Monastary Estate of year 1958, 1966, and 1967 paid in favour of Bhojraj and Jethmull Bank, Gangtok, collected from Mr. Passang Tshering Bhutia erstwhile *Mandal* of Namin village on 29th of January 2012.
35. Tax Receipts of Late Ravilal Pyakurel of Tareythang Busty paid in favour of a Mandal Pahalman Rai in 1965-66.
36. *Sikkimey Janatako Ghoshnapatra* (A manifesto of Sikkimese people) a pamphlet published by Mr. Khada Nanda Upreti on 25th January 1978.
37. Basnett (1974) op cit, p. 151.

Chapter 11

Conclusion

The struggle between the State and the peasantry appears in many forms and it often ends up with anarchy and confusion. The lower stratum of society begin to resist when it found its interest insecure and retaliate the State by adopting a several forms of techniques generally termed as 'Peasants' Resistance'. It is the tacit and unproven social activities of the peasants against the manipulative mechanism by adopting acts of defiance. Their main intention for adopting such impish acts is just to keep themselves in a secured position or to shield them in against the recurrent pressures from their Lords. Similarly, the act of resistance emerges out of the protracted hidden transcripts and such transcripts of the subordinates may appear in various forms. Thus, the hidden and unexpressed feelings of the peasantry are usually loaded with emotions and are usually exposed to manifest their elongated and concealed feelings against the unjust mechanism. Such feelings of the subordinates typically exposes when they feel themselves victims of an unfair arrangement. It is a human tendency to defend him from the unnecessary encroachment or interference of the State. The Sikkimese peasants too had adopted various ways and means during the Colonial period to guard them against the redundant encroachments of the State in their daily affairs. In the battle of survival against hegemony, or what James C Scott refers as 'symbiosis of dependency and exploitation', the Sikkimese peasantry was always the looser and had been compelled to come ahead for compromises. Consequently, peasants' resistance in Sikkim was against the severe moral fibre of what we can consider as 'Sikkimese Feudalism'.

Akin to all others, Sikkimese feudalism too had its root in the process of land grants by the State. Owing to the unavailability of records it is uncertain to ascertain the existence of practice of land grants during pre-Namgyal days. The process of land grants through a *Sanad* was initiated by *Chogyal* Chakdor Namgyal and was continued by his successors till the advent of British. After the ascendancy of the Namgyals the process of land grants began to be considered as esteemed reward that resulted into the birth of many aristocratic families. The influence of such rewarded families was not only curbed within their estates but had also their importance in the State policies.

With the appointment of J.C. White, Sikkim began to experience feudalism in a modern way of interpretation. The colonial idea of ownership brought new changes in the region and the land of the State was given on contract to the '*Elakhadars*' then known as the '*Thikadars*' or Lessee holders. The Nepalese peasants were encouraged to get settled in the Kingdom and the lands of the lessee holders were divided among them. The status of the peasants in Sikkim was also defined accordingly. They were adjusted in these lessee estates scattered throughout the three districts namely East, West and South. North district of the Kingdom was for indigenous Lepcha and Bhutia peasants and the Nepali peasants were kept away from such areas. Further, land at the block level was distributed among some people who became intermediaries between the '*Kazis*' and the '*Raiyats*'. These intermediaries were called '*Bustiwallas*' and '*Mandals*' according to the amount of land they possessed. Such distribution of land allowed several layers of land ownership in Sikkim during early decades of twentieth century and most of the Sikkimese peasants, on the eve of the First World War, were either sharing croppers or the tenants of their '*Kazis*' and '*Thikadars*'. Amidst all other subdivisions, we can categorise them in two significant agrarian classes in the Kingdom of Sikkim: the '*Bustiwallas*', who owned lands and the '*Pakhureys*', who were landless. In the absence of any land record, it was in the whims and fancies of the '*Kazis*' and the '*Thikadars*' to allow a peasant to hold the land. They met woes and miseries at the hands of the officials like the '*Kazis*', '*Mandals*', '*Mukhtiyars*', and '*Karbaris*' who forced them to pay their taxes on time as well as they were also coerced to provide '*Kalo Bhari*', '*Jharlangi*', '*Theki Bethi*', '*Kuruwa*', '*Ghar Lauri*' as forced labourers. Many other unnamed labours had crippled the peasants of the Kingdom to live a scanty life. In addition, the rate of taxation in the Kingdom was excessively high, of which more than 75 per cent of the collected amount went to the private pockets of the '*Kazis*' and '*Thikadars*'. The greedy and gluttonous nature of the lessee holders, who were by any means determined to extract ₹ 6 as House Tax or *Dhurikhajana*, caused anxiety among peasant which gradually reached to the level of intolerance.

The ideas of peasant resistance in the former Himalayan Kingdom flourished with the anti-feudal sentiments can be normally observed as their hidden transcripts. The anger of peasantry and their resentment as a consequence of their humiliation, physical torture, abusive words used upon them by their masters had always forced them to dream for a better world to live in. Being bounded by the social and economic norms, they were forced to be obedient before their masters. During the interaction with their masters, or in some cases, with the officials of their masters, they usually gained hatred, antipathy, and revulsion against the set-up. Such incidents usually culminated in the form of mimicry or in abusive languages during the social gatherings. These acts of the Sikkimese peasantry ought to be regarded as an exhibition of their hidden transcripts against the '*Kazis*' and '*Thikadars*' who had made them to live a life under threats and menace. These offstage activities also involved the acts of cheating, hiding of the grains after harvest, false entry of the land to the concerned office etc. Such acts of defiance were amply practiced by the Sikkimese peasants as a measure to resist the State. Similarly, the hidden transcripts of the Sikkimese peasants were also manifested in the folk songs which were incredibly rational and fervently judicious. Those songs, highlighting the woes and cries of the peasants, had a deep impact upon the villagers to set up their minds against the daily feudal exploitation. With a motive to criticise their masters with a vociferous manner, the Sikkimese peasants had even devise a code language known as '*Palsi Kura*'.

Resistance against the unjust set up is a human behaviour hence; to get rid of harsh set up peasants seemed adamant to follow the dictums of feudalism. Though, in an individual or in a silent manner they objected the monopoly of the State by adopting various practices that includes migration, desertion, fleeing from the village, taking asylum in the British territories, etc. The peasants also offered resistance against the forced labours by sending a substitute in their place. In spite of obligations, a good number of peasants of Sikkim had shown their dissatisfaction through poaching, breaking of channels, ruining of ripen crops of the landlords, creating anonymous threats. Apart from these usual modes of resistance, the Nepali peasants of West Sikkim had devised a new method of safeguarding their interests by changing their caste and adopting the lifestyle of the Bhutias and the Lepchas. This style of peasant resistance is a unique and a new style adopted by the peasants of West Sikkim to counter the feudal oppression. When the level of suppression reached beyond toleration, few peasants openly began to challenge the hegemonic attitudes of the '*Kazis*' and other officials. Violent acts like the killing of a '*Kazi*' scion at Sirwani village of East Sikkim, open rebellion of a peasant of Assam Lingzey against his '*Mandal*', the beating of a '*Kazi*' by the peasants of Bara Pathing and the cases of Namin village where the officials were severely beaten up by their peasants, are few vicious reactions against the asymmetrical feudal set up. At this stage, it appears that, the peasants by now were getting impatient for the elimination of the corrupt and crooked system from their dwelling spheres.

In the everyday forms of resistance, all the struggles made by the peasant commune throughout the world have some basic objectives and among them the objective of bread and butter is the sole purpose of their exercise. Such acts of peasants or resisters, in a truer sense, definitely do not intend to make a revolution or to get pleasure from a colossal change in the administrative machinery. However, the basic element in converting an individual hidden transcript into a mass political movement in Sikkim was the transformation of mediocre thoughts into pervasive observation of the peasantry. When the peasants begin to feel that the class order in front of them is measly an allegory, they begin to get united and exhibited their rhapsody to uproot the unbalanced structure. For the transformation of their thoughts they had considerable grounds in their everyday affairs. The oppression from the above, cheating made upon them by their landlords, forced labours, unjust feudal practices and many other unnamed sketches of feudal hessian played vital role in changing the perception of a peasant. The provoking issues as discussed were in fact the embryos of political consciousness among the Sikkimese peasants.

The politically barren minds of the Sikkimese populace began to take sweeping curves after the foundation *Danthey* Party at Assangthang and Member Party by the youths of Namthang. The process of foundation of such associations continued and by 1946 Sikkim had three more such associations to counter the feudal pressure. It is evident that, their dream to come out of such stifled situation had gained impetus after the Indian independence. Subsequently, on 7th December 1947, all these associations decided to merge to form a political party known as Sikkim State Congress. Thus, after the Indian independence, the hidden transcript of Sikkimese peasantry was taking a shape of a full-fledged political conflict which was a political altercation against the injustice. The nature of the political conflict at this juncture, was direct and very much different than the earlier individually waged everyday form of resistance. The institutionalised politics is apposite and open and has a logical makeover whereas; everyday resistance is casual and related largely with instant and individual achievements. However, the sole objective of both the approaches in Sikkim appeared to accomplish their goals of protection. In this aspect, one can ascertain that, modes of everyday forms of peasant resistance in Sikkim were, in fact, the nucleus of the political ideas which would later precipitate into a political rebellion.

Shield inside the sanctuary of politics, Sikkimese peasantry began to bargain with the State in a full throated manner. The State too, could not act as a bystander and therefore, in February 1949, ruthless measures were adopted to nullify the "no rent" and "no tax" campaign initiated by Sikkim State Congress. The arrest of the leaders was culminated into a huge demonstration seeking the unconditional release of their leaders and for the establishment of a responsible government with a complete elimination of the feudal elements. Immediately after the agitation, on the advice of Political Officer, a council known as '*Popular Ministry*' was set up on 9th May 1949 as Tashi Tshering as Prime Minister. However, due to the absence of clearly defined powers the ministry got dissolved within 29 days of its formation. In lieu of the said ministry, the Government of India appointed John S. Lall as *Dewan* on 11th August 1949 and after prolonged negotiations, the House Tax of ₹ 6 commonly known as *Dhurikhajana* was reduced to ₹ 1. To incorporate the people's representatives for securing a better administration, an Advisory Committee with the *Dewan* as its President was formed.

The introduction of the *Dewani* system of administration marks the beginning of the politicisation of the peasants in the politics of Sikkim. As an outcome of the *Dewani*, it became obvious that political expansion and the establishment of a representative government headed by the peasant leaders in Sikkim had been put into cold storage. After the Indo-Sikkim Treaty of 1950, the *Dewan* was asked to clear up the way for the people's participation in the Government. Accordingly, in May 1951, the matter of Communal representation was discussed and adopted and came to be known as 'parity formula'. Under the supervision of Government of India, five elections for the Sikkim Council were held from 1953 to 1973. The uneven voting procedure, with varied complications in the process of voting and contesting elections, mounted dissatisfaction among the subjects. With the adoption of 'parity formula', a large section of the Nepali subjects were debarred from the process of voting due to their ethnic differences with the Bhutias and the Lepchas. The vagueness kept on escalating that eventually precipitated into a vibrant agitation.

Undoubtedly, a major transformation occurred in the daily lives of the peasantry when they began to get affiliated with Sikkim State Congress and experienced a new way of life yet; they were seriously lacking equality in socio-political sphere. It happened when the party meant to elevate their positions got indulge in pleasing the State. Still large sections of the people were debarred from possessing landed property and equal distribution of lands was merely a word of mouth. They were compelled to live with their hardships due to the lack of roads, communication, post and telegraph etc.

A major alteration on these social issues was the exigency of time and that were to be dealt by their elected representatives. Conversely, accustomed to the royal etiquettes, these representatives kept themselves engaged in pleasing the royal house than resolving the rural despondency. Even during the reign of Palden Thondup, a large number of the peasantry did not possess landed property and the political parties' had a silent approach in resolving the rural issues. Many unsolved political problems like Sikkim Subject Regulations, abolition of 'Parity System', Land reforms, elimination of private estates, eradication of nepotism, and the development of villages were reigning supreme among the rural lives. Such rural issues were overlooked both by the political parties and the State that deteriorated the lives of the villagers. Rather, the peasants were heavily exploited by the political parties and were equally deceived by the State to gain their real interests. Owing to such least bothered attitudes, the rural grievances multiplied and the political parties exploited this baffled situation of the peasantry in a fullest manner. Infused with Indian fascination the political parties once again used these peasants to go against the State that resulted in the agitation of 1973. The political parties made no efforts to eliminate the parity system until they had an amicable relation with the State. When their relationships with the State began to deteriorate, they became pro-peasants overnight and began to criticise the State fiercely. Their furious attitude provoked the rural lots in a wider manner and they supported their leaders against the State that eventually led Sikkim to be a part of the Indian Union.

Reference and Bibliography

Archival Sources

A. Administration Reports

1. Administration Report of the Sikkim State for 1909-10.
2. Administration Report of the Sikkim State for 1914- 15.
3. Administration Report of the Sikkim State for 1915-16.
4. Administration Report of the Sikkim State for 1916-17.
5. Administrative Report of the Sikkim State for 1917-1918.
6. Administration Report of the Sikkim State for 1919-1920.
7. Administration Report of the Sikkim State for 1920-21.
8. Administration Report of the Sikkim State for 1925-26.
9. Administration Report of the Sikkim State for 1926-27.
10. Administration Report of the Sikkim State for 1930-31.
11. Administrative Report of the Sikkim State for the year 1931-32.

B. Letters of Appointment, Petition and Correspondence

1. A request made by *Spyi dpon* (General Officer of Chumbi) *lTum langs rgad po* (Regional Head of lTum langs and the rgad po Nyin ltos zhang phyug to the Sikkim Government in 1796. PD/1.1/004, Namgyal Institute of Tibetology.
2. Appointment letter issued in1932 of a *Mukhtiyar* by Rai Saheb Durga Sumsher Pradhan of Rhenock, East Sikkim preserved at Ramgauri Sangrahalaya Rhenock.
3. Appointment letter of *Karbari* issued in 1931 by Rai Saheb Durga Sumsher Pradhan of Rhenock, preserved at Ram Gauri Sangrahalaya Rhenock East Sikkim.
4. Complaint Letter of the People of Lachung to the Government Officials about the visit of Dr Hooker and Campbell, PD/3.1/004, Namgyal Institute of Tibetology.

5. Complaints of the Raiyats of Sikkim, Land Revenue Department, Dated 21st January 1911, Sikkim State Archives, File No. 37, Gangtok.
6. Correspondence between Sikkim and Tibet regarding the Anglo-Sikkimese conflict of 1889-90, PD/7.3/005, Namgyal Institute of Tibetology.
7. Letter from Sikkim Government to the Sikkimese representative in Year 1871, PD/1.3/008, Namgyal Institute of Tibetology.
8. Letter from *Chogyal* Tsugphud Namgyal to the Tibetan Government, Year 1832 PD/4.2/013, Namgyal Institute of Tibetology.
9. Petition of Sikkim National Party to the Maharaja of Sikkim Sir Tashi Namgyal 1948.
10. Draft Copy of the demands forwarded by the Sikkim State Congress to the Maharaja of Sikkim on 9th of December 1947.
11. Hand written petition of Durga Samsher Pradhan of Rhenock to His Highness Maharaj Kumar of Sikkim P.T Namgyal 24th Nov 1946 for the abolition of *Jharlangi*.
12. Letter from *Chogyal* Thotub Namgyal to the Lt. Governor of Bengal John Woodburn Year 1901, PD/7.4/003, Namgyal Institute of Tibetology.
13. Letter from *Chogyal* Thotub Namgyal to the Secretary to the Lt. Governor of Bengal J.W. Edgar Year 1887, PD/7.3/002, Namgyal Institute of Tibetology.
14. Letter from Edgar to the Sikkimese Year 1887,PD/7.3/003, Namgyal Institute of Tibetology.
15. Letter from Sidkeong Namgyal to the Tibetan Government, PD/3.2/017, Namgyal Institute of Tibetology.
16. Letter from Sikkim *Chogyal* to the Superintendent of Darjeeling Year 1887, PD/7.2/029, Namgyal Institute of Tibetology.
17. Letter from Sikkim *Chogyal* to the Superintendent of Darjeeling, Year 1887, PD/7.2/030, Namgyal Institute of Tibetology.
18. Letter from the *Maharaja* of Nepal to the Kotapas with a grant of an area or *Mana-Chamal*, Year *Vikram Samvat* 1884 (1827AD).
19. Letter from the people of Tibet to the Sikkimese Summer Palace in Chumbi, Year 1831, PD/4.2/007 Namgyal Institute of Tibetology.
20. Letter from the Queen and Prince of Sikkim to the *Chogyal* and Tibetan Government, Year 1890, PD/7.3/006, Namgyal Institute of Tibetology, Deorali, Gangtok.

21. Letter from the Sikkimese Government to the British Officials in Darjeeling, year 1843, PD/7.1/008, Namgyal Institute of Tibetology.
22. Letter from Tsugphud Namgyal to a Tibetan Official (Date Unknown), PD/6.6/015, Namgyal Institute of Tibetology, Deorali, Gangtok.
23. Letter from Tsugphud Namgyal to Lt. Governor of Bengal John Woodburn dated 20th day of 9th month of Iron Ox year (1901 AD), PD/7.4/003, Namgyal Institute of Tibetology.
24. Letter of a Sikkimese Minister to the *Chogyal* Year 1880, PD/9.5/075, Namgyal Institute of Tibetology.
25. Letter of Chinese Amban to the Sikkimese General, Year 1792, PD/6.1/004, Namgyal Institute of Tibetology.
26. Letter of Dr Campbell, date pre 1849, PD/3.3/002, Namgyal Institute of Tibetology.
27. Letter of General Secretary to His Highness Maharaja of Sikkim to the Political Officer for the exemption of *Jharlangi* to Panchdal Rai of Assam Lingzey Dated 11th September 1942, Memo No. 1892/1893 G.
28. Letter of Lepcha Kazi of Ilam to Maj.Gen. Janga Bahadur Rana the Prime Minister of Nepal, Dated Maguh 9th 1921 Vikram Samvat (23rd January 1870 AD). Miss Jennifer Bentley, NIT Complex, Gangtok.
29. Letter of *Maharaja* Sidkeong Namgyal to the *Zam gdong rdzong dpon*, Year 1863, PD/1.1.022, Namgyal Institute of Tibetology.
30. Letter of Sikkim *Maharaja* (Name and Date unknown) to one Nathaniel Smith *aka Rangapore Sahib* asking for his well being. Namgyal Institute of Tibetology.
31. Letter of the *Chogyal* Tsugphud Namgyal to Panchen Lama, Year 1831, PD/4.2/005, Namgyal Institute of Tibetology.
32. Letter of the Sikkim Government to the Tibetan Government, Year 1830's PD/4.2/017, Namgyal Institute of Tibetology.
33. Letter of the Sikkimese Court to the East India Company Calcutta, year early 19th Century, PD/7.1/001, Namgyal Institute of Tibetology.
34. Letter to Sidkeong Namgyal from Panchen Lama dated 1909-1913,PD/6.2/003, Namgyal Institute of Tibetology.
35. Letter to the Governor General in Calcutta from Tsugphud Namgyal Date 1815-1816, PD/9.5/009/Sec/(b), Namgyal Institute of Tibetology.

36. Letter to the Secretary of the Lt. Governor of Bengal regarding empowerment of administrative power of Sikkim to Phodang Lama and Khangsa Dewan, Year 1887. PD/7.2/030, Namgyal Institute of Tibetology.
37. Letter to the Sikkimese *Chogyal* from Chinese Officials Year 1816, PD/7.1/003, Namgyal Institute of Tibetology.
38. Letter to the Superintendent of Darjeeling from the Sikkim *Chogyal*, Year 1885, PD/7.4/006 (a), Namgyal Institute of Tibetology.
39. Petition from the people of Gro gzhi to the Summer Palace in Chumbi, Year 1831, PD/4.2/004 Namgyal Institute of Tibetology.
40. Petition of *Chogyal* Tsugphud Namgyal to the Tibetan Government, Year 1829, PD/4.2/003, Namgyal Institute of Tibetology, Deorali, Gangtok.

C. Tax Receipts and Land related Documents

1. A receipt of *Dhurikhajana* of ₹ 6 paid to the Mandal Dhanapati Upadhyay by the Late Ravilal Pyakurel of Tareythang Busty East Sikkim, Mr Krishna Prasad Pyakurel of Tareythang, East Sikkim.
2. *bcu dpon gi lag 'dzin* a document issuing the sub village leader (bcu dpon) to have control over the tax collection of a number of families in his region, PD/1.1/045, Namgyal Institute of Tibetology.
3. *Da lad Tsong bha ra khel kyi lag khyer* Notification issued to the entire *blon po, rdzong sde pa* and other officials of Sikkim in 1779, PD/1.1/002, Namgyal Institute of Tibetology.
4. Document related to the Nepali Settlement in Sikkim, PD/9.5/041, Namgyal Institute of Tibetology.
5. Family Papers related to land and taxation of Harka Bahadur Limboo *aka* Khukurey Bajey, Ravilal Pyakurel, Chandra Bahadur Basnett, Phur Tshering Lepcha, Passang Tshering Bhutia, and Singh Bir Subba *aka* Phalaichey *Bajey*.
6. Land Grant made to Karma Dargey and Debasang Ringzing, PD/1.2/003, Year of origin 1796, Namgyal Institute of Tibetology.
7. Land Tax receipts collected from Harka Bahadur Limboo *aka* Khukurey Bajey.
8. Land Tax receipts of Ravilal Pyakurel of Tareythang Busty, East Sikkim.
9. List of Tax payers under Ilam rDzong, PD/3.3/001, Namgyal Institute of Tibetology, Deorali, Gangtok.

10. Receipts of *Dhuri Khazana* (House Tax) paid by various people.
11. Tax Receipt maintained by the rTa Sa (village official) of Morang (Nepal), of the year 1819. PD/1.1/001 Namgyal Institute of Tibetology.
12. Tax Receipt of Rumtek Monastary Estate of year 1958, 1966 and 1967 paid in favour of Bhojraj and Jethmull Bank, Gangtok, Mr Passang Tshering Bhutia erstwhile *Mandal* of Namin village, East Sikkim.

D. Resolution, Proceeding and Speeches

1. Resolution of Sikkim National Party to the Maharaja of Sikkim Sir Tashi Namgyal 1948.
2. Resolution Dated 10th April 1975 passed by the Sikkim Assembly.
3. Copy of the Proceedings of the Sikkim Assembly, Extract of the *Chogyal*'s inaugural speech to the Sikkim Assembly on 10th May 1974.
4. Copy of the Proceedings of the Sikkim Assembly, Friday June 28th 1974, from the archival collection of Mr Biraj Adhikari, President Sikkim National Peoples' Party.
5. Copy of the Resolution passed by the Joint Meeting of Sikkim State Congress and Sikkim National Congress on 9th August 1960 at Rangpo.
6. Copy of the Resolution passed by the Joint Meeting of Sikkim State Congress and Sikkim National Congress on 9th August 1960 at Rangpo.
7. Coronation Speech of H.H. Palden Thondup Namgyal, published in Nepali by Publicity Department Government of Sikkim, Gangtok April 1965.
8. Cyclostyle copy of the Special Poll ballot paper issued by Government of Sikkim with the resolution of 10th May 1975, for the referendum conducted on 14th April 1975.
9. Membership Card of Sikkim State Congress issued in 1948 to Harka Bahadur Subba aka Khukuri Bajey.
10. Report of the Fourth Annual Session of Sikkim State Congress.
11. *Sikkim State Congress ko Vidhan* (Constitution of Sikkim State Congress).

E. Circular, Notification and Decrees

1. Acquisition of Land-Payment of compensation in advance before occupation, Circular No. 1/LR (S) Dated 10-08-1970, Gangtok.

2. Blank Forms with direction of Sikkim Subject 1961 issued by Home Department.
3. Lessee form with Terms and conditions issued to the lessees by Sikkim Durbar in 1931.
4. Circular No.1, circulated in Nepali language from the Office of Mr C.A. Bell, Political Officer Sikkim, Gangtok 20th April 1916.
5. General Department Circular No. 5814/G entitled to all the landlords of Sikkim State, Dated 15th July 1924.
6. General Department Notification No. 8146-08/G dated the 19th June 1926.
7. General Department, Circular No. 8545/G, Gangtok, Dated 16th October 1924.
8. Notice of M.P. Pradhan, Land Revenue Secretary to the District Officer Gangtok, L and R Department, Government of Sikkim No. 620/B Dated 30th March 1968, Gangtok.
9. Revenue Order No.1, Central Department, dated the 17th of May 1917.
10. Notification dated 2nd of January 1897 from the Office of the Political Officer.
11. General Department Notification No. 8146-08/G dated the 19th June 1926.
12. Government of Sikkim, Education and Transport Department Notification No. 600-780/E.T Dated 23rd June 1948 circulated in English, Tibetan and Nepali languages.
13. Government of Sikkim, Education and Transport Department, Notification No. 2035-780/E.T Dated 15th February 1949, circulated in English, Tibetan and Nepali languages.
14. Government of Sikkim, Judicial Branch, Notification No. 3054-254/PS, Dated 24th January 1948 Gangtok.
15. Government of Sikkim, Land Revenue and Forest Department, Notification No. 3254-753/G, Dated 20th September 1947.
16. Government of Sikkim, Land Revenue and Forest Department, Notification No. 433-633/L and F, Dated 8th April 1948.
17. Home Department Notification No. 1156/H Sikkim Durbar Gazette (Extraordinary) No.10, Gangtok, Dated 22nd December 1966.
18. Home Department, Notification No. 374/H Dated 30th May 1967, Sikkim Durbar Gazette (Extraordinary) No. 20, Gangtok.

19. *Luga Paune* Ration Card issued to Late Ravilal Pyakurel of Tareythang Busty East Sikkim on 16th March 1948 by the Textile Commissioner Government of Sikkim.

20. Notice for the abolition of Kuruwa Date of publication 31 January 1947. Document preserved at Ram Gauri Sangrahalaya Rhenock East Sikkim.

21. Notice from the Secretary of Land Revenue Department to the District Officers of East, South and West Sikkim, Dated 25th May 1966.

22. Notice from the office of His Highness Maharaja of Sikkim, Notification No. 318, dated 17th October 1950 Gangtok.

23. Notice from the Office of the Dewan, Sikkim State, The Terracing Ordinance 1949, Gangtok Dated 23rd November 1949.

24. Notice issued on 18th December 1945 by Mandal Brihaspati Upadhyay to Ravilal Pyakurel of Tareythang village, East Sikkim.

25. Notice of J.S. Lall, Dewan Sikkim State, issued in 1950 related to power and functions of the Panchayats in Sikkim.

26. Notice to the monks and public of Lachen and Lachung by the *Chogyal* PD/3.1/007, Namgyal Institute of Tibetology.

27. Notification No. 1158/H, Dated 12th October 1962, Sikkim Durbar Gazette.

28. Notification No. 1208/L and R, Part I, Sikkim Durbar Gazette, Vol. I, No. IV, 17th September 1951.

29. Notification No. 1858/L and R, Part II, Sikkim Durbar Gazette, Vol. IV, No. 8, Gangtok 10th January 1955.

30. Notification No. 988/LR, Gangtok 28th July 1958, Part III, Sikkim Durbar Gazette.

31. Order No.11 From the office of the Dewan J.S. Lal, Subject: Collection of Khazana from the Lessees, Dated August 30th 1949, Gangtok.

32. Royal Decree from Bangdutse Palace Year 1880, PD/1.7/002, Namgyal Institute of Tibetology.

33. Royal Order giving Royal authority to Sidkeong Namgyal by his father Chogyal Tsugphud Namgyal Year 1861, PD/1.2/010, Namgyal Institute of Tibetology.

34. Sikkim State General Department Notification No. 3590-4089/G, Ramgauri Sangrahalaya Rhenock.

35. Sikkim State General Department, Notification No. 4816/G(M) dated 31st January 1947.
36. Sikkim State General Department, Notification No. 5186-085/G, Gangtok 3rd January 1948.
37. Sikkim State, Forest Department, Notification No. 5093/F, Gangtok Dated 13th September 1948.
38. Sikkim State, Office of the Dewan, Order No. 4, Revenue Administration, Dated 19th August 1949, Gangtok.
39. Sikkim Subjects Regulation 1961 issued by the Home Department Notification No. 156/S-61.

F. Proclamation, Acts, and Royal Orders

1. Elections Proclamation of 1970 of the *Chogyal* of Sikkim Dated 31st December 1969 (Nepali Translation of English Proclamation).
2. Gangtok Rent Control and Eviction Act 1956, Sikkim Durbar Gazette June 1956.
3. Legal Code of Government of Sikkim Year 1876, PD/9.5/027, Namgyal Institute of Tibetology.
4. Proclamation of H.H. Maharaja Sir Tashi Namgyal dated 7th June 1957 printed in Nepali.
5. Proclamation of His Highness Maharaja Tashi Namgyal, Maharaja of Sikkim, Dated 28th December 1952.
6. Proclamation of His Highness Sir Tashi Namgyal, Maharaja of Sikkim, Dated 23rd March 1953.
7. Proclamation of the *Chogyal* Palden Thondup Namgyal, Sikkim Darbar Gazette No. 09 (Extraordinary) Gangtok 21st December 1966.
8. Rules for advance of loans for agricultural and animal husbandry development, Sikkim Durbar Gazette, Vol. XIV. No. 2, Date (unavailable) July 1964, Gangtok.
9. Sikkim Durbar Gazette (Extraordinary) Proclamation of His Highness Maharaja Tashi Namgyal, Maharaja of Sikkim, Dated 23rd March 1953.
10. Sikkim Durbar Gazette (Extraordinary) proclamation of His Highness, Sir Tashi Namgyal, KCSI, KCIE, Maharaja of Sikkim, Dated 16th March 1958, Gangtok.
11. Sikkim Durbar Gazette (Extraordinary) Proclamation of His Highness, Sir Tashi Namgyal, KCSI, KCIE, Maharaja of Sikkim,

Dated, 4th September 1959, Published by the Manager, Sikkim Durbar Press, Gangtok.

12. Sikkim Durbar Gazette (Extraordinary) Vol. XIX No.19 Proclamation of *Chogyal* Palden Thondup Namgyal on the Laws relating to the election and composition of the Sikkim Council, Gangtok, Dated 31st December 1969.
13. Sikkim Durbar Gazette Vol. XVIII, No.11, notification No. 28/ L.R., Dated 21st April 1969, Gangtok.
14. The Sikkim Panchayat Act 1965, Sikkim Durbar Gazette, Ex. No. 3, Dated 24-12-1965, Gangtok.

G. Pamphlet and Newspapers

1. Tshering Tashi 'A few facts about Sikkim State 1947.
2. Gray, Francine Du Plessix, '*The Fairy Tale that turned Nightmare?*' New York Times, March 8th 1981 Source: www.nytimes.com/ 1981/03/08 Date of Access: 21 September 2011.
3. Himalayan Observer, Saturday, Kalimpong, Vol. 52, 27th December 1969.
4. *Kanchenjunga* Nepali fortnightly Journal, Gangtok, Vol. 6, No. 9, 15th January 1966.
5. *Kanchenjunga* Nepali fortnightly Journal, Gangtok, Vol. 6, No. 2-3-4, 15th September 1966.
6. *Kanchenjunga* Nepali fortnightly Journal, Gangtok, Vol. 7, No. 2/ 3 1st October 1966.
7. *Kanchenjunga* Nepali fortnightly Journal, Gangtok, Vol. 7, No. 9, 1st January 1967.
8. *Kanchenjunga* Nepali fortnightly Journal, Gangtok, Vol. 7, No. 7/ 8, 15th December 1966.
9. *Kanchenjunga*, Nepali fortnightly Journal, Gangtok, Vol. 6, No. 26, 15th November 1965.
10. *Kanchenjunga*, Nepali fortnightly Journal, Gangtok, Vol. II, No. 1, 15th September 1958.
11. *Kanchenjunga*, Nepali fortnightly Journal, Gangtok, Vol. II, No. 3, 15th November 1958.
12. *Kanchenjunga*, Nepali fortnightly Journal, Gangtok, Vol. I, No. 3, 15th December 1957.
13. *Kanchenjunga*, Nepali fortnightly Journal, Gangtok, Vol. II, No. 8, 15th April 1958.

14. *Kanchenjunga*, Nepali fortnightly Journal, Gangtok, Vol. III, No. 23, 1st August 1963.
15. *Kanchenjunga*, Nepali fortnightly Journal, Gangtok, Vol. IV, No. 2, 15th September 1963.
16. *Kanchenjunga*, Nepali fortnightly Journal, Gangtok, Vol. II, No. 5, 15th November 1959.
17. *Kanchenjunga*, Nepali fortnightly Journal,Gangtok, Vol. I, No. 3, 15th November 1957.
18. New York Times, '*The Fairy Tale that turned Nightmare?*' March 8th 1981.
19. Reproduced Copy of Peking Review dated 29th April 1975.
20. Sharma, Sudheer, '*The Pain of Loosing a Nation*', Nepal News (Weekly) published on 11th September 2007- 18th September 2007, Kathmandu, Nepal.
21. Sikkim (Gangtok, Fortnightly) Vol. IV, No. 19, March 11th 1970.
22. '*Sikkim at the Crossroads*', Sikkim National Congress Bulletin No. 2/1972, 26th January 1972.
23. Sikkim Herald, Dated 3rd October 1972, published by the Publicity Department, Government of Sikkim, Gangtok.
24. Sikkim Herald, Gangtok, Vol. 9, No. 61, Tuesday May 7th 1968.
25. Sikkim Herald, Vol. 8, No. 41, July 28th 1967.
26. SIKKIM: Fairy Tale's End, Times Magazine, Monday 5th May 1975. *Source:* www.time.com/time/magazine/article Date of access: 21 September 2011.
27. *Sikkimey Janatako Ghoshnapatra* (A manifesto of Sikkimese people) pamphlet published by Mr Khada Nanda Upreti (Former Education Minister, Govt. of Sikkim) on 28th January 1978, Document collected from Mr Khada Nanda Upreti on 25th January 2014.
28. *Sikkim Today*, April-June 2006, Vol. VI, No. 2, Department of IPR, Govt. of Sikkim, Gangtok.
29. *Sikkimka Pyara Daju Bhai tatha Didi Bahiniharulai Apil* (An appeal to all the beloved Sikkimese brothers and Sisters) a pamphlet jointly issued by Sikkim National Congress and Sikkim Janata Congress on 1 April 1973, printed at Himalayan Observer Press Kalimpong.
30. Sinha, A.C., "*Sikkim of Yesterday*", The Sikkim Times, Gangtok, Saturday June 9th, 2007.

31. The Age, Tuesday, October 3, 1967. *Source:* http://news.google.com
32. The Himalayan Observer, Editorial, Kalimpong, 19th September 1967.
33. Time Magazine '*Sikkim: Hope-La in Gangtok*', Friday April 16th 1965. *Source:* www.time.com/time/magazine /article Date of access: 21st September 2011.
34. India Today online '*Sikkim world's number 1 place to visit in 2014, says Lonely Planet*' New Delhi, October 29, 2013 Date of access 17th December 2013.

Secondary Sources (Books, Articles and Journals)

1. Agarwal, Ajay B. (2003), *India, Tibet and China, The Role Nehru Played*, N.A. Books International, Mumbai.
2. Alley Santosh (2003), *Magar Jati ko Itihaas ani Sanskriti Sikkim ko sandharbha ma* (History and Culture of the Magars in Sikkim) Darpan Publications, Darjeeling.
3. Amin, Sahid, et al., (et al 1996), *Writings on South Asian History and Society*, Oxford University Press, New Delhi
4. Armstead L. Robinson, *Bitter fruits of bondage: Slavery's demise and the collapse of the confederacy: 1861-65*, Yale University Press.
5. Arnold David, (et al., 1994), *Subaltern Studies VIII Essays in Honour of Ranajit Guha*, Oxford University Press, New Delhi.
6. Ashcroft, Bill (ed) (1995, Second Edition), *The Post-Colonial Studies Reader*, Routledge, London.
7. Balikci Anna (2008), *Lamas, Shamans and Ancestors-Village Religion in Sikkim*, Brill, Leiden, Netherlands.
8. Basnett, Lall Bahadur (1974), *Sikkim- A short political History*, S. Chand & Co. Private Limited, New Delhi.
9. Bhadra Gautam, Prakash Gyan, Tharu Susie (Eds1999), *Writings on South Asian History and Society*, Oxford University Press, New Delhi.
10. Bhadra, Madhumita (First Published 1992), *Sikkim: Democracy and Social Change*, Minerva Associates (publication) Private Limited, Calcutta, India.
11. Bhanja, K. C (1993 Re-print), *History of Darjeeling and the Sikkim Himalaya*, Gyan Publishing House, New Delhi.
12. Bhattacharya, Pranab Kumar (1984), *Aspect of cultural History of Sikkim-Studies in coinage*, K.P. Bagniet of Company, New Delhi.

13. Britton, Celia (1999), *Edouard Glissant and Postcolonial Theory: Strategies of Language and Resistance New World Studies*, University of Virginia Press.
14. Bulger, George E. Major, (1869), *Notes of a tour from Bangalore to Calcutta thence to Delhi and subsequently to British Sikkim during the early part of 1867*, Regimental Press Secundarabad.
15. Campbell, A. Dr '*Diary of a Journey through Sikkim to the Frontiers of Thibet- By Dr A. Campbell, Superintendent of Darjeeling- with a Map*' Journals of Asiatic Society of Bengal (1852), (pub 1883) Edited by the Secretaries, Vol. XXI, No. I-VII, Baptist Mission Press, Calcutta.
16. Captain Iggulden, H.A, *The 2nd Battalion Derbyshire Regiment in the Sikkim Expedition of 1888* (1900) Swan Sonnenschein & Co. LIM, Paternoster Square, London.
17. Captain, O'Conner, W.F. (1900), *Routes in Sikkim* Office of the Superintendent of Government Printing, Calcutta, India.
18. Chatterjee Partha, (et al., 1992), *Subaltern Studies VII Writings on South Asian History and Society*, Oxford University Press, New Delhi.
19. Chaube, S. K. (ed. 1985), *The Himalayan profiles of modernisation, and adaptation*, Sterling Publishers Private Limited, New Delhi, India.
20. Chemjong, Iman Singh (2nd Publication 2003), *Kirat Kalin Bijayapur ko sanchipta Itihas*, Kanchan Printing Press, Bagh Bazar, Kathmandu.
21. Chemjong, Iman Singh (3rd Edition, 1982), *Kirat Itihaas*, (History of the Kiratas) Prakash Printing Press, Vishwanath Gali, Banaras.
22. Chemjong, Iman Singh (4th edn. 2003), *History and Culture of Kirat People*, Kanchan Printing Press, Bagh Bazar, Kathmandu.
23. Chopra, P.N. (1979), *Sikkim*, S. Chand and Company, New Delhi.
24. Cohelo, V.H. (1970), *Sikkim and Bhutan,* Indian Council for Cultural Relations, Vikash Publications, New Delhi.
25. Cooke Hope (1980), *Time Change, An Autobiography*, Simon and Schuster, New York, USA.
26. Dahal, Dharnidhar, (1984), *Sikkim ko Rajnaitik Itihas* (Political History of Sikkim), Subha Prakashan, Gangtok.
27. Dahal, Dharnidhar (1998), *Sikkim ko Rajnaitik Itihas Part II* (Political History of Sikkim) Nirman Publication, Namchi.

28. Das Gupta Manas, (first published 1992), *Sikkim- Problems, and Prospects of Development*, Indus Publishing Company, New Delhi.
29. Das, B. S. (First Published 1983, re-print 1996), *The Sikkim Saga*, Vikash Publishing House, New Delhi.
30. Das, Sarat Chandra (Reprint 1970), *Journey to Lhasa and Central Tibet.*
31. Datta, Amal, '*Ethnicity and resource management*' (Sikkim through Periodical articles, reprints, seminar etc.) (Vol. 3 A665-945) North Bengal University.
32. Datta, Amal, (first edition 1991), *Sikkim since Independence*, Mittal Publications, New Delhi.
33. Dewan, Dick B. (2012), *Education in Sikkim, An Historical Retrospect Pre-merger and Post-merger Period*, Published by Society for the Procurement and sales of books, Darjeeling.
34. Dhamala, Jai, (1983), *Sikkim Ko Itihas* (History of Sikkim), Darjeeling, Shyam Prakashan.
35. Dhamala, Ranju Rani, '*Panchayati Raj institution in Sikkim as an instrument of Document*', (Seminar on problems and strategies of Development in the Eastern Himalayas, March 18-19, 1988).
36. Dhar, Maloy Krishna (2005), *Open secrets India's Intelligence Unveiled*, Manas Publications, New Delhi.
37. Dhar, Molay Krishna, '*If not for him, Sikkim would not be a part of India',* Rediff News, Published on 2nd August 2007.
38. Edgar, J. Ware (Re-print2005), *Report on a visit to Sikhim and the Tibetan Frontier*, Pilgrims Publishing Pvt. Ltd, Varanasi.
39. Gaunley Gopal and "priyadarshi" S. Chettri (First published 2002), *History of Democratic Movement*, Department of Information and Public Relations, Govt. of Sikkim.
40. Gorer, Geoffrey (First Published 1938 Reprint 2005), *Himalayan Village- An Account of the Lepchas of Sikkim*, Pilgrims Publishing, Varanasi.
41. Goyal, Narendra (1966)*, Political History of Himalayan States-Tibet, Nepal, Bhutan, Sikkim, Nagaland since 1947*, Cambridge Book and Stationary store, New Delhi.
42. Grover, B.S.K (first edition 1974), *Sikkim and India storm and consolidation*, Jain Brothers, New Delhi.
43. Guha, Ranajit (1999), *Elementry Aspects of Peasants Insurgency in Colonial India*, Duke University Press, Durham.

44. Guha, Ranajit (Ed 1982), Subaltern Studies I *Writings on South Asian History and Society*, Oxford University Press, New Delhi.
45. Guha, Ranajit (Ed 1983), Subaltern Studies II *Writings on South Asian History and Society*, Oxford University Press, New Delhi.
46. Guha, Ranajit (Ed 1984), Subaltern Studies III *Writings on South Asian History and Society,* Oxford University Press, New Delhi.
47. Guha, Ranajit (Ed 1985), Subaltern Studies IV *Writings on South Asian History and Society*, Oxford University Press, New Delhi.
48. Guha, Ranajit (Ed 1987), Subaltern Studies V *Writings on South Asian History and Society*, Oxford University Press, New Delhi.
49. Guha, Ranajit (Ed 1989), Subaltern Studies VI *Writings on South Asian History and Society*, Oxford University Press, New Delhi.
50. Gulati, M.N. Col. (2003), *Tibetan wars through Sikkim, Bhutan and Nepal*, Manas Publication, New Delhi.
51. Gupta, Ranjan, '*Sikkim-The Merger with India*' Asian Survey, Vol.15, No. 9, September 1975.
52. Hamilton, Francis Buchanan (first published 1819 reprint 1971), *An Account of Kingdom of Nepal*, Manjusri publishing house, New Delhi, Bibliothica Himalayica.
53. Harris, Richard Colebrook (1966), *The Seigneurial System in Early Canada. A Geographical Study.* Madison: University of Wisconsin Press.
54. Hasrat, Bikramajit (1970), *History of Nepal as told by its own and contemporary chroniclers*, V.V. Research Institute Press, Hoshiarpur, Punjab, India.
55. Hiltz, Jackie, '*Constructing Sikkimese National Identity in the 1960's and 1970's*' Tibetology Bulletin, Gangtok.
56. Hooker, Joseph Dalton (1854), *Himalayan Journals or notes of a Naturalist in Bengal, The Sikkim and Nepal Himalayas, The Khasi Mountains etc*, Vol. I
57. Jha, Pranab Kumar, *History of Sikkim (1817-1904) Analysis of British Policy and Activities*, OPS Publishers Private Ltd. Calcutta.
58. Jha, Raj Kumar, *The Himalayan Kingdoms in Indian Foreign Policy*, Maitryee Publications, Ranchi.
59. Jha, S.K. and Mishra S.N. (1984), *Sikkim Government and Politics*, Ess Ess Publication, New Delhi.
60. Joshi, H.G. (2004), *Sikkim Past and Present*, Mittal Publication, New Delhi.

61. Karan and Jenkins (1963), *The Himalayan Kingdoms-Bhutan Sikkim and Nepal*, D. Van Nostrand Company INC, New Jersey.

62. Kazi, Jigme N. (1994), *Inside Sikkim- Against the Tide*, Hill Media Publication, Gangtok.

63. Kazi, Jigme N. (January 2009), *Sikkim for Sikkimese Distinct Identity within the Union*, Hill Media Publications, Gangtok.

64. Kotturan, George (1983), *The Himalayan Gateway: History and culture of Sikkim*, Sterling Publication, New Delhi.

65. Lall, J.S. (1981), *The Himalaya Aspects of Change*, India International Centre, New Delhi.

66. Lama, Mahendra P, (2001), *Sikkim Human Development Report*, Published by Esha Beteille, Social Science Press, 69 Jor Bagh, New Delhi.

67. Lama, Mahendra P, (et al. 2004), *Sikkim Study Series*, Vol. I, Department of IPR, Govt. of Sikkim, Gangtok.

68. Lepcha, Nayan Tshering, '*Sikkim Ek Khoj*'(15th November 1965) (Sikkim a Search) Vol. 6 No. 26, *Kanchenjunga*, Nepali fortnight Journal, Gangtok.

69. Lepcha, Sonam Rinchen (2002), *The Wealth of Sikkim*, Mayel Muluk House of Treasure and Citi News, Gangtok.

70. Lesdain, Count De (1908), *From Pekin to Sikkim through the Ordos, the Gobi Desert and Tibet*, John Murray, Albemarle Street, London.

71. Li, Huaiyin (2006), '*The First Encounter: Peasant Resistance to State control of Grain in East China in the Mid-1950*' The China Quarterly.

72. Ling,Trevor- '*Max Weber and the relation of religions to social change, some considerations of Sikkim and Nepal*' (Sikkim through periodical articles, reprints seminars proceedings etc.) Vol.1. A102-339) North Bengal University.

73. Macaulay, Colman (first published 1884 reprint 1977), *Reports of a Mission to Sikkim,* Ratna Pustak Bhandar, Kathmandu, Nepal.

74. Maiti, Provatansu, (1997), *A History of Europe,* 9th Edition, Shreedhar Prakashani, Calcutta.

75. Major Bulger, George, E. (1869), *Notes of a Tour from Bangalore to Calcutta thence to Delhi and Subsequently to British Sikkim during Early Part of 1867*, Regimental Press, Secundarabad, India.

76. Mark McNally and John Schwarzmantel (First published 2009 by Routledge), *Gramsci and Global Politics-Hegemony and Resistance*, Milton Park, Abingdon, Oxon.
77. Markham, Clement R, (1896), *Narratives of the Mission of George Bogle to Tibet, Journey of Thomas Manning to Lhasa*, Trubner & Co. Lud Gate Hills, London.
78. Moktan, R. (first edition 2004), *Sikkim: Darjeeling compendium of Documents* printed by Gopal press, Varanasi, India.
79. Morris, Major C.J. (first published 1933, re- print 1993), *The Gurkhas- an Ethnology*, Low Price Publications, New Delhi.
80. Mukherjee, Mridula '*Peasant Resistance and peasant consciousness in Colonial India Subalterns and Beyond*', Economic and Political Weekly, Oct 8, 1988.
81. Mullard Saul and Wongchuk Hissey (ed) (2010), *A Catalogue of Sikkimese Palace Archive, International Institute of Tibetan and Buddhist Studies*, GmbH, Andiast.
82. Mullard, Saul (2011), *Opening of Hidden Land, State Formation and the Construction of Sikkimese History*, Leiden, The Netherlands.
83. Namgyal, Hope, '*The Sikkimese theory of landholding and the Darjeeling Grant*' Bulletin of Tibetology, Vol. III, No. 2 Dated 21st July 1966, Namgyal Institute of Tibetology, Gangtok.
84. Neel, Alexandra David (1931), *With Mystics and Magicians in Tibet*, Penguin Books, London.
85. O' Malley, L.S.S (First published 1907 re- print 1985 2nd reprint 1999), *Bengal District Gazetteer*, Logos press, New Delhi.
86. O'Connor, W.F. Captain (1900), Routes in Sikkim compiled in the intelligence branch of the Quartermaster General's Department in India, Published by Office of the Superintendent of Government Printing, Calcutta.
87. O'Malley, L.S.S. (1917), *Provincial Geographies of India, Bengal Bihar Orissa and Sikkim*, Cambridge University Press, London.
88. Pathak, Bishnu, '*Federalism: Lessons from India*' p. 12. www.transnational-perspectives .org Article 429 Date of access 17th December 2013.
89. Rahul, Ram, (1970), *The Himalayan Borderland*, Vikash Publishing House, New Delhi.
90. Rahul, Ram, (1978), *The Himalayas as a frontier*, Vikash Publishing House, New Delhi.

91. Raizada, Shefali (2012), *Merger of Sikkim: A new Perspective*, Swati Publications, New Delhi.
92. Ram, N, *Sikkim Story: Protection to Absorption*, Social Scientist, Vol. 3, No. 2 (Sept 1974).
93. Rao, P. Raghunanda (1978), *Sikkim- The story of its integration with India*, Cosmo Publication, New Delhi.
94. Rao, P.R. (1972), *India and Sikkim 1840- 1970*, Sterling Publishers Private Limited, New Delhi.
95. Ray, Sunanda K Datta (1984), *Smash and Grab-Annexation of Sikkim*, Vikas Publishing House, New Delhi.
96. Regmi, Mahesh Chandra (1971), *A Study in Nepali Economic History* (1768- 1846), Manjushree Publishing House, New Delhi.
97. Rev. Graham, J.A. (1897), *On the threshold of Three Closed Lands-The Guild Outpost in the Eastern Himalayas*, Edinburg, London.
98. Risley, H. H. (First Published 1894, re- print 1989), *The Gazetteer of Sikkim*, Bengal Secretariat Press.
99. Rose, Leo E., '*India and Sikkim: Redefining the Relationship*' Pacific Affairs, Vol. 42, No.1 (Spring 1969).
100. Rustamji, Nari (1971), *Enchanted Frontiers-Sikkim Bhutan and Indian North-eastern Borderlands*, Oxford University Press.
101. Rustamji, Nari (1987), *Sikkim- A Himalayan Tragedy*, Allied Publishers Private Limited.
102. Salisbury, C.Y. (), *Mountaintop Kingdom: Sikkim*, Vikash Publishing House, New Delhi, India.
103. Sandberg Graham (1901), *An Itinerary of the Route from Sikkim to Lhasa*, Baptist Mission Press, Calcutta, India.
104. Sandberg, Graham (1888), *Manual of Sikkimese Bhutia Language, De-Jong Ke*, Oxford Mission Press, Calcutta, India.
105. Sankrityayan, Rahul, *Darjeeling Parichaya* (1950), Adhunik Pustak Bhawan, Calcutta.
106. Sarkar, S.C., (1930), *Some Notes on the Intercourse of Bengal with the Northern Countries in the Second Half of the Eighteenth Century*, Proceedings of the Indian History Records Commission, Vol. XIII.
107. Scott, James C (July 1987), '*Resistance without Protest and without Organisation: Peasant Opposition to the Islamic Zakat and the Christian Tithe*' Comparative Study in Society and History, Vol. 29 Issue 3.

108. Scott, James C, '*Everyday forms of Resistance*' Copenhagen Papers.

109. Scott, James C. (1985), *Weapons of the Weak, Everyday Forms of Peasant Resistance*, Yale University Press, London.

110. Scott, James C. (1990), *Domination and the Arts of Resistance Hidden Transcripts*, Yale University Press, London.

111. Scott, James C. (2010), *The Art of Not Being Governed-An Anarchist History of Upland South-East Asia*, Orient Black Swan Private Limited, Hyderabad, India.

112. Sengupta, N., *Sikkim: State Government & Politcs* (1985), Sterling Publishers, New Delhi.

113. Shah, Rishikesh (first published 1990, re-print 1996, re-print in one volume 2001), *Modern Nepal-A political History 1769–1955*, Manohar Publication, New Delhi.

114. Sharma, S. K, Sharma Usha (Eds. First Edition 1998), *Social and cultural heritage of Sikkim and Bhutan*, Anmol Publishers Private Limited, New Delhi.

115. Sharma, S.K and Sharma Usha, (First edition 1997), *Encyclopaedia of Sikkim and Bhutan,* Vol. II, Anmol Publications Private Limited, New Delhi.

116. Sharma, S.K and Sharma Usha, (First edition 2005), *Discovery of North East India,* Vol. 10 Sikkim, Mittal Publications New Delhi.

117. Sharma, Sudheer, '*The Pain of Loosing a Nation*', Nepal News (Weekly) published on 11th September 2007- 18th September 2007, Kathmandu, Nepal.

118. Sharma, Sudheer, "*Twenty Five Years after Sikkim*", Nepal (Weekly) 23rd March 2001-29th March 2001, Kathmandu, Nepal.

119. Sharma, Tulshi Ram (1996), *Sikkim Hijo Dekhi Aaja Samma* (Sikkim from yesterday till Today) Aankura Prakashan, Gangtok.

120. Sharma, Tulshi Ram, (1970), "*Sikkim Pharkera Herda*" (Retrospective view of Sikkim), Kanchenjunga, Vol. X, No. 8/9, Gangtok.

121. *Sikkim- A Concise Chronicle* (March 20th 1963) Published by The Royal Weeding Committee, Printed at The Sikkim Darbar Press.

122. Sikkim Development Report, 2008, Planning Commission, Government of India, New Delhi, Published by Academic Foundation, New Delhi.

123. Singh, G.P. (2008), *Researches Into the History and Civilisation of the Kirâtas*, Gyan Publishing House, New Delhi.

124. Sinha, A.C (2006), '*Peace and Democracy in South Asia*', Vol. 2, No. 1.

125. Sinha, A.C. (2008), *Sikkim Feudal and Democratic*, Indus Publishing Company, New Delhi.

126. Sir Temple, Richard (1887), *Journals kept in Hyderabad, Kashmir, Sikkim and Nepal,* Vol. II, W.H. Allen & Co. 13 Waterloo Palace, Pall Mall, London.

127. Subba, J.R. (2008), *History Culture and Customs of Sikkim*, Gyan Publishing House, New Delhi.

128. Subba, Tanka B, Mishra, Madhu S., (ed) (Calcutta IIM, 1988) Rural Development in Eastern and North eastern India, *'Agrarian Relations and Development in Sikkim.'*

129. Tamsang, Lyangsong (2008), *Lepcha Folklore and Folk Songs*, Sahitya Akademi, New Delhi.

130. Temple, Richard (first published 1887), *Travels in Nepal and Sikkim*, Ratna Pustak Bhandar, Kathmandu, Nepal.

131. Thakur, R.N. (1988), *The Himalayan Lepchas*, Archives Publishers and Distributors, New Delhi.

132. Thotub Namgyal, (Maharaja K.C.I.E), Dolma Yeshay, (Maharani) *History of Sikkim* (un-published type script 1908), Translated by Kazi Dausandup.

133. Turner, R.L., (1980), *A comparative and etymological dictionary of the Nepali language*, Allied Publishers, New Delhi.

134. Waddle, L.A. (1899), *Among the Himalayas*, Bibiliotheca Himalayica Series 1, Vol.18, Ratna Pustak Bhandar, Kathmandu, Nepal.

135. White, John Claude (1909), *Sikkim, and Bhutan 21 years on the North East Frontier 1887-1908*, Cosmo Publication, New Delhi.

136. Zinn, Howard, (2007), *A Power Government Cannot Suppress*, City Lights Books, San Francisco, USA.

Appendices

A brief note on Appendix I: After the murder of a Lepcha Minister Chagzod Bolek in 1827, the other rebellious Kotapas of Sikkim had taken asylum in the Eastern Nepal. The Nepalese Government had granted them a *Zagir* or estate known as *Mana Chamal* in 1827 (1884 *Vikrama Samvat*) to their leader Yug Dathup. The Lepchas were given estate as an endowment from which they could collect land revenue and were also bestowed with the judicial rights.

Appendix I

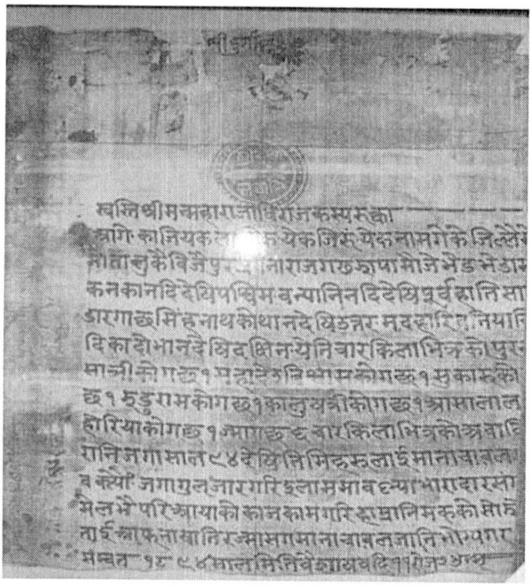

Ditto English Translation of the Land Grants to the Kotapas by the Nepalese Government:

Shree Durga

Swasti Shreeman Maharajadhiraja Kashyarukuwa

Further, Kazi Thukla Thup Dzerung Thek Namguay has been granted the area at Motalu Bijayapur (+- 3 letters) Rajgad Jhapa that includes Bhed

Bheda which is situated at the West of Kanaka River, East to Banyani River, North to Hathisar Bhandar Gach Singhanath Thaan, South of the convergence of Madhari-Banyani Rivers. Inside these four forts include 1 **Gach** of Puran Gosain, 1 **Gach** of Mahadev Bishwas, 1 **Gach** of Sukaru, 1 **Gach** of Jhaduram, 1 **Gach** of Kalu Khatri, 1 **Gach** of Ashalall Horiya, in total 6 **Gach** inside the four forts. We have granted it to you as a Mana Chamal from the year 1884. Make this area suitable for cultivation and inhabit it and maintain a cordial relation with our officials at Illam. You need to work according to the exigencies of time and remain loyal to us and enjoy the grant as **Mana Chamal**.

Samvat 1884 Vaishak 11th Roj (week) 2.

Subham.

A brief note on Appendix II: Letter of Maj. Gen. Janga Bahadur Rana, the Prime Minister of Nepal to Lepcha Kazi of Ilam confirming the exemption from the payment of revenues of his estate granted to him by the Nepal Government. Dated Maguh 9th 1921 Vikram Samvat (23rd January 1870 AD).

Appendix II

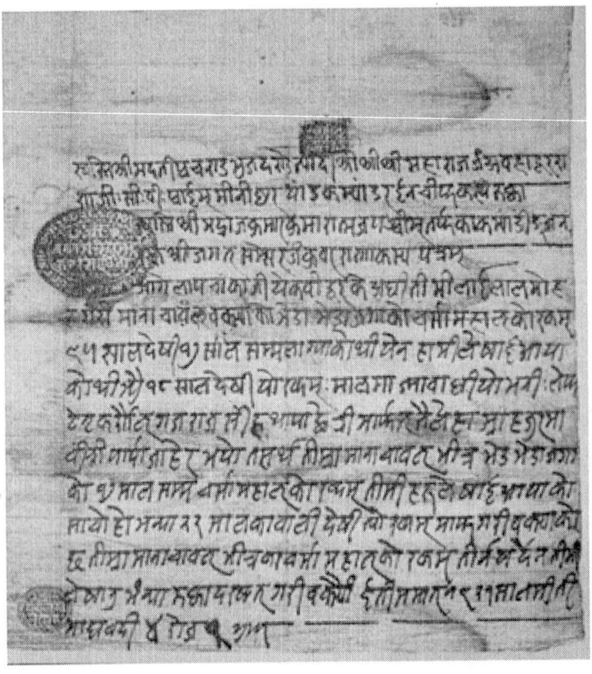

Ditto English Translation of the Letter of Maj. Gen. Janga Bahadur Rana, the Prime Minister of Nepal to the Lepcha Kazi of Ilam:

Swasti Shree Madati Prachanda Bhujha Dhara etc. Shree Shree Shree Maharaja Jung Bahadur Rana G C B Prime Minister and Commander-in-Chief Kasyarukuwa

Swasti Shree Jagat Sumsher Jung Kunwar Ra Ra 1 Kaspa Patram

Previously we had our Lal Mohor (Red Seal) to the Lepcha Kazi Thekvi which had been granted to you as Mana Chamal of Bhed Bheda since 1884. We have not collected the revenue for 1 year which we used to do earlier. You have requested our Lord through Lieutenant Col. Gajraj Singh Thapa Chettri about the matter that from 18th year the revenue was deposited to Maal. Accordingly, it is a fact that the revenue of Burma Mahal of the Bhed Bheda area which belongs to your Mana Chamal was enjoyed by you for 1 year. You are exempted from paying the taxes of the said area from the yield of 22nd year. I have put my signature with the assurance that you do not have to pay tax of Burma Mahal that comes into your Mana Chamal.

Subham!! Samvat 1921 Date Magh 4th Roj (week) 1

A brief note on Appendix III: An attempt was made by the Sikkim Court with the assistance of John C White, the first British Political Officer to put a check on the growing entry of the Nepali peasants into Sikkim. With the issue of a notice mentioned below they had taken a precautionary measure for the protection of indigenous peasants against the irresistible advent of the outsiders by not selling their lands to the new comers.

Appendix III

Notice dated 2.1.1897 issued by J.C. White on selling and sub-letting of land belonging to Bhutia-Lepcha community

I hereby give to all the Kazis and Mondals in Sikkim that no Bhutia and Lepchas are to be allowed to sell or sublet any of their lands, without the express sanction of the Council.

If anyone disobeys this order he will be punished severely.

Gangtok,
Sikkim
The 2nd January 1897

Sd/-
John C White
Political Officer, Sikkim.

A brief note on Appendix IV: The discrepancy created by the Notice of the 2nd January 1897 between the Lepcha-Bhutia peasants and the Nepali peasants was further broadened by Revenue Order No.1 of 17th May 1917. This New Order had forbidden the Bhutia and the Lepchas of Sikkim to sell, mortgage or sub-let any of their lands to any person other than a Bhutia or Lepcha without the express sanction of the Darbar.

Appendix IV

Revenue Order No. 1 Dated 17th May 1917

With reference to the order dated the 2nd January 1897, it is hereby again notified to all Kazis, Thikadars and Mandals in Sikkim, that no Bhutia and Lepcha are to be allowed to sell, mortgage or sub-let any of their lands to any person other than a Bhutia or Lepcha without the express sanction of the Darbar or Officer empowered by the Darbar in this behalf, whose orders will be obtained by the landlord concerned. If any one disobeys the order he will be severely punished.

In this order the term "mortgage" means mortgaging the whole or part of a holding on the *biyaz* or *masikata* system and the term "sublet" means subletting the whole or part of a holding on the *pakuria* system.

Definition

(i) *Biyaz* means mortgaging land to another person who enjoys the produce of the field as interest so long as the principle loan remains unpaid.

(ii) *Masikata* means mortgaging of fields to a creditor who enjoys the produce of the field at an annual instalment towards the loan.

(iii) *Pakuria* means subletting where a ryot allows another new ryot to settle upon the portion of his own holding generally receiving from him some rent in cash and some assistance in cultivating his own fields.

17th May 1917

Gangtok

C.A. Bell Superintendent, Sikkim State.

A brief note on Appendix V: To get rid of the notorious feudalism, the peasants of Sikkim would prefer to get enrol in the army. If they did so, their family members would be exempted from *Jharlangi* and other forced labours.

Appendix V

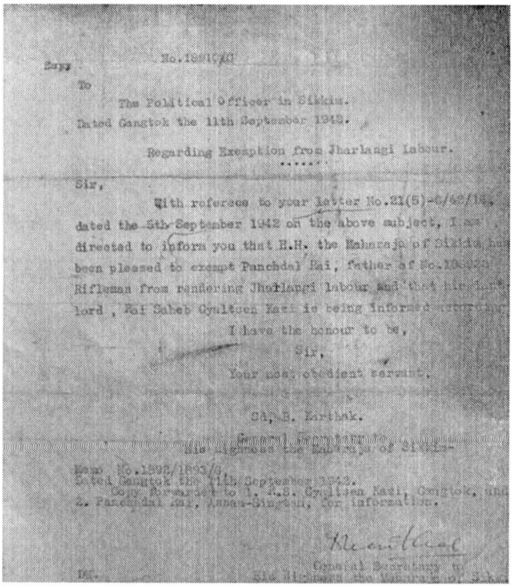

No.18910/G

To

The Political Officer in Sikkim.

Dated Gangtok the 11th September 1942.

Regarding Exemption from Jharlangi Labour.

Sir,

With reference to your letter No.21(5)-G/42/16, dated the 5th September 1942 on the above subject, I am directed to inform you that H.H. the Maharaja of Sikkim has been pleased to exempt Panchdal Rai, father of No.106933 Rifleman from rendering Jharlangi labour and that his landlord, Rai Saheb Gyaltsen Kazi is being informed accordingly.

I have the honour to be,

Sir,

Your most obedient servant,

Sd, B. Karthak.

Letter to the Political Officer of Sikkim from the General Secretary to the Maharaja of Sikkim for the exemption of Jharlangi labour to Panchdal Rai of Assam Singtam

No. 18910/G

To

The Political Officer in Sikkim

Dated Gangtok the 11th September 1942

Regarding Exemption from Jharlangi Labour

Sir,

With reference to your letter No. 21(5)-G/42/16, dated the 5th of September 1942 on the above subject, I am directed to inform you that H.H. the Maharaja of Sikkim has been pleased to exempt Panchdal Rai, father of No. 106933 Rifleman from rendering Jharlangi labour and that his Landlord, Rai Saheb Gyaltsen Kazi is being informed accordingly.

I have the honour to be,

Sir,

Your most obedient servant,

Sd/- B. Karthak

General Secretary to

His Highness the Maharaja of Sikkim

Memo No. 1892/1893/G

Dated Gangtok the 11th September 1942

Copy forwarded to 1. R.S. Gyaltsen Kazi, Gangtok and,

2. Panchdal Rai Assam Singtam for information.

General Secretary to

His Highness the Maharaja of Sikkim

DK

Note on Appendix VI: Notice issued by a Mandal Brihaspati Upadhyay of Tareythang village to one of his villagers Late Ravilal Pyakurel on 18th December 1945 against a report made by another villager Sarvey Bidhyapati Kafley stating that the accused had chopped off a tree.

Appendix VI

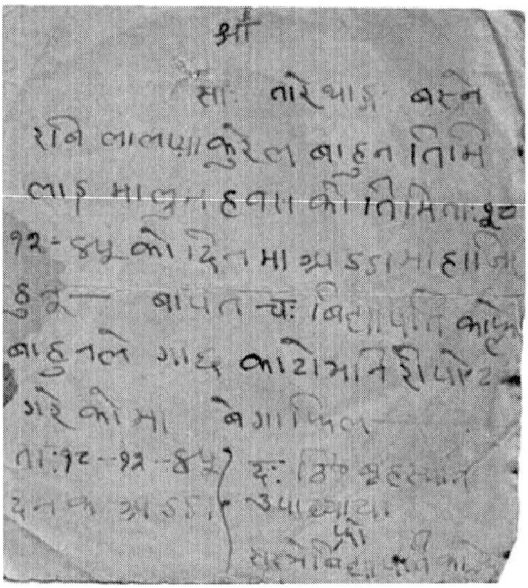

Ditto English Translation of the Notice

Shree

Ravilal Pyakurel of Tareythang Busty is hereby directed to attend Adda Court at Danak on 28-12-1945. A report has been made against you by Mr.

Sarvey Bidhyapati Kafley Bahun for unlawfully slashing a tree and you are directed to attend the Court at Danak Adda without fail.

Dated: 18-12-45 Brihaspati Upadhyay

Danak Adda From,

Sarvey Bidhyapati Kafley

A brief note on Appendix VII: The General Department of the Kingdom issued a notification on 31st December, 1946 for the abolition of Jharlangi labour. Within a month of the passing of this notification, the Sikkim State again issued another notification for the abolition of the *Kuruwa* labour. The Notification of Sikkim State General Department (Misc. Branch) had abolished the awful *Kuruwa* practice with effect from the 31st of January 1947. The Notification issued on a single page in three different languages i.e. English, Nepali, and Tibetan was forwarded to every lessee holders and to the police and patrol outposts. But, most unfortunately, the *Kazis* and the Zamindars who were playing vital role in keeping the king in seclusion had never let the Notifications to be implemented accordingly.

Appendix VII

Notification of the abolition of Forced labour Sikkim State

General Department

Notification No. 3590-4089/G

It has come to the notice of the Sikkim Durbar that there is some confusion regarding requisition of Jharlangi labour resulting in public agitation. It is therefore notified for the information of the public that "whosoever unlawfully compels any person to labour against the will of that person shall be punished with imprisonment of either description for a term which may extend to one year, or with fine, or with both (Sec, 374 IPG).

In terms of Circular No. 5814 G dated the 15th July 1924, read with Notification No. 2756-2955G, dated the 9th October 1937, it is hereby again notified that no Landlord, Manager or their Kamdaris shall employ labour otherwise than by his consent, but for any administrative purpose and ceremonial occasions Jharlangi labour which also includes transport may be requisitioned on payment of wages at standardized rates fixed by the Durbar from time t time. Fuel and fodder shall also be supplied to persons travelling on State duty on payment at rates fixed by the Durbar. Any person travelling on duty is entitled to those privileges.

By Order of his highness the Maharaja of Sikkim

Gangtok
The 31st December, 1946

T. Tshering
General Secretary to
His Highness the Maharaja of Sikkim

A brief note on Appendix VIII: The following Notification of Sikkim State General Department (Misc. Branch) had abolished the awful *Kuruwa* practice with effect from the 31st of January 1947. The Notification issued on a single page in three different languages i.e. English, Nepali,and Tibetan was forwarded to every lessee holders and to the police and patrol outposts.

Appendix IX

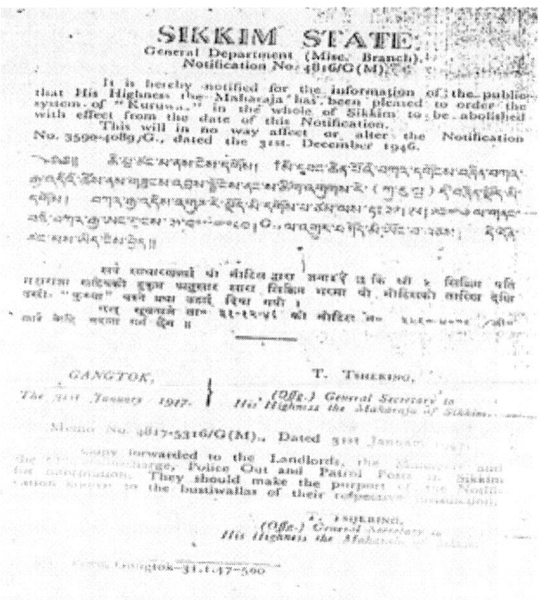

SIKKIM STATE
General Department (Misc. Branch).
Notification No. 4816/G(M).

It is hereby notified for the information of the public that His Highness the Maharaja has been pleased to order the system of "Kuruwa" in the whole of Sikkim to be abolished with effect from the date of this Notification.

This will in no way affect or alter the Notification No. 3590-4089/G., dated the 31st. December 1946.

GANGTOK, The 31st January 1947.

T. TSHERING, (Offg.) General Secretary to His Highness the Maharaja of Sikkim.

Memo No. 4817-5316/G(M)., Dated 31st January

Copy forwarded to the Landlords, ... Police Out and Patrol Posts ... Sikkim ... They should make the purport ... the bustiwallas of their respective ...

Notification of the abolition of Kuruwa

SIKKIM STATE
General Department (Misc. Branch)
Notification No. 4816/G(M)

It is hereby notified for the information of the public that His Highness the Maharaja has been pleased to order the system of "Kuruwas" in the whole of Sikkim to be abolished with effect from the date of this Notification.

This will in no way affect or alter the Notification No. 3590-4089/G, dated the 31st December 1946.

GANGTOK — T. Tshering,

The 31st January 1947 — (Offg.) General Secretary to His Highness the Maharaja of Sikkim

Memo No. 4817-5316/G(M)., Dated 31st January 1947

Copy forwarded to the Landlords, the Managers and Officers-in-Charge, Police Out and Patrol Posts in Sikkim for information. They should make the purport of the Notification known to the Bustiwallas of their respective jurisdiction.

T. Tshering,
(Offg.) General Secretary to
His Highness the Maharaja of Sikkim

A brief note on Appendix X: The formation of the Sikkim State Congress was a landmark in the political history of Sikkim. The smaller peasants' associations were merged into a peasant union with the name of Sikkim State Congress on 7th December 1947. With the inauguration of the party, a resolution was also adopted at the same meeting for political and economic reforms. The petition mentioned below is a copy of the resolution passed by the Sikkim State Congress on the day of its foundation at Polo Ground in Gangtok.

Appendix X

Sikkim State Congress' Petition to the Maharaja of Sikkim Dated 9th December 1947

On behalf of our newly born association, viz. Sikkim State Congress, representing the masses of Sikkim, we are directed most respectfully to approach Your Highness with the following petition praying that it may receive Your Highness' favourable consideration.

Sikkim has been meeting with discontent for many years, as Your Highness must be well aware. The numerous petitions which have been addressed to Your Highness from time to time may be described as legion but it has been of avail. The people's voice has literally and invariably proved a voice in the wilderness. Nothing is further from our intentions than to cast aspersions on Your Highness's integrity and sense of justice as an ideal ruler. It is the form of government, the outmoded autocracy with its twin sister Landlordism which is at fault, which as lent itself to unchecked abuse in unscrupulous hands.

In this connection, we request Your Highness to very kindly take the trouble to go through the paper "**A FEW FACTS ABOUT SIKKIM STATE**" which constitutes one of the enclosures to this letter. Painful as the disclosure may be proved to be, we have not attempted to exaggerate anything may be we have been more guilty of understatement, and we are prepared to prove chapter and verse for every statement made herein.

At the mass meeting of the people of Sikkim held at Gangtok on 7th December, 1947, it has been resolved with one voice that:

1. Popular or responsible government should replace the present non-descript oligarchy with the abolition of Landlordism as *sine qua non* and that no time should be lost in bringing this about;
2. An interim government should be formed and installed as early as possible as a necessary precursor of the democratic form of government to come;
3. And that immediate step may be taken to accede to the government of the Dominion of India, if this has not been done already. The reasons for this are obvious and we need not expatiate on the many advantages accruing from it.

May we request that Your Highness will graciously be pleased to vouchsafe a reply to this petition by 24th December 1947 at the New Year, will see the Interim Government duly installed. We are forwarding a copy of this letter together with the enclosures, among others, to the Government of India and to A.I.S.P.C. for information.

A Few Facts about Sikkim State

Introduction: The object of writing this pamphlet (publication withheld for present) is to air the grievances of the downtrodden ryots (subject people) of Sikkim State consisting of Sikkim Gorkhas, Bhotias and Lepchas, who have suffered untold miseries in the hands of corrupt administration; who have been denied the most elementary justice as against their oppressors, the landlords; and whose condition, through unchecked exploitation and victimisation, have become unbearable. Driven to the state of desperation, but encouraged by the public utterance of Pandit Jawaharlal Nehru and other leaders of the Indian National Congress, a large fully representative section of the people of Sikkim have been aroused to make an attempt on behalf of the masses to achieve their own salvation. It is hoped that the movement under contemplation, which will be launched on peaceful lines, will receive the sympathies and cooperation of the freedom loving people everywhere.

State Council and Secretariat

Sikkim is a small Indian State tucked away in a corner of the Himalayas. Its ruler, Maharaja Sir Tashi Namgyal, K.C.S.I is of Tibetan descent, and so are his personal adherents called Kazis, who formed the majority of the Landlords of Sikkim. His Highness has a State Council consisting entirely of Landlords and a Secretariat which is largely controlled by Landlords. There are few outsiders or non-landlords holding important posts in the administration but they are obliged to pander and knuckle under the influential Landlord party. The more jealous among them had, at some time or other, tried to play the new broom but they soon realised to their cost that it did not pay. A prominent outsider and ex-officio Councillor has long ceased to attend the Council through sheer disgust at the rot prevailing there. The subject people or ryots have no voice in the administration and they have long groaned under the pernicious yoke of Landlordism.

Landlords and Landlordism

The Kazis, who are the leading Landlords, claim to belong to the old nobility and compare themselves with the barons of the feudal system. By long usage they have been accustomed to oppress the people and to expect the utmost subservience from them. They form an exclusive and influential coterie around the ruling family and are able to impose their will on all and sundry. The rest of the Landlords, called "Thikadars", are content to play second fiddle to the Kazi party and thus share in the loaves and fishes of office and other privileges which they have usurped for themselves. Bound by a common policy to oppress the ryots, the Thikadars, especially the more influential among them, have proved as bad as any of the Kazis. Landlordism, as obtaining in Sikkim, has proved the curse of the ryots. It has enabled the Landlords, through coercion and intimidation, to acquire for themselves the best holdings of the ryots. Numerous ryots, especially in the rural areas, have thus been deprived of their patrimonial lands and are compelled to take out a living by cultivating their own disposed fields for the benefit of the Landlords. There are prescribed limits to the possessions of such holdings applicable to all, but the rules and regulations, which are rigorously enforced upon the poor, are conveniently manipulated to serve the interests of the privileged class. The Landlords pay no taxation which consequently falls with greater severity upon the ryots. On the other hand the Landlords receive large unearned commissions from the State as reward for carrying on a thoroughly corrupt administration.

Landlords' Powers

The landlords are vested with magisterial powers in both civil and criminal matters. They are also empowered to register documents for the transfer of landed properties. There are no effective checks on these powers and the Landlords are free to abuse them for their gains. The more fine a landlord can impose, the larger his share of spoils, for he receives one half of the collection as his perquisite while other half goes to the State. When, as has happened, a Landlord forgets to enter a fine in his books, nobody is wiser and he appropriate to the whole amount to himself. A grasping Landlord has no difficulty in dispossessing an uncompromising ryot of his cherished possession, be it a paddy field or a herd of cattle. The slightest delay in the payment of taxation, a matter of common occurrence, enables the Landlord to seize that very property, to the exclusion of any other, and thus the transfer is affected speedily and very profitably to the Landlord. Numerous ryots have thus been reduced to penury and practical slavery. Landlords are invested with different classes of legal powers with due regard to their personal merits and other qualifications. But most of the Landlords live away from their estates and their powers are exercised by the ignorant and rapacious underlings who make no scruple about filling their own pockets besides extracting as much as they can for their masters.

Forced Labour Exacted by Landlords

There are various forms of forced labour to which the ryots are subjected. About twenty years ago, a notification was said to have been issued by the State, based on International Conventions, announcing the application of forced labour. This notification was never explained to the ryots and the practice was never stopped, far less abolished. It is carried on to this day. The notification was a mere pretence of having carried out an unavoidable obligation but was clearly never meant to be observed. Forced labour with minimum, and often without any compensation is usually exacted by the Landlords when cultivating their extensive and mostly ill-gotten private fields and when harvesting their crops. So far the ryots have grudgingly submitted to this kind of exactions through fear of punishment. But such exactions have of late become manifold on account of the ever increasing farming and gardening interests of the Landlords, which allow the ryots scarcely any time to attend to their own affairs. Most of the influential Landlords, who hold important posts in the administration, live at Gangtok. Their estates may be two or three days' journey away. From their ryots have to come all the way to Gangtok and serve their Landlords in turn, in various menial capacities. The ryots get no wage or compensations for such service and they are lucky if they escape from cruelties. The exaction of this kind of service at all times, often accompanied by cruelties, is peculiar to the Kazi Landlords.

Forced Labour Requisitioned by the State

This paragraph applies particularly to the four Landlords whose estates adjoin Gangtok, the Capital, on the route to Tibet. Forced labour is often requisitioned on behalf of the State for carrying loads across the passes (over 15000 feet) into Tibetan territory. To the ryots this means an absence of at least a week from home besides having to provide himself with warm clothes at a prohibitive cost. When he will earn as wages under the prescribed rates for forced labour, he would barely suffice to buy his meagre meal for the journey to and fro. No wonder the ryot would be glad to escape from the liability for a price. The Landlords bleeds him to the limit and sends his own private pack mules to carry loads, for which he is doubly recompensed. A greedy Landlord often seizes upon his chance of making further easy money and calls for double the number of men required. For instance, when only 20 men were requisitioned by the State, he would call for 40 men, thus duplicating his own extortionate demand from the ignorant and unsuspecting ryots.

Transport of "Kalo Bhari"

Kalo Bhari (Black Loads) was the name given to a special consignment compactly packed in black tarpaulin, which gave the name. Huge quantities of these packages were transported overland to China via Tibet during the later part of the War. Such as the demand for transport for this purpose that the wages offered reached unprecedented heights. The cupidity of the Landlords also rose in unison and they stopped to swindling. They falsely requisitioned for force labour "on the authority of the State" to carry packages, which they represented as government stores which the ryots were bound to carry. The ryots would receive the prescribed rates of hire for forced labour whereas the rates offered for these goods were five times the amount or even more. In fact, the goods belonged to private concerns and the ryots were not bound to carry these goods. But the ignorant ryots were completely deceived. Those who could afford to buy off their liability preferred to suffer extortion and paid through nose. The poorer ryots were obliged to carry out the filthy task. They were paid as forced labour and the Landlords pocketed gains. By such despicable means the Landlords concealed for long. When they learnt about it, the victims of the swindle approached the powers that be for redress of the wrongs suffered by them. It was, however, to no effect. As the culprits were all highborn Kazis, the matter was hushed up, and the aggrieved ryots were sent away with a facial advice to "Let bygones be bygones and forgive and forget". The slightest offence, so much alleged, against a ryot exposes him to severe punishment whereas even such downright swindling by the privileged class is treated as of no account.

Deputation of the Ryots

During the later half of 1946, several deputations of the ryots waited on the powers that be to protest against the system of forced labour as well as against Landlords. The ryots expressed their determination not to serve the landlords in future and asked that they should be allowed to pay their taxes into the State Bank direct and not through Landlords. There as nothing unlawful in this approach by the ryots but it was curiously construed as a communal rising and a Notification couched in ambiguous terms was issued by the State to crush it. There are no communal problems in Sikkim. The ryots, who consist of Hindus and Buddhists, live in complete amity. The number of Muslims scattered all over Sikkim is one hundred at most. The only communal question the authorities could have in view is probably that existing between the oppressors and the oppressed, "the Landlords and the ryots". Thus, against all sense of justice, the Landlords were fully vindicated and the ryots effectually suppressed and gagged.

Powers that be

The term "Powers that be" has been advisedly employed in on lighter vein but to denote the real authorities who function behind the Ruling Family. His Highness the Maharaja is of exceedingly pious and retiring nature, although in the prime of life; he leads a secluded life. The Maharajkumar, heir -apparent has started taking an interest in the administration but he is still young and inexperienced. Power is therefore concentrated in the hands of the leading landlords, who are thoroughly committed to uphold the interests of their class at any cost. In such circumstances the ryots could have on justice and have sought for it in vain.

Additional Councillors

Since 1946, when the independence of India (Swaraj) was firmly established, the masses in Sikkim have taken courage in both hands and have started an agitation for the abolition of landlordism for the introduction of reforms long overdue. As a result thereof the ryots, representing the three classes of ryots named in the first paragraph, as additional members of the State Council. This pleasing gesture was apparently made as a palliative to the ryots, but it deceived nobody. After a couple of sessions at the Council, they could do nothing to advance the interest of the ryots and had expressed their desire to resign from the Council.

Conclusion

The abolition of landlordism as the only effective means of removing oppression in Sikkim, in the end aimed at by the masses and they bent on keeping up the agitation until their purpose is achieved. In this they firmly believe that they have the support of the Indian national leaders and the Independent Government of India.

Sd/- Tashi Tshering,

President, Sikkim State Congress

A brief note on Appendix XI: With the abolition of awful Kuruwa, Notification No. 4816/G(M) the Government of Sikkim was running short of the supplies of labourers as the peasants were unwilling to supply labours and transport even for the Government supplies. Therefore, to tackle such situation, the State Government issued a strict order to supply labours during the needful hours.

Appendix XI

Government of Sikkim
Education and Transport Department
Notification No. 600-780/ET

It has come to the notice of the Authorities that people are not willing to supply labours and transport etc. when requisitioned by the Government or Government officials travelling on duty on payment of wages at standardised rates fixed by the Government. The attention of the public is drawn to the last paragraph of the Sikkim State General Department notification No. 3590-4089/G, Dated the 31st December 1946, to the clause which is reproduced below for information and guidance of all concerned:

"But for any administrative purposes and ceremonial occasions labour which includes transport may be requisitioned on payment of wages at standardised rates fixed by the Durbar from time to time. Fuel and fodder shall also be supplied to persons travelling on State Duty on payment at rate fixed by the Durbar. Any person travelling on duty is entitled to those privileges".

The Bustiwallas are again warned that they must supply labour or transport when officially requisitioned through their Kamdaris, Police Posts or any other legal agency, failing which the person or persons concerned will be severely dealt with.

A brief note: To curtail the powers of the landlords a notification was issued by H.H. Maharaja Tashi Namgyal to disqualify the landlords as acting Sub-Registers. From now onwards, their task of registering the public documents was transferred to the Office of Land revenue.

Appendix XII

Sikkim State
General Department
Notification No. 5186-085/G

His Highness the Maharaja Sahib of Sikkim has been pleased to order that with effect from 2nd January 1948 the powers granted to certain landlords for registering documents under the Sikkim Registration Rules will be deemed withdrawn. They will no longer act as Sub-Registers.

Gangtok B. Karthak

The 3rd of January, 1948 General Secretary to

His Highness the Maharaja of Sikkim

Appendix XIII

Office of the Private Secretary to his Highness the Maharaja of Sikkim
Judicial Branch
Notification No. 3054-254/P.s

To

All Landlords, Mondals and Bustiwallas in Sikkim

Whereas several prominent landlords have, in furtherance of the Government's policy on Adda reforms, desired (by registration) to be relieved of their judicial duties-His Highness the Maharaja Sahib is pleased to order that the following changes be made effective for the present.

1. There will be a Panchayat tribunal in every Estate. It will consist of the landlord cum a Government recognised Panchayat of four Bustiwallas of that Estate.
2. In case of the landlord not ordinarily residing in the Estate, his recognised nominee will act for him.
3. The tribunal's judgement will be signed by all five members of the Court.
4. The Panchayat Tribunals are hereby invested the civil powers to hear suits, to the limit of ₹ 100 only in value. Their criminal jurisdiction will extend to petty offences vide schedule below. They are empowered to inflict sentence of fines only, to the extent of ₹ 25.

5. The Panchayat will be selected from the Estate by the following method
   (a) The Mondals will ask for their block people in a meeting called for the purpose, to select four persons to represent the Block in the final selection.
   (b) The four members of the Panchayat will be then selected in a meeting of the Block representatives.
6. The necessary qualifications for selections of the Panchayat will be:
   (a) Age, not below 22 years.
   (b) Literacy in some vernacular of the Country.
   (c) Status of being a payee of land tax of not less than ₹ 15.

   Conviction of an offence involving moral turpitude will be disqualification.
7. The names of Panchayat members after selection and the absentee landlords' nominees will be communicated to the Government for approval and record, as early as possible.
8. All pending cases failing outside jurisdiction of Panchayat Tribunals, as defined in paragraph 3, will be transferred to Chief Court.
9. There will be in future no sharing in fees and fines by Panchayat Courts. They will get remuneration.
10. The landlord courts as at present constituted will cease to function from the date on which the new Tribunals come into being.
11. The term landlord in this notification includes Managers of Estate, Heads of Monasteries, etc.

Index